WATCHING WAR FILMS WITH MY DAD

ALSO BY AL MURRAY

The Pub Landlord's Book of British Common Sense

The Pub Landlord Says Think Yourself British

The Pub Landlord's Great British Pub Quiz Book

AL MURRAY

WATCHING WAR FILMS WITH MY DAD

CENTURY

Published by Century 2013

2 4 6 8 10 9 7 5 3 1

This book is a work of non-fiction based on the life, experiences and recollections
of the author. In some limited cases names of people, places, dates, sequences or
the detail of events have been changed [solely] to protect the privacy of others.
The author has stated to the publishers that, except in such minor respects not
affecting the substantial accuracy of the work, the contents of this book are true.

First published in Great Britain in 2013 by
Century
Random House, 20 Vauxhall Bridge Road,
London SW1V 2SA

www.randomhouse.co.uk

Addresses for companies within The Random House Group Limited can be found
at: www.randomhouse.co.uk

The Random House Group Limited Reg. No. 954009

A CIP catalogue record for this book
is available from the British Library

ISBN 9781780891095

The Random House Group Limited supports the Forest Stewardship
Council® (FSC®), the leading international forest-certification organisation. Our
books carrying the FSC label are printed on FSC®-certified paper. FSC is the only
forest-certification scheme supported by the leading environmental organisations,
including Greenpeace. Our paper procurement policy can be found at
www.randomhouse.co.uk/environment

Picture Credits – Page 126: Macks Aviation Photography,
Page 134: Das Bundesarchiv, Pages 166–168: Author's own

Typeset in Sabon by Palimpsest Book Production Limited,
Falkirk, Stirlingshire
Printed and bound by
CPI Group (UK) Ltd, Croydon, CR0 4YY

For Mum and Dad

Contents

Acknowledgements

Thank you . . .

To Paul Powell for reading the chunks as they arrived.

For the encouragement from Richard, Becky, Dan, Susie herself, and Ben Dunn who saw fit to make me redraft the rambling/ steaming pile I first presented him with. Also to Julia Twaites for helping put this together.

To Nick Austin for his editorial assistance – all mistakes in here are my own, lapses of memory or research or wonky opinions lie with your author. If they're really bad I'll say I was joking.

To Team Total.

To Eleanor for enduring another draft.

To Scarlett and Willow for putting up with history lectures at mealtimes.

Introduction, in which I try to clear a few things up before we get started

1. TRUST ME, I'M NOT AN EXPERT

'Better to know nothing than half-know many things'

Friedrich Nietzsche

If you're familiar with the character I play, The Pub Landlord – and the chances are you might be and that's why we're here together now – you might know he's extremely fond of going off on historical riffs. There's a routine in which he boldly proves that 'Great Britain, World War Champions of the World, have beaten every single country in the world at war – go on, name a country . . .'. He then takes requests for countries and dives into a load of half-remembered baloney, relying on a system loosely based on conkers – if we've beaten this country who've beaten that country then that counts as a win to us. And he can do it: we've beaten everyone, though if someone shouts out Holland I'm in a bit of a pickle. It is, like so much of the history that gets wheeled out to prove a point, partial, thin and laboured. But unlike lots of history wheeled out to prove a point it is at least funny. You can prove anything with half-remembered stuff. As this book seeks to demonstrate.

Now, Nietzsche was a smart man, a cripplingly, self-consciously clever wise man, a man who stared out of the window and thought about loads of stuff an awful lot, a prolific writer, a man who declared God dead because the idea just wasn't good enough. Wow. Opinions are nevertheless divided on Nietzsche, as well they might be what with the Nazis being so keen on him, albeit posthumously, though it was largely down to his sister sucking up to them because they were powerful. Nevertheless, he was so very clever that he's someone we ought to pay attention to – and he's a mine of quotes. This one is his clever spin on something you've surely heard a lot: a little knowledge is a dangerous thing.

But on this quote I can't agree, and if you stick with this book maybe you'll disagree with Friedrich too. This book contains a great deal of half-known stuff. No matter what you might learn from this book you're not learning it from a historian, merely from someone who likes history, is interested in it and can half-remember a fair bit of it. With the internet helping to jog my memory (apart from that day when they switched Wikipedia off in protest and the creative industries in the UK ground to a halt and everyone else got loads done) I have been able to flesh out a great deal of what I half-know. The alternative – knowing nothing, no matter how much Nietzsche might like that idea – wouldn't make for much of a book, and would be a lot less interesting. And let's be honest, most of us half-know many things – I'll bet you can drive but have no idea how the sodding car actually works, but that doesn't stop you getting in the car, does it? Real historians or proper specialist fans will be tearing their hair out reading this book. That's fine, to be honest. A sale's a sale. But I'm a consumer of history, not a historian – calling me a historian would be like calling someone who likes fish and chips a trawlerman.

2. HINDSIGHT: AN ARSEHOLE'S VIEW OF EVENTS

'Hindsight is always twenty-twenty'

Billy Wilder

This book is, to some extent, a memoir. However, what you won't get is poor me, we only had a black and white telly, I had to turn the laughter of the bullies against them and that's why in the end I became a sad clown dancing for joy at the laughter of strangers. Sorry. One reason for this is that I'm not from the North. The other is there's lots I don't want you to know, mainly because it's not at all interesting, not even interesting enough for me to recall. This is a memoir about fascination, and hindsight. Fascination I'm all for, really, it's good to be interested in stuff, don't you think? But hindsight, with which we write memoirs as well as history, is dangerous stuff.

Hindsight is, to my mind, an arsehole's view of events, both figuratively and literally. In writing this book and remembering stuff I've used hindsight to make unconnected things connect, events cohere and, as a result, attain significance. Writing a thing like this, you cast yourself as the hero, or clown, of the hour. Why wouldn't you? There's every chance I've given myself some of the best lines – it's my book, get over it. That's fair enough, I think, when you're writing a frivolous book like this, but in writing history it's like napalm spewed liberally all over the truth

4

of what really happened. If you'll accept my hyperbole. It's going to be that kind of read, I'm afraid.

There's a thing called the Historian's Fallacy. Basically it says that when studying history we need to remember one simple and blindingly obvious thing: people in the past could not see into the future. The information that we have today to weigh up what happened back then (and importantly, and very interestingly, what might have happened) simply wasn't available to the protagonists at the time. Of course it wasn't. And even if it had been, who says they'd not have made the same decisions? In other words, just because we won the Second World War doesn't mean we were always going to.

As a fan and consumer of history, and military history in particular, it seems to me from what I've read that an astonishing amount of military historians (naming no names) seem to forget this, often in the hunt for book-selling controversy. Not only that, you'll also see them disappearing down embarrassingly partisan wormholes to make their point, forgetting that when you don't know what's around the corner, you don't know what's around the corner. In other words, why did Hitler start World War Two when it's obvious he was going to lose?! Well, from where he stood he thought it was a good idea at the time – and for an awful lot of it it wasn't at all obvious he was going to lose. It's fair to say we've all been there (having good ideas at the time: not starting World War Two, obviously). You may have heard of confirmation bias, when you find what you're looking for in the thing you're theorising about. Hindsight is a major partner in crime of confirmation bias – it nudges you along into finding exactly what you're looking for. No one's immune to it. And because I've decided that I'll find it to be true wherever I look.

The French have that excellent expression: l'ésprit de l'escalier – the wit of the staircase. It's the perfect witty remark that comes to you as you're on your way down the stairs after the dinner party. Comedians build careers on experiencing, remembering and recycling exactly that – many, many killer routines are fantasy re-enactments of what the comic concerned could or should have said. I've tried not to use too much of it in recollecting how my fascination with things military and historical has panned out over the years, and I've done everything I can to avoid hindsight. And now I've reread the manuscript I realise that I've failed, and frankly I should have seen it coming.

3. A NOTE ON FOOTNOTES[1]

'Existence is a series of footnotes to a vast, obscure, unfinished masterpiece'

Vladimir Nabokov[2]

It's a well-worn cliché that things end up as footnotes to history, as if this is a fate worse than death. This book promises wholeheartedly to embrace all forms of cliché but in history books footnotes are slightly different. If you, like me, read regular popular and proper real history books like what they have in academic libraries and which sometimes, very rarely, escape into the outside world, you will inevitably run into footnotes. Tons of them.

These pesky things at the bottom of the page – sometimes pointed out with an asterisk like so * – crop up everywhere, especially when your historian needs to let you know which published authority he got the bit he's telling you about from. If he has to do another, he might use this symbol †, whatever it's called – probably a crucifix – and in the event of yet another reference, this one ‡, which implies a double martyring (you wouldn't want to be the one on the bottom much). Very often when reading a serious history book you'll find three-quarters

---

[1] This is a footnote, this thing here that you're reading. Carry on.

[2] He means this book, obv.

to four-fifths, more even, of the page taken up with the footnote(s), cramming the actual main body of text up into the top of the page like it's an unwelcome intruder. Sometimes it will even continue over onto the next page. Historians do tend to qualify a great deal of what they say.

So, in this book I offer you in the manner and style of, though definitely not in the spirit of, the serious historian, numbered, hopefully brief footnotes. I promise that at no point will the text find itself squished up against the top of the page. I also guarantee that only once or twice (maximum) the stuff you're reading below what you should be reading will be more interesting than what's up above. Some of them might even contain extra jokes, like deleted scenes from a DVD. For reasons similar to those detailed so far, I don't like glossaries one bit, so I'll do my best to explain some of the technical stuff as we go along. Forgive me if I slide into familiarity with some of the terms used – like lots of jargon they partly exist to keep outsiders outside.

4. ON HISTORY

'History will teach us nothing'

Sting

I mean, what a doughnut.

By the way, if you haven't read the introduction that's fine, no one does, there isn't a test.

5. AND ANOTHER THING

'Now this is not the end. It is not even the beginning of the end. But it is, perhaps, the end of the beginning.'

Winston Churchill

A great deal of this book (though not all of it) talks about World War Two, the Second World War, WW2 whatever you might call it – and as we'll see later what different people call it and why varies widely through the world. But I grew up calling it 'the War', because that's what my parents – who were both children during it – called it. I still call it 'the War' and sometimes get asked 'which one?' but smile sweetly and explain which one. 'What, Hitler's war?' is the question I was asked that on one occasion took me to the brink. So – mainly for purposes of brevity and because all varieties of names for the War seem to be such mouthfuls – in this book I'll mainly be calling the War the War. Other wars come up but they're not the one I'm mainly on about.

1. Watching Private Ryan

WATCHING WAR FILMS WITH MY DAD

If ever you want to ruin something properly, and by 'something' I mean a war film, watch it with my father. Though actually, if ever you want to ruin something (I mean a war film again) properly and he's not available you could always watch it with me. Maybe 'ruin' is a bit strong, but certainly derail, bouleverse, scupper, traduce would cover it. Neither of us can help ourselves. It just happens. Not doing it requires monumental self-control, actual lip-biting.

In our defence I think that it's obvious why we can't help ourselves and that really it's not our fault at all. Because war movies contain representations of real events, real equipment and of course real people, they are ripe, low-hanging fruit for the very worst kind of nit-picky pedantry. And the worst kind is the kind that fills you with a morbid thrill of the delight at being right. Put on a war film and I start to seethe reflexively at the damned thing. Because the film can't answer back it's like being able to shout 'I told you so' at someone powerless to respond. I know we're not alone. War is hell, yes, but war films are worse. Just try watching

The Battle of Britain with someone who knows their Spitfire types, it is torture, and as for the German planes in that . . .

. . . well, they're not German planes, they're Spanish planes made under licence after the war, which in an odd twist are powered by made-under-licence British Merlin engines (the fabled engines that powered Spitfires, Hurricanes, Mosquitos, Lancasters). The planes standing in as the German Heinkel He 111s are CASA 2.111s. So the German aircraft have the wrong-shaped noses (especially the Messerschmitts) and make the wrong noise. But I digress. All too easily, you may find. The reason they were powered by British Merlins was that the German parts were hard to come by after the war, and what with the Germans having lost and Germany's military exports having been somewhat curtailed, the best engines on hand were British. Even as Britain scrapped its air force, dumping huge numbers of planes in the sea, this was going on. And of course you don't mind selling the stuff that's obsolete, if it comes to it your own stuff is better: at this point the RAF had gone over to jets almost completely. So you have Fascist-owned Nazi airframes powered by Allied engines.

Anyway, I grew up on this stuff. War films were a mainstay of British male popular culture when I was growing up in the Seventies. To some the Seventies is all about flares and disco, or Mohican haircuts and punk or, worst of all, ABBA – but to me the Seventies is war films on the telly. I was blissfully ignorant of the idea that these movies were a way of British culture processing what had happened to it during World War Two: the nine-year-old me had little sensitivity (or even an atom of it) to what my grandmother who had lost her husband and brother in the war might make of my enthusiasm for war films. Or my mum, who'd never known her father or her uncle. They were made for men, about men, with men in them. That's certainly

12

how I saw them when I was a boy – though I know I didn't think about it too hard, either.

How else was I supposed to see them? Sometimes they'd have girls in them, but as a lad you'd wonder why they were in them at all. Pilots would leave wives at home, wringing their hands, men on secret missions might take a break from evading and/or slaying Germans to snog the female radio operator or Resistance contact (to then discover often enough that she was a spy and then have to slay her too). I remember pretty much resenting the presence of the women in their pointy-boobed jumpers and the accompanying feminine treachery in *The Guns of Navarone*, its subplot as brimful of original sin as the Garden of Eden. This was boys' stuff! No girls allowed! These Sten guns are cool!

As well as being unreservedly masculine, many of the Fifties war films plainly depict a post-war self-image of reserve and stiff upper lip, essential to the temperament of the time and how the country was telling itself the story of how it had got through the war: but my nine-year-old self didn't register any of this. At all. A friend of mine had a war-film-themes record that we would listen to; often as not I knew the music long before I ever saw the film. Playing with Action Man with the theme to *633 Squadron* on the record player in the background was a fairly standard afternoon in the holidays. And ace. But on top of this boyish fun, from an early age I also took on the mantle of war-film pedant, a skill I learned eagerly at my father's knee.

There's one film that is central to all of this, pivotal in my development as a war-film pedant and then as an enthusiastic consumer of history (complete with a brief detour into doing an actual degree in history, an academic episode best described as dismal and distracted), and it is the classic film *A Bridge Too Far*. I'll be coming back to the film and the events it – how shall we say?

– represents, again and again in this book. It was where I became aware, very early on, of the collision of storytelling, history, myth, war and its undeniable glamour: even in a film that is squarely pitched as a 'war: ain't it a waste?' film. And how important tea is.

I have a clear memory of being taken to see *A Bridge Too Far* at the cinema when I was nine. It was a really big deal – we didn't go to the cinema much, and this was a major dad-and-lad event. I think we went to Bletchley but I could be wrong. It might have been the bright lights of Aylesbury, possibly Luton. These were the days of the B-feature, huge cinemas that you could stay in of an afternoon and watch the whole programme all the way round again. I remember seeing *The Eagle Has Landed* like this: we'd missed the start so stayed and caught the painfully slow first half of exposition and plotting. That was definitely in Luton. And the B-feature was a short about trains.

Now a Sunday-afternoon teatime staple, *A Bridge Too Far* tells the story of Operation Market Garden. Every male human of my ilk has seen this star-studded war epic, a tale of British pluck and tea, American guts and glory, immaculate German uniforms and ruthlessness, lofty failure, etc., etc. And when I say star-studded I mean star-studded: Connery, Redford, Hackman, Bogarde, Caine, Hopkins, Caan, Olivier – and loads of other people you need the first names for. And Cliff from *Cheers* in a cameo that irresistibly draws the eye away from Robert Redford, proving that a spud-faced bloke is better than any handsome git any day. Directed epically in an epic style by Dickie Attenborough, with an epic script by William Goldman,[3] it tells the epic tale of the failed

---

[3] Goldman – who amongst other things adapted *Misery*, wrote the Butch and Sundance pictures, etc., etc. – has written about writing this film and is completely upfront about the need to (cough) abridge stuff. He is particularly interesting about the 82nd Airborne boat assault on the Nijmegen Bridge, but it's not my story to tell and I'm sure he'd like the inevitable sales pick up when you follow up this footnote.

Operation Market Garden at a personal as well as, um, epic level. It has tons of guts, tons of glory and stars vying for screen time. It ends poignantly, asking us to ask: why? And it is, like all historical films, shot through with inaccuracies, riddled like a machine-gunned evil Nazi's corpse. Some of them proper howlers.

And *A Bridge Too Far* was a big cinematic event for my father, too; living, as we did, in a village in Buckinghamshire with one bus a week. It also wasn't dad's thing much – he has always had a restless energy and concentration that didn't suit the essential passivity of sitting in a cinema seat.

My dad was an airborne sapper (engineer) officer from the 1950s through to the 1970s and the battle at Arnhem is probably the central event in British airborne culture and history. He knew many of the men who'd been there – he did his National Service in the 1950s and then stayed on in the TA. The senior officers in the post-war airborne set-up were men whose names resounded in the accounts of the war – there's been many an occasion when I have asked dad, 'Well, what about him?' and he has proceeded to give me his own personal impression of the man. So how Arnhem was represented on the big screen was a properly big deal. He also knew and still knows the battle backwards. An essential truth, how the men fought at Arnhem – bravely and against increasingly overwhelming odds – is in the film, no doubt about it. But it has to be right. Aged nine, I was a willingly thirsty sponge for all of this. But old habits die hard. When first I broached with my father that I'd be writing this book he muttered about how he'd seen *War Horse* the night before and how most of that was wrong. So watch a war film with me or my dad – or, worse still, me *and* my dad – at your peril.

Don't get me wrong. This shouldn't preclude your enjoyment of the motion picture. We're not like sci-fi deniers who say ah yes well nothing can go faster than the speed of light, and there's no sound in space and anti-gravity is impossible – to which there is one simple answer: 'Yet'. Or 'Shut up!' We understand that stories need to be compressed, of course, situations précised – after all, it's not a documentary, and even documentaries – especially documentaries – have to compress information. It's also not a problem with actual continuity errors – reappearing props, that sort of thing, or goofs like being able to see a plane flying away in the distance after it's supposed to have crashed. It's the inaccuracies, and if you're like me there's probably a moment, maybe several, when you say 'Oh, this is bullshit!'

Maybe – like with my dad – it's simply the way actors salute like civilians and not like soldiers. That one gets him every time. He always mutters on about their haircuts too, like he used to mutter about my haircut.[4]

Maybe it's the scenes when the 1st Airborne Division jump into Arnhem – an amazing piece of film, entirely authentically done, shot with the Parachute Regiment, appropriate aircraft, the right drop zone. There's a fabulous sequence shot from an on-board camera with a parachutist (unremarkable now with helmet-cams and camera phones everywhere, but really quite breathtaking in the 1970s, the guy who's being filmed gets his canopy lines tangled when he first jumps and everything).

These scenes are all very well *except* some of them are jumping 'clean fatigue', without any weapons or equipment. An infantry parachutist would typically jump with his Lee-Enfield rifle, plus about 100 rounds for a rifleman as well as an extra magazine for the section Bren gun, grenades, maybe some mortar rounds, an entrenching tool, water bottle, two 24-hour ration packs, mess tins, etc. – it would come to about 200 pounds of

---

[4] I used to have a haircut.

equipment, in a very heavy bag that they'd lower beneath them once the parachute had deployed safely. Also they are, strictly speaking, jumping with the wrong parachutes. They're an update of the 'chutes the men jumped with at Arnhem.

This stuff matters to the pedant – as a pedant in a pub argument might say 'no, look, listen': the parachutes in the film are the PX 1 Mark 2 with fringes that were introduced much later, and though safer than the 1944 'chutes they are quite wrong for the period, even if they're not as wrong as modern 'chutes would be. Yes, they're direct descendants of the right 'chute, but they're still wrong; add to this the fact that men are jumping with reserve parachutes and there's plenty to start chewing your lip about from this one scene alone, impressive as it is. The fringes on the PX 1 Mark 2 prevent oscillation – terrifying swinging-around to you and me, difficulty in controlling the 'chute to the person dangling beneath it – and make the parachutes more stable. Doesn't matter: they're inaccurate.

But the use of reserves is a real howler. British parachutists didn't jump with reserves during World War Two for all sorts of reasons: they would jump from so low and so heavily laden that there'd be little time for them to deploy the 'chute, and it was deemed better to use the weight for carrying more ammunition and weapons – a reserve was regarded as an unnecessary expense. You'd probably not get to pull it anyway, especially if you were jumping at night and couldn't tell what was going on – you wouldn't know what height you were being dropped from and most likely wouldn't be able to see the ground. American paratroopers were fined if it was deemed they'd used their reserve 'unnecessarily', which meant they would tend not to use it. That's one way of finding out whether it was necessary to pull your reserve; I don't know about you

17

but that seems pretty tough. Would you go splat in order to save $25, or was the dead man who didn't open his reserve intent on not having his pay docked . . . ? But then parachutists are meant to be tough. Of course, what I'm asking for here is that for the film to be accurate the parachuting has to be less safe and that's an altogether unreasonable demand, but you know what? It's still annoying.

Maybe it's the (possibly understandable) confusion about which German formations were at Arnhem; the film calls them II SS Panzer Division, when in fact they were 2 SS Panzer Corps (this is enough for a full war-pedant embolism amongst some). These kinds of mistakes abound in war films. Of course, the British airborne soldiers on the ground might not care particularly which German was from which unit, just that there were tanks there that they hadn't been told to expect. Or had they? There is a riddle at the heart of the Arnhem battle about military intelligence and its uses and dissemination that no one comes out of very well. The movie touches on this – the intelligence officer who blows the whistle on the presence of German tanks is told he's working too hard and needs a break (confusingly, he had the same surname as Major General Roy Urquhart, one of the main players in the battle, so they changed his name in the movie) – but the way the information was dealt with, and who decided essentially to turn a blind eye to it, is properly scandalous.

Depending on how you look at it, those at the top simply didn't care enough about their men's lives, or were spectacularly overconfident and discounted the bad news. This had also happened to the other British Airborne Division, 6th Airborne – so called to make the Germans think there were Airborne Divisions numbers 1 through 6 – which had not been entirely clearly briefed about the nature of the German armoured forces they faced on D-Day. But because D-Day worked out successfully (pretty much) this part of the story has faded from importance. But it is fair to say that a big part of what went wrong at Arnhem can be put down to generals and their ambition (one in particular, possibly General Browning – but this bit is all about nit-picking rather than naming names).

Maybe it's the misattribution of quotes in the film: the German general looking at the approaching air armada says something along the lines of 'If only I had forces like this at my disposal' but it wasn't him who said that, it was someone else.

But maybe you're just like me and the moment is when the Leopard I (!!!!!!!!!!!!!!!!!!) tank comes indestructibly careering across the Arnhem Bridge, crushing the debris from an earlier battle, and blasting the hapless paras' positions. It's meant to be a Tiger tank, I suppose, or maybe a Panther, but it's neither. It resembles both in that it's a big grey metal thing with tracks and a turret, but it's the wrong tank, with the wrong paint, the wrong gun, the wrong everything. By God, it's the wrong tank – it's from 1965 for Pete's sake. It turns up momentarily earlier in the film but it's at that point I want to walk into the film, wave a flag and say, 'Stop! Stop! Wrong wrong wrong!'

It's not that the story up to that point is any more or less inaccurate than any other war movie (in all honesty it's not that far off a passable approximation, especially within war-film constraints, and it's not up there with Errol Flynn's infamous *Operation Burma*):[5] it's just that the tank looks so glaringly wrong, fifty tons (that's a guess) of incongruity. It jars, rends

---

[5] Flynn, though Australian, had decided that the war was not for him. His good friend David Niven quit Hollywood and went back to the UK to rejoin the army. *Operation Burma* featured Flynn as an American soldier parachuted into Burma and winning the war, which must have been news to the one and a half million British Empire troops in the Fourteenth Army.

asunder any pretence that the film is realistic – it's unmistakably from the wrong era and that's that. And it's a great shame, because plainly so much effort has gone into making the film look as good as it does. Loads and loads of effort. It was the first war movie to have a boot-camp approach to making the actors act a bit more like soldiers rather than work-shy show-offs with bad haircuts. They put in the effort. But sadly, wrong tank, game over.

However, no matter how wrong the Leopard might be in *A Bridge Too Far* it's not like the story-shattering and mind-bending *Battle of the Bulge*, a true classic of who-cares-what-really-happened film-making. For whilst its central scene of General McAuliffe, surrounded in the town of Bastogne, replying to the German demand of surrender with the one-word answer 'Nuts' is there, feeling like a weird nod to truth, in this film the Germans go to war in thinly disguised American tanks against other American tanks. Robert Shaw, playing implacable Nazi Colonel Hessler, talks (to other Germans) in accented English, but his men sing the Horst Wessel song in German – this is a moment maybe best described as more than a bit creepy; in *A Bridge Too Far* everyone speaks the language expected of them, though the Brits are all 'what-ho' and 'old boy' and the Americans talk ever so slightly less 'gee whiz'.[6] Shaw spends a great deal of time standing upright in the turret of his tank, looking chiselled and decisive against a lurid blue screen. God, it's terrible. In *Battle of the Bulge* you get the feeling no one is all that bothered about any of that stuff, really – it's 1965, after all, World War Two was ages ago. It's as if making a slapdash film is really just kind of OK, y'know?

The real, gripping story of the Ardennes offensive, the futile

---

[6] I blame Goldman who, great as he is, must have not been able to resist.

last-ditch attempt by Hitler to derail the Allied advance in the West by pushing them back to Antwerp and splitting the British and American armies with a bold surprise attack, is swapped instead for Robert Shaw's (wrong) tanks racing for an American petrol dump and being thwarted at the last moment. The Battle of the Bulge was a moment when the Allies were well and truly caught out: the Germans achieved complete surprise – because no one on the Allied side believed that you could get tanks through the Ardennes, even though the Germans had done just that in 1940, and because the Germans had been scrupulous about keeping the attack secret. Hitler had miscalculated what his armies would be able to achieve, but his aim – as it often was – was political: the Ardennes offensive was as much intended to knock the Allies' confidence and cause the alliance to fall apart as it was to gain territory.

If you like war films but know even a tiny bit about what happened in the Ardennes you might find yourself kicking over a telly. Or, indeed, writing a chapter like this. Henry Fonda is in this film, himself a naval war veteran, enlisting in 1943 and saying, 'I don't want to be in a fake war in a studio', which raises the question of how he reconciled appearing in this tripe that at best disrespects, if only by being really fucking lame, the people who fought in the Ardennes. The film does feature Otto Skorzeny, a sort of Nazi super-commando, and his unit who, dressed as Americans, drove American vehicles and infiltrated the American lines, but it seems to bung them in for entertainment value rather than for accuracy. The Ardennes battle was also characterised by atrocities committed by both sides: 84 American prisoners of war were shot by the SS at Malmedy. With grim inevitability, perhaps, the Americans also shot around 60 German POWs on New Year's Day 1945 in the village of Chenogne.

Skorzeny was the man whose unit rescued Mussolini from

his mountain-top prison in a glider raid in September of 1943: daring, audacious, faintly pointless. Gliders in World War Two had cornered a fair slice of glamour, despite being spectacularly dangerous.[7] They did a lot of the jobs that helicopters do these days and the Germans had led the way with them. Between the wars when the Luftwaffe was illegal they'd kept their piloting skills going in gliding clubs, and then when the war came they innovated and began using these unpowered aircraft to seize strategic targets.

A glider full of soldiers was a good way of delivering men somewhere unexpected in an altogether unexpected way. The successful capture of the fort at Eben Emael at a crucial strategic point on the Belgian-Dutch border on 10 May 1940 meant that suddenly everyone had to have gliders. The Germans had landed on the roof of the fort, and with 78 men and some explosives were able to keep the 650 Belgian troops inside cooped up and unable to use their guns to stop the German invasion. Gliders had the advantage over parachuting – if they landed safely and in the right place – of delivering a concentration of men all in one go, whereas parachuting would scatter men who would then have to form up. The British looked long and hard at the lesson of Eben Emael (Churchill firing demanding memos left, right and centre), took it to heart and in response used gliders enthusiastically, embracing them as the solution to the problem of how to deliver heavier weapons by air. In the end they built gliders called Hamilcars big enough to fly in small tanks or large anti-tank weapons, and landed men behind enemy lines and captured bridges – most famously Pegasus Bridge – and so on: though at

---

[7] There are way too many incidents of gliders slipping their tow ropes over the sea and ending up in the water, long before they got anywhere near crashing or landing upside-down or the anti-tank gun coming loose and crushing the men in the glider for anyone to say that they were a softer option than parachuting.

Arnhem this had been deemed too dangerous, a decision you can pretty confidently look back on as utterly wrong-headed.

Skorzeny, who sported a spectacular duelling scar on his left cheek and had been hand-picked by Hitler to spring Mussolini from captivity, had landed his gliders on a mountain top and overwhelmed Mussolini's guards without firing a shot – maybe the Italians guarding him had decided the Duce wasn't worth anyone getting killed over. A light plane then flew in and extracted Mussolini and Skorzeny. His next mission – which failed because Russian spy Nikolai Kuznetsov got an SS man drunk and persuaded him to tell him all about it – was to assassinate Churchill, Stalin and Roosevelt as they met at the Tehran Conference in October 1944. Their cover blown, the plan was abandoned.

After the war Skorzeny was tried for fighting in American uniforms – a war crime – and was saved by the testimony of the legendary Allied agent 'The White Rabbit', Wing Commander Forest Frederick Edward 'Tommy' Yeo-Thomas, who said he'd often worn German uniform as a disguise. Skorzeny briefly crops up at the start of *The Eagle Has Landed* rescuing Mussolini, prompting Hitler to demand a feasibility study on the assassination of Winston Churchill. Michael Caine's character Colonel Steiner is a sort of Skorzeny-lite; he intervenes and tries to save Jews on their way to the death camps, and has to go on the Churchill assassination mission as a kind of suicide-mission-type penance. His squad dress up as Polish paratroopers, in an echo of Skorzeny's Ardennes skulduggery.

However, if you want real drama, and from the actual as-it-happened Ardennes campaign – drama as in personal conflict, pride before a fall, vanity bringing a man close to ruin, overweening hubris – you could do a lot worse than the horrendous press conference that Field Marshal Montgomery gave shortly afterwards where he claimed to have rescued the

Americans. By this point in the war – having pulled off the biggest seaborne invasion the world has ever seen as well as the battle that followed it – he'd got pretty, no, incredibly big-headed (and pretty good at dealing with the Germans, especially in defence) and saw no reason why he shouldn't let everyone know how clever he was and how well he'd done. Once the German offensive had petered out in the Ardennes, Monty took it upon himself to hold a press conference to explain what he thought had happened. It was a disaster. Planting his foot firmly in his mouth – actually, it would be fairer to say he paced out the distance and then took a run-up – Monty said that the battle was 'the most interesting, I think possibly one of the most interesting and tricky battles I have ever handled'. He then said that American soldiers were 'as good as any others'. Ouch.

Montgomery would probably have got away with it too if there hadn't been a grain of truth in what he'd said – he had shortened and tidied up the Allied lines, consolidated positions and stopped the Germans breaking through to the river Meuse. However, the real set-piece scene-stealing heroics had been General Patton's efforts to relieve the American troops stranded in Bastogne, a mad dash, turning his army around in record time. Given how the Americans had first crumbled when the Germans attacked – 7,500 men from the 106th Infantry Division had surrendered – the way they had then sorted themselves out, turned themselves around and stopped the German advance was truly extraordinary. Monty had completely misread the mood, entirely living up to Churchill's description of his greatest general: 'Indomitable in retreat, invincible in advance, insufferable in victory.' The journalists who packed the tent sensed Monty's mistake instantly and set up about doing him over in the American press. His American rivals, who he'd been rubbing up the wrong way since D-Day, sensed a chance to have him sacked and almost succeeded in doing so[8] – threatening to resign unless Monty was replaced – something Eisenhower couldn't do politically. This would make a great drama with some ball-breaking American actors, an effete Brit, you could set the whole thing in a series of olive-drab tents . . . maybe I can see why this hasn't been made into a film. Maybe a telly play, then.

In order not to fall to the floor and foam at the mouth, I won't bother engaging with films like *Where Eagles Dare* which is, after all, an action movie, set in World War Two (in the same way that the critic-splitting, wish-fulfilling *Inglourious Basterds* was. I loved *Inglourious Basterds* because it completely wanted you not to take it as a war film but rather as a loony piece of film-making – a piece of art, even – the same way *Pulp Fiction* isn't a proper crime drama – um, no cops, anyone?). But when it comes to *Where Eagles Dare* there's no point trying to argue that Richard Burton is way too old and out of shape to be on a secret mission, it simply doesn't matter – it's not as though this is anything to do with the true history of SOE, or anything much. The fact that Clint Eastwood fells Germans like ninepins as they keep running up a staircase while he plasters it with bullets from his MP-40 is nothing to do with combat and its realities;[9] Clint dispatches something like 80 Nazis in this film, cars blow up when he so much as looks at them. That the Germans speak English and the English speak German without any discernible change in how they sound is, well, to help us

---

[8] Maybe the last word about how Monty handled things could go to the Germans, who credited him with stabilising the Allied front, thus making it harder for the Germans to press home their breakthrough (which sounds like he got things right to me, but hey, I'm a Brit and I would say that, wouldn't I?).

[9] I say this as someone without any experience, but a lifetime as a coward tells me that they wouldn't just keep running up the stairs after, say, the first one of their buddies was dispatched.

all to keep up. Don't panic, *Where Eagles Dare* is entertainment, don't panic, the good guys won – chill, everyone; the film's message is good guys win, even if they're puffy and out of shape and even though the German army consists of ninepins.

In a similar category, though nowhere near as preposterous, is *The Guns of Navarone*. The fact that David Niven was a veteran of the war, fighting with the Commandos and a shady outfit called Phantom, maybe adds gravitas. Or tells you that maybe, like Henry Fonda in *Battle of the Bulge*, he wanted the work and wasn't too bothered about the story being hokum. Niven himself said he wouldn't reminisce about what being in action was like, and that the US war graves in Normandy gave him 7,000 reasons for this. These films aren't worth tackling because they never made any historic claims. Therefore, the ones that stick in the craw are the ones that claim to be history.

In short, it must have been torture for my dad taking me to see *A Bridge Too Far*. How he didn't leap to his feet hollering 'Bollocks!' when the Leopard I tank appeared I've no idea – it would have been out of character, sure – but I do remember him pointing it out to me at the time. It must have been eating away at him then and there in the cinema. Because he is a war-film pedant, and so am I.

My last proper experience of paternal war-film ruination was when I tried to introduce dad to *Band of Brothers*. Not strictly a film, the TV series *Band of Brothers* sprang from the self-consciously gritty loins of *Saving Private Ryan*. There's loads wrong with *Private Ryan*, mainly in the form of plot holes, but the look of the thing and the effort that went into making sure there weren't any blundering Leopard I tanks shattering scenes was laudable. Shot in dulled colours, it sort of half-plays at being historically accurate. The visceral opening scene at Omaha Beach is unforgettable, though it is worth remembering that in the film the carnage lasts 20 minutes while at the real Omaha it lasted from first light through till the early afternoon when the Americans were able to stabilise their front. The landing-craft door opens and the murderous fire spews into the platoon, and the sense of the horror of the landing is palpable. Though really they're all too old to be Rangers (I can't help myself). There's no need to explain the story, everyone's seen it and the title is the one-line pitch for the movie anyway, as Tom Hanks and his perfectly-selected-for-maximum-character-conflict squad set off to, um, save Private Ryan (an incredibly ungrateful Matt Damon: if I were in his position I might find it hard to refuse as adamantly as he does). On their way to finding him they run into all sorts of what would be called scrapes if this wasn't a gritty war film that Steven Spielberg wants taken seriously. In many ways it's a very old-fashioned action movie going about its business in the guise of a war movie – or at least it would be if it weren't for the scene at the start on Omaha Beach.

Omaha Beach has rightly become the central feature of American understanding of the sacrifice in Normandy. The landing there, on the stretch of beach between Sainte Honorine-des-Pertes and Vierville-sur-Mer – 'Omaha' is just the code name – got off to a disastrous start. Like so many places that are almost notorious for their history, visiting Omaha Beach it's hard to disentangle what you might know about what happened there from how you see the place: maybe that's my way of saying it's one of those places where if there aren't ghosts, and even if you don't believe in ghosts, you bring some with you anyway. The bluffs where the German beach defences had been built are imposing, and if you stand where the German emplacements were the whole strand is laid out in front of you – you can see miles up the coast even on a dull day, all the way to the cliffs at Pointe du Hoc. At Omaha Beach the casualties were the highest suffered by the

Allies on D-Day. *Saving Private Ryan* has cemented its position at the heart of American – and certainly popular – cultural understanding of what happened on D-Day. As a result, what could be called myths have swirled around it and grown up to the point where even discussing it is tricky. Omaha Beach was very heavily defended, we're told. The German troops there were crack troops. Yet compared with what the British faced at Ouistreham-sur-Mere – or Sword Beach as it was called – Omaha wasn't the most heavily defended, and the landings at Omaha, being further west than Sword, didn't have the prospect of nearby German armour turning up and counter-attacking. There is a strong case for saying that the problems the Americans faced on 6 June were mostly of their own making: failed bombing runs, muddled tactics, disbanded squads – they'd broken up regular squads into landing teams under sergeants the men didn't know: it doesn't sound like much but it must have undone a lot of the training. Amphibious tanks were lost in mistimed approaches to the beach, depriving the Rangers of armoured support. (Voicing some of this stuff is controversial, to say the least.)

The landings turned so sour that for a period General Omar Bradley, who was in command of the American armies on D-Day, considered aborting them and diverting his effort to the other American landing site, Utah Beach to the west. Here things were going much more smoothly, partly because they'd landed in the wrong place that was less well defended than the intended sector. (That one always leaves me scratching my head: why not plan to land on the less-defended bit in the first place?) While the casualties are the thing that grabs your attention about what happened that morning, the truly amazing thing about what happened on Omaha Beach is how the Americans turned around this dire situation, overcame their momentary paralysis and took the beach, overpowering the German defenders and breaking out into the land behind it. This was down to the officers and men who'd survived the initial onslaught by being incredibly brave, and having the resolve, guts and energy to get themselves out of trouble. The ones we know about are the ones who were seen by men who survived. Brigadier General Norman Cota set the tone, going up and down the sea wall, waving his swagger stick and rallying his men with stuff like 'Gentlemen, we are being killed on the beaches. Let us go inland and be killed!' Eventually the Rangers were able to get themselves inland.

Naturally, *Saving Private Ryan* hasn't got time for all of this as it has a tale of rescue and redemption to tell. But the story of Omaha Beach is one that has huge resonance and has come to represent what happened on D-Day; and it's interesting to compare it with the 1960s star fest *The Longest Day* which attempts to tell, pretty straightforwardly, the whole of what unfolded on D-Day. *The Longest Day* is scrupulous in its account of D-Day, and while stuff has to be left out you do get a sense of the sheer scale of things, of the involvement of all nations on the Allied side (the French certainly get a very fair crack of the whip, their commandos seizing the casino at Ouistreham) and of the context of each component of the invasion. It's particularly good on the glider attack on what's now called Pegasus Bridge. It's probably worth noting that it came from a book by the same author that *A Bridge Too Far* was based on, Cornelius Ryan, who had perfected the style of telling war history by showing the personal set amidst the epic.

Band of Brothers, based on the personal memoirs of members of the US 101st Airborne Division, was what they call landmark television. It is, in my view – and in saying so I'm hardly breaking ranks here – excellent, though (let's be honest) there's no way Damien Lewis won the war on his own, in slo-mo with

29

haunting orchestra or not. Shot again in the grimy style of *Saving Private Ryan*, huge attention to detail went into the series – Tiger tanks were Tiger tanks not bloody Leopard Is (well, actually, they were brilliantly adapted Russian T-34 tanks, the chassis retained because it's very similar, but clad with a false body to be at a distance a dead ringer for the real thing, the driver's the wrong side is how you can tell, oh God, there I go again). The series follows the men of Easy Company from the Normandy landings right to Berchtesgarten, where they find the homes (and quite a bit of the stuff) belonging to the Nazi top echelons. Tom Hanks produced the series, clearly as some sort of long-term penance for *Bachelor Party*. (Exactly the kind of film and freedoms the Greatest Generation didn't lay down their lives for, though surely they wouldn't have minded some of THAT action before they embarked for Anzio – it's something you don't want to watch with my dad. Or, increasingly, me.)

Courtesy HBO®

Problem number one with *Band of Brothers* is the poster, the artwork, whatever you want to call it – the cover of the DVD. Look at these idiots. They're standing on the horizon, in plain sight. If you were the Germans, or even the Cossacks who found themselves fighting in Normandy against the 101st Airborne you'd have no problem shooting these suckers, or at least knowing where they were. I think there isn't a war film that has been able to resist the temptation of the skyline or horizon shot: they get all their best vehicles and line them along the horizon probably so the backers can see all their money up there on screen. In *A Bridge Too Far* the Sherman tanks in the background were fibreglass outline shells bolted to Land Rovers, so there was no other option than to film them in the distance in silhouette, like armoured hieroglyphs they could only go from side to side. Another classic war-film error that features in amongst others *The Bridge at Remagen*, a truly unfaithful telling of the truly amazing[10] story of the capture of the only intact bridge across the Rhine in the spring of 1945, is waving a white piece of paper or a map about at night, usually lit with the white light of a torch. This would not only destroy your night vision, it would be visible from the other side of the Rhine or wherever, inviting trouble. You just wouldn't do it, and if you did you'd be mad. Or in a movie.

But back to the *Band of Brothers* artwork: not one of them is porting their weapon properly in case of trouble, and they are all WAY TOO CLOSE TOGETHER. One hand grenade would do for half of these guys. This is a standard war-film problem that comes up again and again, but if a platoon spread out the way it might in the real world there'd be not a lot to film, even in IMAX. There'd also be scant dialogue – one thing that is

---

[10] And it *is* truly amazing. Look it up.

certain about *Saving Private Ryan* is that the whole platoon would've made it home alive if they'd just stopped bloody yakking. The Germans must have heard them coming a mile off, certainly in the scene when they attack the radar station. But then there'd be no drama, no story without the yakking, no moral dilemma openly discussed – no film. Spielberg might well be the master of visuals but if the characters don't say stuff to each other who knows what the film would be like. Like people going hiking invisibly and the occasional burst of frenetic violence.

But I'd bought the box set, and trusting in the very genuine-looking Tiger tanks I'd decided to try *Band of Brothers* on my father. The opening episode is the usual stuff about the training being tough and the martinet out of *Friends*. That's right, the martinet out of *Friends*. As a comedian I long to play serious roles, though I have every suspicion it's something I just can't do, and clearly David Schwimmer wanted to stretch himself with a serious, tough, chewy role, playing someone who is less eager to please than maybe Ross was (my dad didn't know who he was, by the way, not a clue, nor his monkey). Captain Herbert Sobel is the martinet who is incredibly tough on the men during training and in the end is called back to the US to carry on training new soldiers and is not given command. He seems to be brimming with tears the whole time – the episode seems to be suggesting that war brutalises all men, no matter the extent of the contact they have with it. When he's sent home he's heartbroken, but it seems fairly obvious that he is good at instruction, so it's all pretty understandable – the army values his training skill. The guys from Easy Company don't like him, but that is a classic way of instructing people in the military: you bind them together through hardship. Practice hardship, not actually the real thing, they're going to get plenty of that later. Maybe if they'd listened to Ross from *Friends* they wouldn't all be stood along the horizon like a bunch of idiots.

But I sat dad down to watch the episode when the men of Easy Company take part in Operation Overlord. They parachute into the Cotentin peninsula to capture the causeways connecting the landing beaches and the rest of Normandy – there are important crossroads to capture and artillery sites to suppress. The landing was disrupted – bad weather, inexperienced pilots (the Allied air forces very much saw the transport part of their job as unglamorous and wanted their best pilots for combat missions) and the general chaos of things happening for real, like enemy fire – and the men of both of the American airborne divisions ended up scattered all over the western end of the Normandy beachhead. It was so chaotic that the Germans were for a day or two completely bewildered by what was going on, the law of unintended consequences really doing its bit for the Allies. *Band of Brothers* amply conveys all of this, it does its best to get inside how the men felt, and all for the small screen, with the added bonus that it all really happened.

We'd never make one of these things in the UK. First of all, we don't have the money. Secondly, we can't quite bring ourselves to say they were all brothers and that. For us (and to my taste, to be honest) the war is best remembered with the doddering dignity of the Cenotaph, rather than high-production-values firefights with extreme close-ups and slo-mo of men looking doubtful and possibly hugging each other. After all, in Britain we know all too well the problems that an accurate film like *The Dam Busters* can throw up. (The Dog.) I want to talk about that but it's complicated and a hostage to people who actually really want to be able to say 'Nigger' out loud. I don't so I won't and that's the end of that. The fact that in reality almost half the bomber crews died gets forgotten somewhere along the line . . . ah, well. And they certainly didn't do it in order to be able to say 'Nigger'. There I go again. God.

That aside, *The Dam Busters* is a great, great war film, given that it was made in 1955 and that the whole thing was top secret – the Upkeep mine (rather than 'bouncing bomb') was something entirely unknown to the public and the movie had to come up with something that would fill the gap: unlike the ball in the film it looked more like a huge metal barrel. Similarly, edges were taken off Guy Gibson's character – he was very tough, very demanding, pushy, condescending towards non-commissioned officers (even pilots) and hadn't picked all of the crews himself. Not that that makes him and his achievements any less heroic or extraordinary, and he'd probably have stressed that there was a bloody war on – he was only 24 at the time of the raid, with huge responsibilities. But otherwise it is a very straight account of the raid, of Bomber Harris's reluctance to go ahead with it – the film serves the viewer a pinch of Bomber Command politics – of the bravery and ghastly sacrifice of the crews. Given that Bomber Command and its war had essentially been airbrushed from history, to have a movie such as *The Dam Busters* that was unflinching about the losses and the effects of the bombing campaign makes the war-film pedant's task a grimy, shameful one. So for people to bang on about the dog is, basically, not good enough.

Anyway. I sat my dad down to watch this episode of *Band of Brothers*, having enthused possibly a bit too much about the realism, etc. And it's fucking good, *Band of Brothers*. If a bit mawkish at times, but you can't complain. I thought I was onto a winner. And as they parachuted into Normandy and before they'd so much as landed dad got going. 'They're exiting that plane far too slowly.' Forget that the scene shows planes going down in flames, men baling out on fire, the pounding flak, the atrocious weather, the tension, the bravery, the men's resolve to go ahead and do the extremely dangerous thing because the world is at war – they're exiting the plane far too slowly. The thing is he was right. Dad used to be a parachutist. They try to get out of the plane as fast as they can so that when they land they aren't all scattered, especially at night. But it's not a great start, is it? I could feel tension rising in my parents' sitting room.

A couple of minutes later we hit the moment when I know there won't be any more *Band of Brothers* for this father and son. The impossibly chiselled, handsome and natural leader Dick Winters gathers together the men he can find in the darkness (these people did a night drop – incredibly dangerous, each of them carrying 200 pounds of equipment) and proceeds to try to figure out where they are and what to do. And that's when it happens. Winters's group of stragglers form up and make their way down a railway line. My father was unable to take the programme seriously after this. A railway line!! Never! It's noisy! It's obvious! There's no cover! You're visible! You'd be ambushed! They're all talking! They're too close together! And while this may convey the chaos of the night, the staggering about lost in the dark, the dispersed landing, the whole plan going wrong from the outset, even before contact with the enemy that no plan survives, as the saying goes, it's still plain wrong. Ross from *Friends* would be doing his nut.

Many of the men who dropped into Normandy that night found themselves lost, isolated from their units. They wandered about looking for other American soldiers, fighting the Germans they came across, or exercising discretion and avoiding them. They returned to their units over the next few days. How the 101st and 82nd Airborne Divisions acquitted themselves during

35

the Normandy landings is truly extraordinary, given how disorganised they found themselves after the drop and how lightly armed they were. But that first night a lot of them did a lot of wandering around which, if you put it on film, may well come out like a whole lot of nothing. And this brings us to another classic problem with being interested in war. In lots of ways it's like the solar system: for something so interesting it has huge great big swathes of empty dull nothing in it.

This is the thing. For every massive clash of tank armies on the broad Russian steppes there was the 400-mile trudge to get there. For every daring convoy ship evading the U-boats there were the days and weeks of sailing with nothing much happening (though this isn't to say these times would not have been full of tension and fear, just very little of what a film crew might call 'Action!' for). Before you graduated to bomber crew you spent months in training. For every daring parachute assault there were fifteen cancelled operations,[11] with men sitting around a lot, disappointed. If you visit the Cabinet War Rooms in Westminster what you will find is an underground, map-covered nerve centre, yes, complete with rows of different-coloured telephones, but before you get to it you are greeted by the War Cabinet committee room, the business end of Churchill's war. Where committees met and argued and discussed and harangued and settled on policy. And let's face it, endless committee meetings trying to decide what to do aren't interesting (which is why Hitler's way of doing things, ranting at people and relying on his intuition and bullying and sacking people, overruling his Chiefs of Staff – something Churchill never did – even though it lost Hitler the war and destroyed his country – even though

---

[11] This was certainly the case with Arnhem, which may be why the men of 1st Airborne embraced such a half-baked plan with such enthusiasm.

he had the best army[12] – is the thing everyone is interested in rather than the great big boring Allied committee meetings that won the war).

That this gets left out of war films is fine by me. But it's worth mentioning. In fact I feel duty bound to comment on it. I can't help myself. It's how I was raised.

---

[12] Or so we're told.

2. War, what is it good for?

ABSOLUTELY NOTHING?

So hang on, you're thinking. He likes war? Surely this is unremittingly boysie and puerile. Well yes, certainly, my interest began as a puerile boy (as if there's any other kind). And war is without a doubt a bad thing. It's good for absolutely nothing. Unarguably.

'War! . . . Huh! Yeah!' hollers Edwin Starr, and the 'Huh!' is indisputably the greatest 'huh' in all of pop music, far greater than any 'Huh!' that James Brown might have uttered: his were trivial, sex-oriented, man's world-ish, ultimately frivolous, indeed increasingly frivolous the more seriously he sang. Edwin's is political, indignant, righteous. All in a 'huh!' He sets the bar high with this opening 'huh', the 'yeah' that follows it isn't quite so interesting – pop music is littered with 'yeahs' and in all honesty this feels like a pretty standard 'yeah'. Perhaps Edwin needed to cut the 'Huh!' with something milder, given its great power and force, or he knew there was no point wasting anything extra on the 'yeah'. In Sixties pop music 'yeahs' are two a penny, there are 'yeahs' left right and centre, so maybe he thought the 'yeah' could only do so much. Perhaps the 'yeah' was him lowering expectations, given the fact that the meat of the thing is just around the corner. 'What is it good for?' Edwin chides: to be honest this is a rhetorical question, which nevertheless Edwin bundles in and answers anyway. 'Absolutely nothing! . . . Say it again!' If a rhetorical question is worth answering once, it's worth answering twice, yes? Yes?

The first time I heard this song was on The Tube, the long-gone but toweringly influential Channel 4 music programme in the 1980s. We would watch The Tube in my boarding house on Friday evenings, after tea before 'prep' (sitting silently doing homework in an orderly manner, crowd control dressed up as schooling – it worked for me, no complaints, learned my French regular verbs by rote, hasn't left me) and the hosts Jools Holland and Paula Yates beamed skinny-legged anarchy into the big telly we were all sitting around as if from another planet. As we sat in our pecking-order-arranged jumble (finishing your tea early meant getting a decent spot near the front, larger, tougher lads would sit on chairs up on the tables) what were we to make of all of this? Why were Duran Duran on again? Why did The Jam have to retire, they didn't look much older than the lads in the sixth form? Was this Malcolm McLaren fellow really claiming to have invented hip-hop? Was it meant to be this, um, sloppy? I mean, I liked Jools, he always seemed like someone who'd be a laugh to hang out with and Paula was undeniably foxy, but really? Could we not just finish an interview properly for once? This is doubtless my memory playing tricks, and as it came before the epoch-making wobbly-camera fest that was Network 7 (I think that was the name) it might not have been as loosely anarchic as I remember but I do remember Edwin Starr. In a self-conscious groovy soup of knowing winkiness, Starr seemed suddenly serious, earnest. Sincere, even. It stuck out like a sore thumb. It almost seemed gauche.

This is the greatest anti-war anthem of the lot. And it's an anti-war anthem too, not a pro-peace anthem. It's an important distinction: he's not shilly-shallying around and asking that we *Give Peace A Chance*, no, he's telling us what war is good for.[13] If ever there was a flawed proposition *Give Peace A Chance* is it – you *Give Peace A Chance*, it doesn't work out for you, Peace fails to deliver whatever it is you want from Peace (John and Yoko offer no clues as to what *Giving Peace A Chance* is going to deliver apart from Peace) and no one is ever going to *Give Peace Another Chance*.[14] After all, when bombing doesn't work they tend to switch to something else. More bombing, usually. Lots more. Despite the fact that the first lot of bombing didn't deliver whatever it was meant to. (It is something that vexes me endlessly that, having been bombed and stood up to it and been proud of the Blitz Spirit, the British expected the Germans to react any differently. Or the Serbs. Or the Iraqis. Or anyone else.) But if that doesn't work out, sometimes Peace might not even live up to expectations. It tends not to or war wouldn't keep breaking out – history is littered with people giving peace a chance and then giving up on it. Whatever, Edwin Starr has made his mind up and isn't going to plead with anyone over anything – he knows how he feels about war and is going to tell us straight. 'Listen to me!' he hollers, even though we already were listening – how could we not? Edwin is burning with his message and we are going to goddam listen.

This record bristles with anger, indignation, it crackles – though not like a bowl of Rice Krispies. And that's all the actual music writing I'm going to do. Writing about music is incredibly

---

[13] Absolutely nothing.

[14] Lennon is similarly vague about all this in his Christmas song, *Merry Christmas, (War is Over)* in which he and Yoko suggest that 'war is over, if you want it'. That'll make the Iranian Revolutionary Guard stand down, won't it? King Jong Un now thinking twice.

difficult, and music journalists all over the world make it look very, very hard every single day; it's rare you read a review of a record that leaves you any clue as to what it might actually sound like. You'll note I keep saying record, that's because records are records and always shall be. (This is non-negotiable). Talking about music is hard enough: and now that we live in the *X Factor* age where what gets talked about is tracks rather than songs, and vocals rather than singing (what else would the singing be? Anal? Elbowed?) it's got even harder.

Maybe the problem is an essential shortage of words that half-adequately describe music. Drums clatter or thud, I guess, they get bashed or whacked, but that's about as far as you can go with describing them. Guitars chime or growl, bass lines can be nimble or they can be throbbing. Keys tinkle, synths bleep or swell. Singing – how the hell do you describe singing? Soulful? Impassioned? Lifeless? Flat? Sharp? Wobbly? Shouty . . . ? I don't know. In all honesty you have to salute anyone brave enough to take on the mantle of music writer – they are doing their best, I'm sure, but it's still not telling you that much, is it? So to say the record bristles with anger and indignation probably isn't good enough, though it might get me a job at *Q* magazine. It's raucous, it's not smooth or delicate or light or namby-pamby. (Adjectives versus music we could call this bit.) Either way, it's impossible to describe (at least for me) so go and listen to it. Basically it sounds like a classic old Motown record before their stuff got all smoothed and blanded out, which I think coincided with them buying a real studio. Besides, you've heard it, everyone has.

Originally recorded in 1969 by the Temptations, *War* is a classic Motown track, in that it was recorded quickly, tried by one artist, passed on to another, rearranged, re-recorded and re-released until it was a hit. This was a pretty standard way of doing things at Motown and also, it's worth noting, at Stock Aitken and Waterman. (Remember them? It's about 20–25 years ago, they must be due some kind of horrible revival, surely.) The fact that this is how things worked at S.A.W., by the way, does not make them 'the same' as Motown. No, it doesn't. No. Sorry, Pete. The Temptations version did well on campus, as they say in America, but Motown sought to duck any controversy involving one of their biggest groups; The Temptations weren't in the business of causing a furore, no matter how tempting they might be. That meant that, briefly, *War* was a hit without a singer – Edwin Starr got wind of this, fancied a go, and that's the version we know now. With the Vietnam War at its height and Motown springing from black American culture and plugged directly into the mainstream, it's little wonder it was a huge hit. It's little wonder he looked so damned sincere on The Tube. And there was plenty for him to be sincere about.

During the Vietnam War,[15] African-Americans made up 11% of the US population but 12.6% of soldiers in the US Army, mainly serving in the infantry (and therefore doing most of the fighting, unlike in World War Two when they were pretty much kept away from any dangerous actual fighting for all sorts of absurd racist reasons, whilst their government was seeking to defeat a murderously absurd racist enemy). The US Army in Vietnam had a very long logistic 'tail' – people involved in getting the fighting men and the means to fight to the front, also known as REMFs, Rear-Echelon Motherfuckers – so if you were 12.6% of the army and in the infantry, that meant you were at the front line. That's progress for you, eh? Vietnam was an infantry war – the close country wasn't the kind of place for great columns of tanks – so the infantry, the 'poor bloody

---

[15] Which in Vietnam is called (roughly) The American War, naturally.

infantry', were having to do the fighting and take the casualties. The figures bear this out further. 1967 through to 1969 were the heaviest years for the US in Vietnam, and across the war the ethnic breakdown of casualties saw 'negro' soldiers at about 12.5% of the 58,193 killed. *War* went to number 1 for three weeks in the summer of 1970. Edwin Starr followed it up with a song called *Stop The War Now*, which sees him getting off the fence and recommending actual policy. I don't have the words to hand, but I'm betting it has a 'huh' and a 'yeah' or two in it, and a firm, no-nonsense call for the war to be stopped.

But the trouble with Edwin Starr's classic record is the rhetorical question that he then insists on answering. It was a question that bothered me the first time I heard the thing, growing up as I had done on war films and the righteous defeat of Hitler. After all, the Vietnam War had certainly been portrayed as a ghastly and wicked event, but one we definitely weren't part of. To my teen-brain he was singing 'The Vietnam War, what is it good for?': absolutely nothing, obviously. After all, it was nowhere near here, and *Rambo* was a piss-poor movie. The Vietnam War, in 1980s Bedford at least, seemed to belong to the 1960s and movies that we had to watch for some reason. It's not as though *Chariots of Fire* and *Gregory's Girl* on a double bill were addressing the horror of Khe Sanh. And why would they? Part of the problem with the Vietnam War belonging to the 1960s was that the way young people protested against it was used as a sort of litmus test of youth and my generation – it felt like we were being made to feel lousy for not having gone through anything so exciting. Like, thanks, grandpa. Not that there was much you could practically do about that on Pemberley Road in Bedford if you hadn't done your French prep.

But Edwin's question in general, well . . . And here's my

problem: on some level I reckon it can be pretty convincingly argued that war isn't good for nothing, and that it hasn't got only one friend, the undertaker[16] (and you have to admire the song's poetic licence there, really – there aren't many top-hatted chaps with tape measures on battlefields scouting for custom) and that if we're honest, no matter how many times you say it again, war isn't good for absolutely nothing. The obvious and cynical answer is that war is good if you're someone who lends money, makes weapons, profits from the economic distortions that the calamity of war brings; the military-industrial complex, you might say, the bankers, the finance houses. The undertaker, even. But war is good for some things: top of the list must surely be the destruction of Nazism.

This is, I'd say, undeniable. At the beginning of World War Two the most powerful European state was Nazi Germany – the Greater German Reich or whatever grandiose title they'd given it. By the end of the war it was gone. In ruins, destroyed, never to return and, it could be said, Nazism with it. When modern Western governments ask themselves whether foreign interventions work the answer is there: yes, Germany, 1945. And the answer offers a price tag, and a clue to how it is done as well – you rout and destroy its armies and materiel in the field, completely and utterly smash the place to pieces, burn its cities down, cut the country in two, re-educate the entire population, if necessary quietly rehabilitate some of the people you were fighting, hold show trials to make it clear exactly who's won and where the blame for the whole thing lies, then save its economy and rebuild it and occupy it for decades (in other words you have to do more than knock a statue over). This is how the most successful military intervention in recent history was achieved. Not that

---

[16] By which I'm sure Mr Starr means the chap who buries you, not the WWE wrestler who bears an uncanny resemblance to my mate Dom.

45

there was much of a choice during the Second World War. Hitler was determined not to repeat the defeat that Germany had suffered in the previous war – Nazism had its heels well and truly dug in – and as a result Germany was going to (have to) suffer a far worse defeat than in the previous war.

Hitler's government, well, Hitler – they pretty much did what he wanted, as well as 'work towards' what they reckoned he wanted – wasn't going to roll over easily, indeed he wasn't going to roll over at all. He had made it clear over and over again that his mindset was firmly wedded to Götterdämmerung one way or another, and that his country was going to go down with him. This hadn't always been the case, he hadn't necessarily got the war he'd been after in 1939 – development of weapons in the Third Reich was aimed at coming to fruition in roughly 1943 so he was ahead of schedule with his major European war. Hitler liked to rely on brinkmanship to win cheap victories, but once he'd got over his anger with the British for declaring war – he turned to his Foreign Secretary von Ribbentrop angrily and said 'Now what?!' – he'd embraced the business of taking on the world. When, after Stalingrad, it was becoming clear that his gambler's luck had well and truly run out he took to the idea of his country going down in flames with terrific gusto. Despite the occasional burst of wishful thinking that the Allies would fall out and the Cold War would come early, going to the bitter end seemed to be his preferred outcome. His army had sworn an oath of allegiance to him, he frequently called for his men to fight to the last round, and the spell held the Reich in his thrall right to the end. Even though by August 1944 it was obvious to any German with any nous that the war was lost, Hitler was able to insist that it wasn't over till it was over; he took this even further by saying finally that he'd put the German people to the test and that they'd failed, they'd let him down and that they had had what was coming to them. With war the only option for overthrowing someone like Hitler, democracies also have a real problem in that once they've started a war they're snookered by their own internal politics into staying in it (anti-war tickets are extremely hard to run on once a war is up and running). Yes, democracies can change their minds and reverse their way out of wars, but once they get fighting in the name of freedom they find it very, very hard to stand down. Afghanistan, anyone?

This means that amongst the myriad of miscalculations Hitler made was that he took on two major democracies and their allies, who then used him to define themselves against. It's worth remembering that in 1940, once France had fallen, there were only fourteen democracies left in the whole world: Great Britain, Eire, America, Canada, Australia, New Zealand, Sweden, Finland, Iceland, Switzerland, Mexico, Columbia, Costa Rica and Uruguay. What some call the current 'triumph of democracy' was never a foregone conclusion, and the 1930s had been a time of real doom and gloom about democracy's viability. Influential people in Great Britain occasionally shot admiring glances at the way that Mussolini[17] 'got stuff done' and wondered aloud whether the country needed a strongman leader to sort the country out. The apparent vigour of the German recovery under Hitler (flawed though it was, being based on rearmament) led some otherwise perfectly sensible people to wonder whether democracy had been superseded. The war intervened at the precise moment when democracy was going to have to have a firm word with itself and figure out what it stood for. And it took the Americans a little longer than everyone else to figure that out, too.

And this is another thing war has been good for. Because the

---

[17] Mussolini had described his brand of fascism as 'The Third Way'. Never heard that before or since, have we?

Second World War became this ideological clash between democracy and fascism (and I'm only leaving out the Soviet Union from this equation because everyone else did as it makes the whole thing easier). Hitler's legacy was a heightened sense of what democracy means and stands for, and how it needs checks and balances and protections against its own potential for fascist excesses – it must have surely been on every democratic politician's mind that Hitler had proved *his* democratic appeal in two elections before he seized power and then ditched elections, as promised, and proceeded to deliver on his manifesto. So war is straight up good for at least two things: destroying fascism and redefining democracy – it's no exaggeration to say that our understanding of human rights springs directly from having had to defeat a regime with such contempt for them.

Don't get me wrong: this isn't the reason Britain went to war in 1939, and it's certainly not why the Americans entered the war in 1941. It's a by-product. We didn't enter the war to save the Jews of Europe, or even to liberate Poland, and we had all sorts of reservations about defending France (there was a great deal of fatalism in political circles in 1930s Britain about how being allied to France wouldn't work out, and vice versa). We went to war because appeasement had failed. Appeasement had failed, in that it had neither satisfied Hitler nor had it prevented a war. It had also been wildly popular right up to the moment when everyone changed their mind and decided it wasn't – Churchill really had been a voice crying in the wilderness. Neville Chamberlain's government had been humiliated by the collapse of the Munich Treaty (having not really spotted that he'd already been humiliated by signing it) and the political consequences of not declaring war in 1939 could have seen his government fall. So to war we went. But the unforeseen consequence of Britain finally deciding that enough was enough in its dealings with the

Fuhrer, and entirely traditionally[18] siding with the other major European power against an over-mighty near neighbour, was that it found itself – once it had finished fighting for its survival – fighting for democracy. And for a lot of the time since then having to live up to what fighting for that ideal entailed – in many ways it raised the bar. So war is good for that.

War is also good for cat food, more specifically canned food. I'm allergic to cats but love baked beans so I can approach this one with proper balance: even so, perhaps less profound than the rebirth of democracy but nevertheless a hugely important by-product of war is canned food. War is good for that. During the Napoleonic Wars (and they're called that because he started them, yet somehow the French think he's just dandy) the French government found itself with huge citizen armies, and problems with how to feed all of their *citoyens*. A prize was set up with the winner bagging the grand total of 12,000 francs – a lot of money back then but, then again, money back then always is a lot of money back then – for a successful method for preserving food. In 1810 there was a winner, Nicolas Appert, who had figured out that food that had been boiled and bottled and the bottles then sealed would last. It had taken him something like 15 years to figure this out. 15 years. Appert had won great acclaim by preserving a whole sheep with his method. What he spent the prize money on I don't know. Glass wasn't ideal for transportation, let alone having cannonballs fired at it. But meanwhile, over in Britain France's enemies were taking the idea one step further – a merchant called Peter Durand earned himself a patent for tinning food in August of the same year.

---

[18] England/Britain/the UK has been going to war for this reason – along with making sure that the Lowlands (Belgium, the Netherlands, often the Channel ports) were in the hands of a power we were aligned with – since at least the time of Elizabeth I.

He sold on the patent three years later, but the idea had made it back across the Channel and the French army adopted tinned food with some slight problems: the can opener[19] hadn't been invented and cans had to be opened with bayonets or smashed open with rocks.

When the Napoleonic Wars ended it fell to the Royal Navy to carry on with the development of canned food, because it needed to feed its crews on long journeys, was open to innovation (we all know why Brits are called Limeys, of course) and because the process was too expensive for regular folks to afford. Eventually, thanks to the Crimean War, the American Civil War and the Franco-Prussian War the technology was perfected and became more affordable. So it's pretty much thanks to Napoleon's insatiable lust for military glory, the collapse of Anglo-Russian relations, the internal tensions between the Union and the Confederacy and Bismarck's realpolitik scheming that you can feed the cat the delicious juicy chunks she loves when you get in of an evening, heat up some baked beans and drink a cool beer. War, what is it good for, eh? Cat food! Say it again! Just don't ask me to look after your cat – or, if you invite me to dinner, provide a warning and/or antihistamines.

Then there's holidays. World War Two started more than 70 years ago with technology that looked like it really was from 70 years ago – open-cockpit biplanes for fighter planes and binoculars as early-warning systems – and ended with ballistic as well as cruise missiles, jet engines and in-plane radar. In six years flat most of the technology we take for granted in getting around the world was developed (which does make you wonder what could be done about global warming if people got their act together, or if, from another point of view, it was a crisis

---

[19] That took another 30 years.

WATCHING WAR FILMS WITH MY DAD

they were prepared to take entirely seriously rather than an excuse to try to get us to recycle).[20] Aircraft went from being made from fabric and sort of blunt to being made of metal and pointy, cabins were pressurised, guidance systems invented, navigation perfected. World War Two with its soundtrack of Glen Miller and air-raid sirens seems at this distance quaint and antiquated, but the breakthroughs in aviation design (and the massive spending that went into it) are how you can go on your package holiday.[21] Every navigational aid for getting bombs on target, every radar device designed to track incoming hostile aircraft means your flight can find its way to Malaga and then air-traffic control can bring your plane into the airport. One of the things that gave Britain the edge in the Battle of Britain – radar – means you can lie on a beach gargling warm bottled beer. From a can, too.

This extends to all technology. I'm typing this on a PC – a machine with which I have a typical if unoriginal love-hate relationship – and I have no idea how it works. At school I thought that the BBC Micros – that you had to code yourself – were a dead end. But they were of course the future. And where did the computer come from? Well, as untold stories go, Bletchley Park and Alan Turing is now one of the most told. 'The British went and invented the computer in order to crack the German codes' pretty much covers that (though of course because it was so Ultra secret[22] the UK was then unable to benefit from it commercially as the machines were destroyed

---

[20] The juice in the bottom of the food bin? The most disgusting substance on the planet.

[21] Read that last phrase in a clipped Pathé newsreader voice for the full effect.

[22] That's a wink towards those of you who know about Ultra. There's no real point me explaining Ultra and Colossus here, there will be something on Channel 5 about it shortly. Tuesdays, normally.

and the lessons and know-how deliberately repressed, along with the notion that any homosexuals were involved). The not-told-quite-as-much story of Tommy Flowers, the engineer who designed and built the Colossus computer, is pretty good too: at one point he was paying for much of the work himself – he was an expert on valve switches and became convinced he could build a machine with valves and had to get his hands on as many as he could. After the war the government gave him £1000 to recoup his costs – it wasn't enough and anyway he shared the money with other staff members who'd worked on the machine. When he went to the bank to get a loan to build computers they didn't believe the machine would work, and because his work had been as Top Secret as anything possibly could be, he wasn't able to tell the bank he'd already built one and done much to win the war in doing so. Ah, well.[23]

The trouble is, we are so blasé about computers: this one I'm writing on I frequently yell at, curse and slap, watch porn on, play games, listen to music, record music, watch TV, read the news and still take utterly for granted, so the idea they had to be invented is obscured by not really giving a shit due to their ubiquity and actual brilliance. This paragraph could now go on for several volumes as I spell out every ramification of the invention of computing (I won't). The song you might write in reply to Edwin's could go on for weeks, and would have iPhones, laptops, digital watches, modern cars, tamagotchis, televisions, those novelty electronic staplers, drum machines, sprinkler systems, broadband, tumble dryers and so on and so on. Aside from keeping the Allies one step ahead of the Germans, or

---

[23] I'm sure that neither Flowers nor Turing nor anyone else involved imagined that 70 years later computers would enable those emboldened by the anonymity of the internet to write to comedians online so they could say 'your an unfunny fat bald c*nt' let alone introduce them to hot singles in their area.

rather inside their decision-making loop, the cracking of the Enigma code (and others) by the invention of modern computing gave us everything else. Pretty much.

By now you've probably got my point, and I haven't even bothered with talking about medicine which always takes great leaps forward in times of war. The number of lives saved by the effective industrialisation of antibiotics, principally in the form of sulphonamide, probably run into the tens of thousands – American soldiers carried a first-aid kit with antibiotic powder in it that they would sprinkle into wounds. At a battle like Waterloo, the wounded (unless they were posh and/or officers, and pretty much no one posh wasn't an officer) would lie around groaning, clutching their guts or stumps and generally be left to their fate. If you broke ranks to tend to the wounded at Waterloo you were regarded as having deserted. To us this might seem barbaric, but infantry formations had to hold their shape and form to work effectively, and men leaving the line or square might cause a panic and the collapse of the formation and a rout. Descriptions of what Waterloo was like – and Napoleonic warfare in general – mainly boil down to whoever stood their ground the longest in the face of utter horror and/or manoeuvred their way through the hideous carnage tended to win. Having marched around chasing each other, even trying to run into one another and thus confront one another, armies would form up opposite each other and blast and blat and snipe and charge at each other, firing cannonballs into infantry lines or squares to try to destroy and disrupt the formations, crumbling away at the other's lines until something gave way. (The Duke of Wellington's answer to this was to try to hide at least some of his men in the lee of the downward slope of a hill – at Waterloo they lay down in the wheat, keeping them out of range of the enemy cannon and fresh for later in the day to do something

53

decisive.) Huge blocks of infantry would march and fire at each other, trying to force each other back, or when they were charged by cavalry they'd form squares bristling with bayonets to repel their attackers. A man breaking ranks to tend to a fallen comrade would undermine the formation's shape, and one man running, for whatever reason, might cause others to run. A square that disintegrated in the face of a cavalry attack was lost. So the wounded were left where they were.

A hundred years later there had been a revolution in how the wounded were treated, via Florence Nightingale, Mary Seacole et al., and in World War One you might win a medal for rescuing the wounded (often under fire). Two centuries later and you have battlefield medicine in Afghanistan that would be unimaginable to the men at Waterloo, and post-operative care and physio way beyond anything that men in the Second World War, even the Falklands War, might expect. This stuff is all pretty obvious, perhaps.

A not quite so obvious medical thing that war is good for is the rave scene. I was twenty during the so-called Second Summer of Love in 1988 (just the title put me off: the first one had looked grubby when I was a teenager, and at more than 45 years' distance the 1967 Summer of Love looks grubbier and more embarrassing than ever, what with all the participants now being ancient) and missed it entirely for a variety of reasons. I was in Edinburgh performing in a thinly attended sketch show. This was just fine by us at the time: my first day at university I had run into Richard Herring and Stewart Lee fresh back from Edinburgh – they had returned garlanded with success and acclaim, and their sketch group was playing to packed houses. What they omitted to tell anyone (wisely or maybe they just didn't see why they should) was that in Edinburgh they had actually been performing to up to as many as seven people on a daily basis. This didn't matter to them, it seemed, and hadn't dented their confidence one bit, so a year later my sketch group was quite content to play to tiny houses. If I recall correctly we were only outnumbered by the audience on one occasion; there were five of us, in case you're wondering. The show went on. You've no idea how exciting it was.

While we were serving this gentle invisible apprenticeship everyone else was raving. At least, this was the impression you'd have got if you watched the telly fragments about it – if you read the music papers then it was wall-to-wall raving. And at the heart of the scene was E. My attitude to drugs when I was at Uni was one of basically petrified conformity: in this I am best described as scared and square. Now it's more enlightened, best summed up as petrified-you-can-do-what-you-like-within-reason-please-be-careful. Added to this I am not a fan of dancing. Dancing is the moment where self-consciousness about lack of coordination trumps all show-off instincts I undoubtedly possess.[24] So the idea of a drug that made you want to just dance all night could not have more perfectly cross-referenced my purest anxieties. The basic worry that it might kill me whilst doing something utterly cringeworthy was enough to make me grateful that I'd counted myself out of that summer's youth revolution performing to next to no one in a basement, but the dropping-dead part was never really the problem. Not for me rushing around the M25 (at the time a highway of utter novelty) from phone box to phone box to find out the secret location of that night's rave. Yes, phone boxes. They organised this game of cat and mouse without mobiles or social media. Not for me dodging the cops and necking handfuls of pills. No, we had a sketch show to do, thank you very much. As well as rather

---

[24] This is why no matter how powerful my show-off urges might be there is no way on earth you'll ever see me on *Strictly*. It's not even the sequins.

delicious sandwiches from a particularly good deli on the Royal Mile. And a drug that was an abbreviation? No, thanks.

And E wasn't its only name, of course. Or its only abbreviated name. E – ecstasy – is also known as MDMA. A friend of mine who is an enthusiast for the stuff and is amused and bemused by my twitchy refusal to join in is adamant that MDMA is the proper stuff, and won't even consider so-called E. The military are fond of abbreviations and acronyms – that's an understatement, they simply wouldn't be happy without them – NATO is only the tip of the iceberg. If you visit militaryacronyms.net you'll find something like two hundred on the A page alone. The supreme commander of NATO is called SACEUR – Supreme Allied Commander EURope. That one is at least decipherable. But when you immerse yourself in the world of the military acronym they offer acronyms within acronyms, like Russian dolls: for instance – SEDSCAF. SEDSCAF stands for Standard ELINT Data System Codes and Formats. So to understand that acronym you have to know what ELINT is (don't worry, I looked it up, it's Electronic Intelligence). There's a whole book in the culture of military acronyms, and you're not reading it. MDMA's origins, real and mythical, are mixed up with the military, and this may or may not be the reason it's called MDMA, it could just be that Methylenedioxymethamphetamine is a bit of a mouthful.

Originally conceived by German drug company Merck to treat abnormal bleeding, MDMA according to myth was then used on German soldiers in World War One. From our perspective this seems odd: why would you give a drug to soldiers that would make them dance in an unabashed and foolish manner? But since time began armies and navies have relied on various substances to get them through combat. Vikings would go into a berserker rage by eating magic mushrooms and drinking loads of booze. Booze, after all, makes you brave (or, if you're being technical, lowers your inhibitions): this applies to the singles bar as much as it does to the battlefield. Rum was a central part of the Royal Navy's culture until 1970. So I suppose MDMA's mood-altering powers – cheering people up whatever the horrors around them might be – makes sense. Except it didn't happen. The patent lapsed – and it wasn't until the 1950s that the US military started trying it on people.

But other drugs ran rampant. LSD and the CIA (hooray! more acronyms!) is well-worn conspiracy-theory territory, a great deal of it true, and because of lysergic acid's freak-out properties it has long hypnotised and fascinated clever people. More prosaically, amphetamine – speed – in the form of Benzedrine was regularly doled out to Allied soldiers during the Second World War for obvious reasons: it keeps you awake and alert. Though it can also make you jumpy and see things: probably not so brilliant if you're armed. The Germans, meanwhile, were dishing out methamphetamine, under the brand name Pervitin (it must not sound pervy in German). Because there was a war on and because it does keep you awake and alert the side effects were something that no one was particularly interested in; someone who might have wanted to know what the side effects were was Hitler, who had regular injections of methamphetamine during the last three years of his life. Given that all the footage of Hitler from before 1942 shows us a jerky-limbed, carpet-chewing, swivel-eyed loon it's a wonder that his doctor thought he needed it.

The Japanese had a similar attitude and millions of Philopon tablets were handed out to workers to improve their productivity. This carried on into the 1950s and at the same time a huge military stockpile of the stuff got into the hands of the Yakuza. Speed went from being something for soldiers for winning wars to being an illegal stimulant and around the world it went underground. Cheap and in pill form it was a working-class drug: Northern Soul Mods – especially when written about by sensation-hungry newspapers – were into speed. Having been to Wigan it makes me wonder what it would be like being in Wigan and on speed: like living in two separate time streams, perhaps. When you watch footage of The Who at the Isle of Wight Festival the audience are stoned, lying in a puddle, dressed in grubby cut-price kaftans. They're listening to music that stoned people themselves simply couldn't make – Keith Moon's whirling-dervish drumming isn't the sound of navel-gazing giggles and the munchies, it's the sound of someone who simply can't stop.

If the 1960s counterculture achieved one thing, apart from spawning acres of tedious reminiscence and hideous self-importance on the part of its participants (I mean, really, stop going on about it, grandpa, you didn't invent sex, logic says you simply couldn't have, and you're not the first people to have got out of your tree or showed your bums), it made drugs normal. Not socially acceptable, not legal, but normal, usual – existing side by side in a parallel reality that politicians aren't allowed to acknowledge.[25] By the late 1980s I might have been petrified, square, numb with silly fear, but more importantly the stuff was out there if I fancied it. I didn't, I couldn't, but for those who wanted to when MDMA showed up again at this time, speed, along with marijuana or whatever you want to call it, coke and scary scary heroin, it seemed cuddly and charming by comparison (I suppose: it terrified me – dancing! Help!). We had been told that heroin would not

---

[25] I was cannon fodder on a pilot for a panel show a while back, where some political types argued about drugs. When the cameras were rolling they churned out the usual dull drivel about prohibition. Off camera they were perfectly sensible about it all. It was entirely dispiriting and unsurprising. The thing wasn't even for broadcast.

only kill us, it would turn us into ugly vampire types. On reflection this was probably preferable to what MDMA could do to you, and I'm sure if it hadn't been so very, very scary I'd have tried it (obviously not).

But the other thing war is good for is entertainment. It has sat at the centre of entertainment for as long as there have been stories to tell and plays to perform. Homer. Shakespeare. Cinema (more on that later). Marching music. The 1812 Overture, and pop music too – songs. Anti-war songs, even. So even those who don't like war, who think that war is good for absolutely nothing (say it again) can turn it to their wheel – and have a number-one hit record that then haunts them for the rest of their career.

None of this, of course, is a reason for starting a war. The notion that the US President sits in the Oval Office and while he decides where next to invade or generally blat with bombs or drones from a vast distance he also weighs up the potential side benefits is a silly one at best. Now nobody thinks that except maybe Noam Chomsky, Oliver Stone and those people who say that absolutely everything that happens in this world is a 'false flag' operation because – in a nutshell – they're idiots. You may well have decided some three or four thousand words ago that this chapter is drenched in wearying cynicism and you want it to stop. War is bad, of course it is, I'm not one of those idiots saying that what would sort the younger generation out is a nice spell in the trenches. But just because it's bad doesn't mean good might not come out of it – it's an ill wind, etc. Just ask its only friend, the undertaker. And the films! The books! The toys! The TV!

3. You only sing when you're winning

N-N-N-NINETEEN

Although I was unaware of it as I painted model Spitfires with my tongue sticking out of the side of my mouth, American war films in the 1970s were undergoing a radical change of gear. Instead of simply looking back at World War Two like British war films did they had a war happening right there in front of them to deal with. While we were still telling ourselves how plucky and persevering we had been back in the 1940s, America was addressing the godawful mess it had got itself into. Aged eight, I have to say I was unaware of the new wave of Hollywood auteurs – *Taxi Driver* hadn't made it into the Home Counties' collective junior consciousness as far as I remember. Jodie Foster was Tallulah in *Bugsy Malone* and that was about it. Post-Watergate disillusionment and cynicism were creeping into everything and throwing up the generation of great directors who now stalk the cinema (if I remember any signs of this at all it was a huge *Jaws* poster in Caracas where we lived for a few months at this time). But there was no way I knew about

61

Francis Ford Coppola's epic *Apocalypse Now* and if I had known about it I expect I'd have thought it was a bit long and why was there a tiger in it anyway?

Apocalypse Now is an amazing film, no doubt. The classic scene of Robert Duvall's Air Cavalry swooping in to deliver fiery mayhem – the whole movie unarguably drunk on its portrayal of the glamour of war and men's love of war, of the hot thrills of firepower, the problems of divided loyalty and conscience, the line between heroism and lunacy – is thrilling stuff. As 'The Ride of the Valkyries' blasts out of the helicopters' speakers and the choppers bank in to attack you almost wish you were there and you are hugely grateful you're not. It's quite a trick to pull. It's a hard film to get too war-film-pedantic about – the events are fictional but the attitude and the whole dramatic thrust are so powerful that it makes it easy to stop worrying about whether the soldiers have the right carbines or the helicopters aren't quite the right models for the Air Cavalry. As Duvall's Colonel Kilgore seems to be running his own kind of private army cum surf club, I'm loath to get too picky about the whole thing. And it is all excellently done. But for all the pyrotechnics the whole point of the film is to tell us that war is bad. Very bad. It's so bad that it is an obscenity. In fact, it's so obscene that it's made Marlon Brando hide in a shack upriver somewhere and mutter to himself endlessly in the dark about just how bad it is. Without having bothered to learn his lines or read *Heart of Darkness*. That bad.

Now, none but a pinhead would argue that war isn't bad (I'm relying on you having taken the last chapter of this book at more than face value, obviously). But why were American war films saying this all of a sudden? Sure, war had been depicted as hell, tough, grim, pitiless, merciless, bloody, capricious, terrifying, brutal and dangerous in Hollywood movies up to this point, but out and out bad? Evil? Wrong? Epic war caper *Kelly's Heroes* was, for all its US-soldiers-robbing-a-bank-of-ill-gotten-Nazi-gold grooviness, utterly sure that they were the good guys and the Germans were the bad guys. Similarly, films like *Catch-22* – a noble attempt to cram Joseph Heller's hilarious zigzag novel into a film with a sort of beginning, a kind of middle and something resembling an end (and added Art Garfunkel) – makes it clear that the Americans for all their corruption, licentiousness, insane regulations and careless destructiveness were still not as bad as the Germans. Not quite. (That's the way I see it, to be honest – I could be wrong.) But by the time *Apocalypse Now* comes along, and certainly by the time Stanley Kubrick has got his teeth into *Full Metal Jacket* war had gone literally from good to bad.

Neither of these films is about the Second World War, of course – unless you regard them as about all wars in a chin-stroking allegorical manner. Their setting is most resolutely that of the Vietnam War. And the crucial thing about the Vietnam War – and I think the reason why all of a sudden war isn't such a jape, with Frank Sinatra riding trains and Clint Eastwood dispatching endless scuttle-helmeted stooges or Donald Sutherland groovily helping himself to Nazi gold – is because the Americans weren't winning. Why they were there was muddled, what the point was was seemingly obscure and the enemy were proving extremely difficult to deal with (and not fighting battles in an orderly manner like the Germans did despite being led by an identifiable loony with a civilisation-sized death wish) – and losing was indigestible. The Vietnamese were making the Americans do the thing that superpowers can't stand: doubt themselves. And a war you're not winning might somewhat undermine the idea that war could possibly be good, or at the very least worth it. You only sing when you're winning.

63

There had been a major starry attempt at making a pro-Vietnam war film, *The Green Berets*, which is as watchable as anything with John Wayne in (not very). I don't get John Wayne. His is a mysterious charisma: he's stiff, he has tiny dead flinty eyes and his delivery isn't what you'd call versatile. To be honest, you have to admire an actor who uses one flat tone all the way throughout his career. Perhaps it's the ultimate kind of versatility in an actor: no mucking about, I can do this and I can use it for everything, happy, sad, excited, sarcastic, romantic, whatever you want.

Respect to the Duke. Is this how one day Tom Cruise will appear to our grandchildren? John Wayne is way too old in this movie to be running around assaulting enemy positions and cracking wise with much younger men, but there he is, staggering around with a rifle tucked up under his armpit like it's a Winchester and he's out hunting Redskins, and generally being completely unbelievable. He's even older and more absurd than he is in *The Longest Day*, where at least he'd got a part playing a parachuting colonel who'd broken his ankle on landing so he could be hauled around on a cart, an artful disguise for his altogether unathletic demeanour. But *The Green Berets*,[26] shot a fair bit on a sound stage[27] and for some of the action scenes in that 'we've put a filter on the camera so it looks like night but we all know it's broad daylight' look, when put up against *Apocalypse Now* looks prehistoric. It also suffers from a sort of goody-two-shoes feel. It is in favour of the Vietnam War and war and soldiers in general, and hey – how could it be? Although the war wasn't yet lost it certainly wasn't cool. It's a square film for squares, and no amount of drawling Duke-action could make up for it.

As well as being all literary and being based on Joseph Conrad's

---

[26] Pronounced 'Burr-ays'. Ugh.

[27] There's that unmistakable sound of their voices and footsteps off the back wall.

Heart of Darkness right down to its plot of a special mission upriver to find an AWOL VIP,[28] *Apocalypse Now* drew on *Rolling Stone* writer Michael Herr's experience of Vietnam for some of its attitude. Coincidentally, at school we had read his book *Dispatches* for O-level English – we had been doing war and literature, so had also had our compulsory 1980s English-teacher dose of George Orwell doing his bit in Catalonia. But Herr's book was much sexier – it had Jimi Hendrix records in it and soldiers whose helmets said stuff like 'Yea though I walk through the valley of death I shall not fear for I am the meanest motherfucker in the valley'. Fifteen-year-old lads in Bedford were suckers for this stuff. Herr's prose was direct and frank, about death and injury and tension, as well as American soldiers' self-medication and disillusionment with the war. It was unvarnished in the way men spoke; it didn't shy away from the casual racism of American officers and men towards their own soldiers as well as their enemies and their allies: 'the Gooks and the Dinks'. It was pretty clear he enjoyed the excitement of it all – but then, he never had to do any actual fighting so maybe that helped. It would have certainly helped me. His writing was sparse and gritty – a long way from Orwell's deliberations and realisations in Spain about the true nature of POUM and all the conflicting factions on the Left. *Dispatches* was exciting because it was exotic, peopled by 1960s crazies and potheads and Marines with thousand-yard stares, tales of battle tinged with dope and rock 'n' roll: impossibly exotic. Herr was at Khe Sanh, where it seemed the Americans were going to repeat the earlier French disaster at Dien Bien Phu – surrounded, supplied only by air, trying to draw the North Vietnamese Army into a decisive set-piece battle – and he paints a vivid picture of a strategy teetering on the

---

[28] I've always felt I'd be good at writing those very short film listings.

brink of disaster and no one really knowing why. In a World War Two book men might grumble and bitch about the rations and that but they'd fight to the last round to get the job done and so on, because they knew what the job was (and we know in our hearts it was worth it because – you got it – we won).

More than this, unlike Orwell in Spain which seemed like really old news, *Dispatches* was also about a war that had just happened and that everyone said America had to 'get over'. It was a fresh wound. No one ever seemed to earnestly wonder whether Vietnam would ever get over it, whether they were making movies that might help them 'move on' but there you are. Mind you, you do want your superpowers to get over stuff that's bothering them, it tends to be best for everyone if they're happy. Even now things get compared to Vietnam – Afghanistan has been required to stand in for Vietnam for both the Soviet Union and NATO. God knows how the Vietnamese must feel about that. I don't suppose anyone has asked them.

I saw *Apocalypse Now* at my friend Mike's house. We were probably doing some light skiving from the CCF or cross-country. We used to sign up for more than two sports and play them off against each other – it was a genius scam worthy of a duo of master criminals, you'd say you were at the other, and do the odd token run to show willing. It bought us Tuesday and Thursday afternoons to muck about. Mike's family were right there on the cutting edge and had a VHS. Mike had a copy of the *Thriller* video and having marvelled at it maybe once or twice we then began to find it increasingly hilarious, and then once we'd laughed ourselves out we would put on *Apocalypse Now* as our main feature. I don't remember getting to the end: I'm sure we watched it up until they went upriver and the film slows down and they talk about making sauce and then the tiger appears and then we rewound to the bit with

'The Ride of the Valkyries'. This was because we were callow youths and that whole sequence functions very well as a big-explosions action movie but when it then turns elegiac and philosophical it gets, um, a bit boring. But we had seen *Apocalypse Now*, its message had made it to Bedford. War was bad, man!

Then, in the late 1980s, we were all told breathlessly that the war film had yet again been revitalised and saved and rebooted (though no one called it that then) with Oliver Stone's *Platoon*. This time it was internal, personal, not epic (read 'cheaper', perhaps). I went to see it two or three times when it was released and I definitely thought it was unlike many of the war films I'd seen before. It was compulsory viewing. *Platoon* smouldered with self-righteous anger and fury, self-conscious brooding, and absolutely no real regard for what on Earth it might be like for the Vietnamese having a paranoid superpower smash the place up for more than a decade. The movie is all about how bad it was for GIs, how sad it made them, how the whole thing was rotten to the core and how it made the men feel alienated and disillusioned. It drew directly on Oliver Stone's experiences. I mean, I get that it might well have been terrible for Oliver Stone, but did we need to have to feel so terrible too? Sheesh.

I may well be wrong, but if the Americans had won in Vietnam would this film have even been made? Perhaps it's precisely because this is where American war films and culture had ended up, dismayed at how Vietnam had turned out, that they found themselves burrowing further back in time to World War Two to make themselves feel better about war. To resolve their feelings about it. *Saving Private Ryan* feels like it is an antidote to *Platoon* – there's no doubt at any point that Tom Hanks and his men are doing the right thing: even though they earnestly debate it for what feels like three-quarters of the film it's not seriously in doubt. The clue is in the name of the film, after all. It's not an anthem to doomed youth. The film ends with everyone convinced that they're doing the right thing, from the hardbitten sergeant played by Tom Sizemore, through the whole cynical section to the wide-eyed peacenik interpreter played by the skinny bloke off of *Lost*. Regardless of the gory soul-sapping horrors of war as depicted in *Saving Private Ryan* war is a good thing – Tom Hanks may have the shakes but it's all worth it. It's for defeating Nazis. Perhaps Spielberg felt that having brought dinosaurs back to life from traces of their DNA in *Jurassic Park* he could do the same with the World War Two movie. It's as if *Saving Private Ryan* is Hollywood getting over Hollywood getting over Vietnam. You can't imagine this film being made about the Vietnam War. And then there's *Rambo*.

Yes: *Rambo*. The first movie – *First Blood* – is a good enough poor-sod-comes-home-from-war-can't-fit-in-goes-ape-shit-with-a-machine-gun-turns-out-he's-been-betrayed-by-those-in-the-know-blah-blah potboiler. Mike and I saw this at the cinema – when Rambo stitches his arm back up I remember Mike hissing, 'I thought this was meant to be a fifteen?' Stallone's wounded-animal stare and huge knife made for a strangely gripping film, though there's the astonishing and incomprehensible breakdown scene at the end which I bet no one has ever sat through and said 'Ah yes, old chap, marvellous, I got all of that.' Yet somehow this brand of boss-eyed baloney became seen as a legitimate expression of post-Vietnam angst. God, America's odd. Or complicated. Or oddly complicated. Or complicatedly odd. Again: what we were meant to make of these films in mid-1980s Bedford Christ alone knows. The big British films at the time were the likes of *Gregory's Girl* and *Chariots of Fire* which I saw on a double bill – as mentioned in chapter 2 – and while they were deeply British movies, and said some deeply British stuff about Britain, as well as getting off with girls in Scotland and running in slo-mo on a beach, you could hardly say they were trying to exorcise national angst in an exciting entertainment form the way Stallone's films were. There's a sad lack of explosions filmed from several angles and cut together rapidly in either. Nor a montage with a pumping rock soundtrack. And anyway, as if a few bombastic movies could fix a thing like a country's broken heart?

'And if the Americans find losing a war difficult' as the Pub Landlord has been known to remark, 'they should try winning one and then fading into obscurity while their ally takes all the credit.'[29] As the Rambo films got bigger and noisier and crazier – and there's no way they fall under the umbrella of war films, you're right – and as Stallone also battered the shit out of various Cold War stooges in his other guise of Rocky (another series of films that started out reasonably enough) it seemed that the way America was going to get over the Vietnam War and through the Cold War wasn't by chin-stroking heavy voice-overed introspection like in *Platoon* but by the braying rattle of a machine gun you didn't need to reload, deafening explosions and monstrously heavy-handed not even bloody allegory. It is perhaps a relief that we aren't permanently bombarded with how terrible the Vietnam War was for America any more: though it's taken Iraq and the War on Terror to displace it. It did always have me wondering what it had to do with me: the people from the 1960s didn't half like to bang on about how their decade was the coolest – making it pretty clear that they thought we were living in a crap one. Yeah, well, thanks a lot.

In British popular culture what we got in response to the

---

[29] We do, every now and again, agree on stuff. This is one of those occasions.

Vietnam War was quite different. What we got was Paul Hardcastle and *19*. 'The average age of a US soldier in combat in Vietnam was 19 n-n-n-n-19'. That stuttering sampled voice, cheesy keyboards, blippety drum machine, mention of Khe Sanh. Britain took the whole barrage of American culture trying to process its tragic experience and fed it into the ever-reliable British pop-music grinder and out popped a number-one dance floor filler. And on the back of this huge smash came Simon Fuller, Paul Hardcastle's manager, who in honour of their breakout hit called his management company Nineteen. Who in turn discovered The Spice Girls and now manages David Beckham, Lewis Hamilton and Andy Murray.[30] So if ever you want to know how the Vietnam War affected us – there it is, right there, in black and white. JFK's decision to back the South Vietnamese government with military advisers and the Johnson government's expansion of this effort and the draft and Agent Orange and the rest led directly to David Beckham on a billboard in his underpants. War – what is it good for?

---

[30] Every year the good luck messages come to me on Twitter, and this year I spent a good week being congratulated on my win.

4. Armchair Generals

TEA, CAKES AND FLANKING

MANOEUVRES

The First Gulf War? Remember that? Operation Desert Storm (catchy American code name right there – the British name for it was Operation Granby, dear oh dear, not snappy at all). It was at the start of the 1990s, a decade that when I was a lad seemed impossibly far into the future. After all, the Tom Baker *Doctor Who* used to be set in 1980, an unimaginably distant and unrealisable time, and the eye-popping *Two Ronnies'* nightmare-vision-of-the-future-sketch 'The Worm That Turned' in which women ruled the world was set in – gasp! – 2012. Pictures of the early 1990s which at the time didn't look or feel dog-eared at all now show an era that's decidedly dodgy. Mainly my hair.

We'd just had the fall of Margaret Thatcher and the arrival of her successor John Major, who radiated a sort of benign cluelessness and was seen as a kind of welcome light relief after more than a decade of *Sturm und Drang*. Though the last thing she'd done, pretty much, was persuade the not at all gung-ho

George Bush senior (a former head of the CIA and a far more worldly and seemingly weary figure than his alarmingly lively son) that he needed to stand up to Saddam Hussein and not accept the invasion of Kuwait: 'this aggression will not stand' was his catchy slogan at the time. Soundbites have got snappier since. Well, the First Gulf War coincided with when I was living in a post-university house. We were a bunch of paint-still-drying-graduates arriving in South-east London to try and get our careers going/figure out what on Earth we were supposed to do, whilst doing our damnedest to maintain a student lifestyle. (I'm not just speaking for myself here, it was all of us, even those of us who ended up in really rather serious jobs.) It was one of those houses in which people would deep-fry eggs, leave the front door open, and if we ran out of toilet paper no one would do anything about it, except maybe wipe their arse on some newspaper. Happy days.

Several things strike me about Desert Storm. First of all, compared to many events that followed it, it all seemed pretty clear-cut: the Iraqis, protesting that Kuwait was in fact part of Iraq actually, had invaded Kuwait and wouldn't leave, so the concerned nations (concerned about the oil price, but you know, if everyone drives a car, uses plastics, relies on oil, of course they might well be concerned, the fact it leaves you feeling all grubby about it is an added bonus, surely?) decided to boot them out. It seems so straightforward, so simple. Compared to the collapse of Yugoslavia that ran across the decade it was black and white: unlike the maps of Yugoslavia, a sort of ethnic crazy paving, even the borders in the Gulf were straight. Perhaps because it all appeared to be so clear-cut it probably meant that no one seemed to imagine that it might open a massive can of unfinished-business worms.

Secondly, this war took place before the internet – before

dial-up, even. The cutting edge of tech in our house was a fax machine and a dot-matrix printer that would burp and rattle away. One of the guys I was living with, an alarmingly bright character called Danny, was one of the (probably) seven or eight people in the UK who, in 1991, knew that the internet was coming. He would talk about .exe programs and we would nod and hope that we understood and that he might be right. I would shake my head in wonder at the idea of 16-bit sampling, he'd tell us about the possibility of watching telly on our phones and living in a *Star Trek*-like world and we'd all look at him as if he was some crazy dreamer. It sounded brilliant, and nothing like what we've ended up with since. He certainly never mentioned the prospect of meeting lots of hot singles in our area. Him and Turing both. So we had to read newspapers and watch TV to find out what was going on rather than relying on tweets headed BREAKING.[31] And the other thing I remember was a hideous kind of glee getting hold of me. And probably not just me.

Wanting to keep up with the story we had stacked up the three TVs we had between us into a futuristic Bond-villain-style wall of information. The top one was one of those small bedside-alarm-clock tellies, its tube running down inside its body – with a screen 6 inches by 4 at the most it was black and white and you had to squint at the picture simply to make out anything at all. In 1991 24-hour news, the grinding hideous repetition machine, hadn't quite made it to the UK – the planes crashing into the World Trade Center on a repeating loop were at least a decade away; the news Daleks hadn't quite taken control of the BBC. This meant the existing channels would just carry on after close-down and harvest

---

[31] I'm entirely aware that even mentioning Twitter firmly plants this book in the 18-month window it was written in.

the news as best they could. The land campaign proper, with Stormin' Norman's armies swinging around the Iraqis and outflanking them, lasted 100 hours, ending with the slaughter of the Road to Basra, Highway 8. But the build-up – oh the build-up.

In fact, because the mass-of-manoeuvring-tanks-charging-into-the-desert part of the war was over so quickly the build-up was where the war got fought (and won) on the TV and in our lounge. Coverage resulted from journalists being made welcome by the military: Kate Adie had been out to see 'our boys' firing artillery at the distant Iraqi lines – though there's no doubt she wouldn't have called them that, she was very stern and serious then, though I seem to remember her looking much more animated at being around when something was actually happening (perhaps she was excited to have an exclusive scoop?). ITN would turn itself over to – if I remember rightly – CNN. Reporters stood on hotel roofs as the cruise missiles – previously so shy, what with all the fuss at Greenham Common – made their exciting and unforgettable TV debut, hurtling in around the Baghdad ring-road looking for their exit into the city. We would switch from telly to telly as the coverage shifted, using the tiny telly with its CCTV-esque image to warn us of new developments: the screen would white out if there was a big explosion to be shown.

Many of the things we have become possibly too familiar with in the last two decades – war looking like a video game, military press conferences (a response to the perception on the American side that they had lost the Vietnam War as much on the TV as they had in the field), Iraqi ministers lying outrageously, night-time cityscapes that light up suddenly and then go BOOM!, 'Allied' or 'Coalition' press being taken to see things that had been bombed – all of this stuff was pretty much on its first outing during Desert Storm. And maybe because it was new, maybe because we had the time on our hands to order a takeaway and sit down and watch it all of a Friday evening, maybe because it was War! Live! in our lounge, it was undeniably thrilling. Hence the grim glee.

The previous media war experience we had had was the Falklands War, a more austere affair. We'd had to make do with Brian Hanrahan counting them all out and counting them all back, and the rather dour fellow at the Admiralty relaying what had happened after it had happened. No slick PRs in 1982. Attempts to control the news were pretty clumsy – as the attack on Goose Green was about to start the World Service announced it on the news, to the dismay of the British soldiers approaching their start line. Imagine that nowadays? Well, actually it would probably have been scooped and the Argentine defence minister asked for his reaction to the news. The lads in my boarding house had to make do with the artist David Ace's (real name? surely not) drawings in the *Daily Mail* for any kind of visuals. So the Gulf War, this multi-screened rolling-news event, this war that was priding itself on being hi-tech and all out in the open, had our house gripped.

There were, of course, the usual arguments. 'Why were we siding with American aggression?' I found that one a little hard to call, what with it not really being American aggression,[32] at least not as far as I could tell. 'The West is only protecting its interests!' Um, er, yeah? Who else's would it protect? 'We've sold Saddam tons of weapons!' Um, nothing like as many as the Russians – no, really, nothing like as many as the Russians, not even close, those Scuds weren't made in Bolton or Hemel Hempstead . . . The dread question of Israel, sure to destroy

---

[32] This book has not been run past John Pilger prior to publication.

any dinner party, loomed. This was all conducted very good-naturedly as the five-week air campaign to 'degrade' – that was another thing that was new with Desert Storm, all that strange not-very-euphemistic language – the Iraqi command-and-control structure (sometimes stuffed full of civilians to make the Allies look like they were wantonly slaughtering civilians)[33] got under way. The Iraqi air force had scarpered, of course: they had flown next door to arch-enemies Iran – puzzling, yes – and so the Coalition was able to get on with their 'degrading' at leisure. The West's freedom of action, with the Cold War having ended, was very hard to get used to: it wasn't how things were done at all. As the UK shipped our stuff over from Germany and painted our tanks yellow it seemed that the collapse of the Berlin Wall only a couple of years previously was unpeeling the world and the way that it worked like a geopolitical onion. Had the Ostis who had wanted blue jeans and television seen this coming? And anyway, Kuwait? Where the hell was that? Ooh, look at the straight borders! What do they mean? What about Israel? But aside from the armchair politics there was a fair deal of armchair general-ing, mainly from me.

'Well, of course we need to gain air superiority before we can even think about getting things going on the ground,' I'd say. 'And that could take some time, which is just as well as all our tanks need refitting to cope with the desert climate, what with them being built for a European war.' My housemates would nod for a bit, and then in their boredom go and buy bog roll. Whenever I'd read an article in the paper that mentioned armchair generals I'd think oh not me, not really. But the business of being the chap at the top, the business of making those incredibly difficult decisions fascinates me. And I'm not alone.

---

[33] . . . Yes, I know, Mr Pilger . . .

But I think the thing that often gets forgotten is how some of the people at the very top, making all those decisions, life-and-death decisions, get a pretty short end of the stick from history. Understandable when they fail, maybe, but it seems they really cop it if they're successful. A good example of this is Monty: Field Marshal Bernard Law Montgomery.

Monty is a controversial figure. He was controversial during the war, so it's no surprise that he continues to be. Alongside 'Bill' Slim, who brilliantly commanded the Fourteenth Army in Burma, Monty made it to the top of the tree as a general under Churchill – no mean feat, given the Prime Minister's fondness for sacking generals who didn't deliver the results that the PM needed. I have a soft spot for Monty, even though I know perfectly well what a monumental arse he could be, and how he had a habit of rubbing people up the wrong way as well as not being entirely honest after the event about what had gone on. He was, as I mentioned before, incomparably big-headed – he certainly saw himself as the heir of Wellington and Marlborough; but even this appeals to me: after all he'd done why wouldn't he? To me it seems unreasonable to expect him to emerge modest – after all, one thing we needed was a general who we could tell our troops and their families was a war winner. Maybe it's because he has been comprehensively rubbished by history, lambasted for his woeful lack of diplomacy, mocked for his mistakes and (justly) damned for the astonishingly tactless bridge-burning memoirs he produced in the late 1950s.[34] Maybe it's because he was, for better or worse, a genius of democratic warfare: he somehow knew how to get what was

---

[34] In his memoirs, which caused outrage at the time, he said, 'I would not class Ike (Eisenhower) as a great soldier in the true sense of the word' OUCH OUCH OUCH! 'but he was a great Supreme Commander – a military statesman'. OUCH! And extra ouchy for being pretty much right . . .

an essentially civilian army to work so professionally, alienating in turn some of the professionals. For this I think he deserves a little bit more credit than perhaps he gets sometimes. For many experts he is the watchword for undynamic, cautious battle, to others he is the British general who finally figured out how to beat the Germans. Like most either/or questions, the answer contains a bit of both. Did I mention he was bad with people yet?

Monty was a peculiarly English type. I say this knowing that [a] he was an Ulsterman – sort of, his dad became Bishop of Tasmania and was often absent, leaving his children with their keen-on-beating mother – Monty fell out with her completely, even to the point of not going to her funeral; and [b] I have no idea what other nationalities have to offer in the way of eccentric characteristics for senior officers. Perhaps he is a good example of the peculiar people that the British Empire at that time could produce. Outwardly effete yet extremely physically tough, seemingly ruthless yet often sentimental, incredibly professional but capable of basic blundering – a showman who kept his true nature well hidden – he makes as much sense to us today as would anyone born in 1887, or anyone bearing that kind of responsibility, or both. He did not do well at school and joined the army against his family's wishes: an early sign of the man going his own way. He didn't do that well at Sandhurst either, almost getting expelled for setting fire to another cadet's breeches with a hot poker. Yes. That's right (anti-Monty types always like to bring that one up). His battalion was sent to India, where Monty, a serious fellow, found the slow, gin-drenched, polo-playing kind of officer culture a colossal wind-up. Serious about his military career he was dismayed with how things were done, saying in his memoir: 'As for the officers, it was not fashionable to study war and we were not allowed to talk about our profession when in the Officers' Mess.' On his battalion's return to England, Monty sought out like minds – talking privately with a friend about 'what was wrong with the Army.'

Then came World War One.

The Great War shaped Monty's fate, the way it did for the whole generation who became Britain's leading officers in the 1940s. On leaving England he was told to get his hair cut and sharpen his sword. The early stages of the war left Monty aghast, his battalion taking on attacks without any reconnaissance, 'no plan or covering fire', orders as simple as his CO arriving on his horse and saying the Germans are at the top of that hill, go get them. Up the hill they went and then back down again. (His CO was sacked, you may be relieved to hear.)

In October 1914 in an attack on a German position he found himself facing a huge German, and despite having taught rifle and bayonet drill all he had on him was his recently sharpened sword – the only sword work he'd ever done was saluting drill. He kicked the German in the stomach and took him prisoner. Later in the same action he was horribly injured. Montgomery was shot through the lung, the soldier who came to help him was shot through the head and killed by the same sniper who'd got Monty, and lay dead on top of Montgomery for hours as the sniper carried on pumping bullets into his corpse. Another round hit Montgomery's knee. Both men were left for dead. When night fell stretcher bearers went out to find any wounded left behind. Monty's memoir says drily, 'I was in a bad way'; when he was rescued and taken to the aid station that night they dug a grave for him. Having recovered from his wounds he became a staff officer, and learned the organisational skills he would excel at later in his career. This combination – a keen understanding of the necessity to manage carefully the relationship with his men (in other words leadership) and a profound understanding of how to organise armies – made him the general he was. But he was also bad with people. Terrible with people. Did I mention that yet?

After the war Montgomery continued his career as a professional soldier, trained as well as taught at the Staff College, involving himself in the intellectual end of soldiering. He was in Ireland during the Irish War of Independence, doing what we would now call counter-insurgency, and showed a firm grip on the limits of what could be sustained politically. Brutality would be the only thing that would work but it could only damage Britain politically: subtle for a soldier? Or maybe a political touch that was to desert him in later life? Possibly both.

But wherever he went as he worked his way up through the reduced peace-time army Montgomery's insistence on talking shop made him unpopular. If you read David Niven's autobiography *The Moon's a Balloon*, his description of inter-war soldiering in Malta gives a fair impression just how uninterested British Imperial officers were in talking shop. Niven's tales of boozy high jinks and light-hearted cricket matches are just the sort of thing that would have made Monty's blood boil.[35] This and his insistence on discussing soldiering in the mess meant that he was regarded as not quite a gentleman. His domestic life was ill-fated: though he had married and had a son his wife of ten years died as a result of an infected insect bite. Montgomery threw himself back into soldiering and became staggeringly distant from his son – so distant that it was remarked upon even in the more emotionally austere 1930s and 1940s. At the end of the 1930s before war broke out again he had

---

[35] Curiously, one of Niven's fellow officers in Malta was Roy Urquhart. Niven found the army essentially trivial and, after asking a lecturing general if he could hurry up as he had a date to get to, decided to leave under a cloud.

been in Palestine dealing with an Arab rebellion, a war he said he had 'enjoyed'. There speaks the professional.

But a lot of his success came down to luck, and Monty was as lucky as he was talented. His injury in World War One meant that instead of being killed in the trenches as a lieutenant like so many were he found himself doing staff work. Similarly he was lucky that he recovered from the illness that cost him his command in Palestine in 1939 – the lung problem that had troubled him lifted during his cruise home and his career was saved. He acquitted himself well during the collapse of the BEF in France when the Germans attacked in May 1940; his division handled well because he'd been insistent on them being fit and practising for night manoeuvres. In this aspect other generals' failings were his good fortune – on return to the UK he got on with offering his opinion about what had gone wrong and made no bones about what he thought of his superiors – and his forthright manner and insistence on professionalism got him a job commanding preparations for the expected German invasion. His men noticed, all right: suddenly, physical fitness – one of Monty's training trademarks – became a big issue. With the British Army reeling from the catastrophic defeat of the BEF in France his self-assurance must have seemed almost too good to be true. His pronouncements on filling his troops full of 'binge' (whatever that was, only Monty seemed to know) had a magical effect.

Peacetime career rules and customs were suspended. Montgomery's luck took his career forward. He was lucky that he got the job with the 8th Army: the man originally chosen for the job, William 'Strafer' Gott, was killed hitching a flight. The Germans were at the end of their supply lines and overstretched and, most importantly, the new and better equipment had come online, as well as a big reorganisation of the 8th Army itself, all initiated by Monty's predecessor, General Claude Auchinleck. This short, chippy and chipper man's luck would have rubbed people up the wrong way, let alone his manner. But again, yes, Monty was lucky to be in the right place at the right time in North Africa, and lucky to have the resources he needed for his style of battle to work, but he was also lucky to be good at galvanising those around him. Alan Brooke and Harold Alexander – his boss in London and his direct boss in the Middle East respectively – were astonished by how much Monty had transformed the previously war-weary atmosphere in the 8th Army in just a week. He was also lucky to have ULTRA decrypts that told him what the other side were up to more often than not (something that General Slim in the Far East viewed with great envy). From my armchair, I can't really see how hurting feelings and sacking those he deemed no good is so bad when there was a war on. But then, it's comfy in my armchair, I suppose, and no one will fire me if I underperform.

Most importantly, though, Montgomery's luck extended to having the sponsorship of the one man who could get him out of trouble, the Chief of Staff Alan Brooke – in turn, Alan Brooke was lucky that Monty was as good as he was, considering the trouble that Montgomery could have made for him. Monty knew his boss's personal side – on the beach at Dunkirk on 29 May 1940, overcome with the shock of the BEF's defeat, Brooke had broken down in tears. Monty had put his arm around Brooke's shoulder and turned him away from his staff. They trusted one another, though Montgomery did everything he could to test that trust. Alan Brooke knew what Monty was like, and with this in mind Brooke appointed staff officer Freddie de Guingand as a sort of diplomatic bodyguard for Monty to extract his boss from whatever strain of shit he'd landed himself in, political, military and diplomatic. This task drove de

Guingand to a state of nervous exhaustion. And the oddest things could come up.

Probably the most bizarre challenge to Montgomery that Brooke and de Guingand had to see off was a charge of corruption surrounding a pig. After the D-Day invasion in June 1944, Montgomery was running the Allied land battle. (It may come as a surprise to some, after years of D-Day anniversary coverage, that there was a battle that followed the invasion.) His every move was subject to relentless scrutiny. He had enemies in high places – Air Marshal Tedder, in charge of the air component of the invasion force, had the ear of Supreme Commander Ike Eisenhower and loathed Montgomery. Montgomery had fostered close relationships with the RAF in the desert – forging an excellent working partnership with the New Zealander Arthur 'Maori' Coningham, who had developed the close air-support tactics that had helped the 8th Army defeat Rommel[36] and became indispensable in winning the Normandy campaign. However, Monty's return to the UK before D-Day and his subsequent PR campaign as the all-conquering British general alienated Coningham, and relations with the RAF had soured. In July 1944 it was this atmosphere in Ike's court that was the most potentially dangerous threat to Montgomery's position, far more than the high-profile rivalry with George Patton. With Ike's headquarters in the UK, journalists asking him difficult questions about Allied progress, and Tedder and Coningham politicking against him, Monty's position was extremely vulnerable. (Sometimes this stuff seems literally

---

[36] Coningham was a genius at managing air-power – he invented a system called the 'cab rank' of fighter-bombers permanently on radio call. To make for closer cooperation he moved his HQ into Monty's tent. Though this raised the question: two whole years after the Germans had humiliated the BEF with devastatingly close air-support, why hadn't it been there in the first place?

incredible when viewed at this kind of distance.) Enter a pig.

Looting was, of course, both strictly forbidden and a fact of life. Soldiers would scrounge stuff to supplement their rations or, if they didn't scrounge it, they'd take it. A veteran I spoke to once talked of pinching chickens and butchering cattle. He also told me a story about blowing open a bank vault in Germany with an anti-tank weapon – the blast burned all the banknotes 'which were Reichsmarks and useless anyway'. After D-Day, Normandy, with its lush dairy products and cider, depopulated in anticipation of an invasion and because French men had been taken by the Germans to work abroad, must have seemed like a land of plenty to British soldiers straight from ration-hit Blighty. Well, Monty's TAC HQ (Tactical Headquarters) was no exception. TAC HQ would set itself up wherever Monty felt best in touch with what was going on, starting in Creullet in Normandy two days after D-Day and ending up in May 1945 at the Elbe in Luneburg where he took the German surrender. He surrounded himself with young liaison officers, most of them men who'd only come into the army for the war and were therefore free of army career politics. They had carte blanche to go wherever he wanted them to go and find out from the different HQs on the ground what was actually happening. He described them in his memoirs as 'a gallant band of knights'. No doubt he found their company more stimulating than a traditional mess where no one spoke to him about matters military. The atmosphere was 'collegiate' – they'd argue at the table, and while the boss remained the boss it was all very relaxed. But as well as running the battle Monty had the locals to deal with.

In July he had received several letters from concerned parties, including Foreign Secretary Anthony Eden's Permanent Under-Secretary, asking him that he do something about looting. General de Gaulle's office was also concerned. However, by the time TAC HQ had settled at Blay in Normandy he had 'six canaries, one love bird, two dogs' that can't have appeared magically. The dogs were called Rommel and Hitler: 'Hitler and Rommel both get beaten when necessary . . . both coming 'to heel' well.' With questions being asked about looting at the highest level TAC HQ found itself being checked up on. Visiting – well, let's be honest, snooping – from London one colonel, the Hon. Leo Russell, spotted a pig, covered in blood, running through the camp. When he sat down to eat that evening he realised that the fresh pork in front of him was from the same pig. He declared – to Monty – 'I'm not going to eat that: it's loot!'. He investigated further and found a coop of chickens, ducks and more pigs as well as a piano behind the TAC HQ mess. He also discovered that the farmer – on whose land the TAC HQ was camped – had been offered £2 to pay for the pig. This was all too much for Colonel Russell, who complained immediately and vociferously. The men of the TAC HQ thought he was, basically, being silly, but Russell was deadly serious.

This does sound scandalous (ish), but if you consider what was going on around him, you'd be right in thinking that Colonel Russell had no sense of proportion. In mid-July Montgomery and his staff were preparing a huge thousand-tank offensive – Operation Goodwood, more on that in a minute – and possibly weren't that bothered about Russell's pig-based botheration. It was also a crucial time for Monty's critics, most of whom were back in the UK, who were looking for anything to bash him with, convinced as they were that the battle for Normandy had stalled (you can only assume they weren't paying proper attention to what was going on or what he'd told them might happen). When Russell challenged Monty at first the general tried to brush him off, then asked Russell if he was accusing his personal staff of looting. Colonel Russell went the whole hog, so to speak, and said he was going to pursue it all the way to a court martial. Sensing a personality clash at best, a scandal at worst, de Guingand phoned the next day, advising Russell to drop it, suggesting looting was normal and it wasn't worth throwing away his career over a 'couple of pigs'. 'A matter of principle,' Colonel Russell replied. And so de Guingand got to work and made sure that the six-page report Russell had compiled, of every spoon, fork, pig and hen's egg he could find, would not find its way up the chain to Alan Brooke. The issue faded. Monty's luck held.

And then came Operation Goodwood.

By mid-July consternation was growing on the Allied side about the way the battle was progressing, how it had become static and seemingly stuck. Whispering in Ike's ear grew louder, impatience became the general tone of the papers. The notorious Operation Goodwood,[37] a battle mired in controversy and used to lambast Monty by Monty-bashers who use the benefit of hindsight to full effect, is a prime example of how the Normandy conflict was played out, but it also shows how decisive these numbers were. It doesn't help that Monty in his memoirs said that Normandy had all gone exactly according to plan, but the battle and how it turned out had been his approximate scheme – it's just that he had rubbed everyone up the wrong way so comprehensively there weren't many who would admit it. The Germans' main problem in Normandy was that while it was perfectly clear what the Allies were trying to do – break out of the invasion beachhead, push further into France and most probably head for Paris – they were unable to second-guess where the main thrust would come from. The initiative was

---

[37] I'd simply lose it, it's a relic.

dwindling the longer the Allies were caught in the beachhead – obviously they were going to try to break out, but their options were fairly limited. However, crucially the industrial advantage lay with the Allies. Goodwood, though arguably a disaster – an argument that continues to this day – demonstrates this advantage very clearly.

Operation Goodwood consisted of a huge thrust of tanks at the British end of the beachhead – the eastern end, to the south-east of the city of Caen, which had been bombed flat, no exaggeration, as the British and Canadians prised it from the Germans' grasp. The countryside to the south-east of Caen opened out into wider fields, unlike the smaller fields and hedgerows[38] in the land closer to the sea – it looked like it presented fewer hold-ups for the Allies' tanks. The Germans knew that if the British broke out of this end they were in real trouble so, if the British decided to push, the Germans would have to do everything to try to resist it. Consequently, the bulk of their tanks were at this end (not to forget that this eastern end was at the short limit of the Germans' supply lines, hampered as they were from the sky by Allied air attack). This of course left them vulnerable at the western, American, end of the beachhead. The controversy around Operation Goodwood centres on whether Monty was planning to break out or simply apply pressure: though whichever he was trying to achieve, or did achieve, made things much, much harder for the Germans. The Americans also launched an offensive at the other end of

---

[38] The *bocage*. This word crops up in every Normandy book, often in italics. For some reason the British, from a land of small fields and hedgerows, were utterly flummoxed by the Norman landscape of small fields and hedgerows. The Americans doubly so, until they figured the best thing to do was to stick an improvised bulldozer's claw on the front of a tank and drive through the hedgerows and across the fields rather than up the heavily defended roads, thus bypassing the Germans' intricate defences.

the Normandy beachhead – 'Cobra' – almost simultaneously, but against less armour: a question is, was Operation Goodwood intended to prevent the Germans from responding to Operation Cobra? Cobra got off to a bad start when the USAAF 'precision bombed' their own men waiting on the start line, and killed a general. Chaos, confusion, carnage – it's with these things that historians find and foster controversy.

The aftermath of Operation Goodwood is telling – the Germans lost something like 100 tanks, the British around 300. The British didn't break out, but the Germans couldn't repair the damage done or replace the equipment lost, and then couldn't drive back the Americans when they then broke out in the west. Operation Goodwood is controversial because Monty made various confusing (at the time and with hindsight) and contradictory (given how things turned out) statements about what he was trying to do and how. The meat of the controversy centres on the orders he gave and the impression he seemed keen to make before the offensive began – did he or did he not see it as a possible breakout, and did the plan he set in motion reflect this? This is one of the most bitterly fought controversies concerning the Battle of Normandy, reflecting how acrimoniously it was all argued about 70 years ago. It's very hard to call – persuasive arguments are made on every side of the debate, mighty tomes have wrestled with the whole issue, but one thing has always struck me: I can imagine Montgomery giving orders to his tank men along the lines of 'Well, this isn't really a breakout, you're not putting your necks on the block to get us to Paris but to relieve pressure at the other end of the Allied line' – it might not have sounded all that inspiring. They might even have tried to disobey or bend their orders, as some had done in the desert. With a cavalry ethos informing a great deal of the tank men's fighting philosophy (the old cavalry regiments had swapped horses for armour) many tank men believed that once they were out of the Normandy hedgerows and into wide-open fields to the south-east of Caen they'd be able to swoop in grand charges and roll up the Germans.

What happened was far from a glorious swooping charge: as the British tanks rolled over the open plain, uphill towards the Bourguébus ridge, the Germans picked them off before they were close enough to attack properly. There had been a huge cloud of dust from behind the Allied lines as the tank force had joined up in preparation for the attack – though from the Bourguébus ridge on a clear day you can see well beyond Caen and almost all the way to the landing beaches. The Germans fought as grittily on the wide-open fields as they had in the closer hedgerows. This despite Bomber Command having lent a hand and bombed the German positions with its heavy bombers (some German tanks were tossed over by the force of the bombing). Operation Goodwood marked the last offensive hurrah by the Imperial Allies in Normandy – their tank forces had been hit too hard, even if the Shermans were replaceable. Montgomery may also have talked up the aims and objectives of Operation Goodwood in the press because he knew perfectly well that the Germans were doing everything they could to divine his intentions. Maybe Monty was having to balance all these elements and played it pretty well. Or not. Don't take it from me: I'm a comedian who's interested, that's all, not an authority.

For historians a major problem with investigating this battle is that Miles Dempsey, the general who executed Monty's grand plan, insisted that his papers should be destroyed on his death, so we'll probably never know for sure. This is worth knowing, though: on the eve of Operation Cobra, the American breakout, the British had fourteen Divisions facing fourteen German

Divisions with about 600 tanks; five of these divisions were relatively fresh in the line. General Bradley, the American commander in the west of Normandy, had fifteen Divisions, with four more in reserve under Patton, facing nine German Divisions with 110 tanks. This with British resources dwindling, its stock of manpower running low, lives becoming increasingly precious. Monty had often spoken, before the battle, of drawing the German armour onto the British Second Army Group in the east – these figures seem to suggest he'd done just that.

I've stood at the top of the Bourguébus ridge and talked to a veteran who had fought his way almost to the top: he commented on how different the view was from the German perspective, that his officers must have been mad to have picked such a place for a battle, and then said in a voice best described as miffed, 'as I look across the plain . . . I just wonder how in heaven's name did we make it?' Well, I said, the German soldier was a good soldier and he replied, 'we were just that bit better.'

From my armchair I'd say that Montgomery was a genius at democratic warfare, commanding the last conscript army in the last major war. I'd also say he deserves better than being endlessly and pointlessly compared with Patton – Omar Bradley would be a better general to weigh Monty against, if you have to do this sort of thing. Exciting, flamboyant and outspoken as he was, George Patton[39] could never have masterminded D-Day: he would never have had the patience to fight the attritional Battle of Normandy that followed it. For all his reputation as a great attacking general, Patton's true moment of brilliance came not

---

[39] If you have to compare Monty and Patton this is the best way of looking at it: the British Monty was a very British general with a very British way of doing things that worked well with British armies made up of British men – the American Patton had a pair of shiny pistols.

in attack but in defence when he rode to the rescue of the 101st Airborne Division at Bastogne during the Battle of the Bulge; after all, his great breakout in Normandy came after Montgomery's plans to hold up German armour in the east of Normandy had come to fruition and Germans were pretty thin on the ground.[40] In fact, I won't say anything else about the Monty/Patton comparison, it's silly. For all Monty's much criticised cautious generalship, he almost fell out with Ike completely over Eisenhower's cautious 'broad front' strategy – Ike, needing to balance the contributions of the Allied armies, rejected Monty's calls for a single more dynamic thrust (which, um, he was going to command, of course). Market Garden illustrated what happened if you threw caution to the wind.[41]

Also, Montgomery certainly shouldn't be remembered for the intense and odd relationship he had with a teenaged Swiss pen pal. Maybe the prurience directed at that relationship says more about the times we live in than it does about Monty. Nor do I think he should be remembered for the terrible things he said about apartheid. Or Labour governments. I think he should be remembered, for all his faults and mistakes, for having his heart in roughly the right place what with all the pressures and vicissitudes of his job, as demonstrated, I think, by this

---

[40] You can write to complain all you like about this bit but I won't reply. This is my armchair general view, so lump it.

[41] Strangely enough, for someone supposedly unable to admit his mistakes, this is what Montgomery had to say about Operation Market Garden: 'It was a bad mistake on my part – I underestimated the difficulties of opening up the approaches to Antwerp . . . I reckoned the Canadian Army could do it while we were going for the Ruhr. I was wrong . . . In my – prejudiced – view, if the operation had been properly backed from its inception, and given the aircraft, ground forces, and administrative resources necessary for the job, it would have succeeded in spite of my mistakes, or the adverse weather, or the presence of the 2nd SS Panzer Corps in the Arnhem area. I remain Market Garden's unrepentant advocate.' Oops. Big footnote.

encounter: in 1944 just before D-Day he stood on the bonnet of a jeep to address some troops. He asked one of the soldiers a (possibly trick) question: 'What's your most valuable possession?'

The soldier, well trained, replied, 'It's my rifle, sir.'

'No, it isn't, it's your life, and I'm going to save it for you. Now listen to me . . .'

Monty then went on to detail how he was going to fight his battles, with due care and caution, in order not to place his men at any unnecessary risk – the very qualities his opponents are still harping on about even now. He never claimed to be anything else.

So – you might be wondering – what does this have to do with the First Gulf War, with this house of layabouts using newspaper to wipe their bums and scoffing Chinese takeaways in front of their stack of rolling-news televisions? Well, from my armchair something about Montgomery and his 'over-cautious' style that so infuriated many of his Allied contemporaries strikes me, especially given the Gulf War and how it turned out. Desert Storm was built around a massive build-up, a long air campaign, careful positioning of coalition forces and massaging of egos, the destruction of the enemy lines to the point where an attack could go in in relative safety. Modern American military tactics aren't like the arguably profligate techniques used during the Second World War – Vietnam taught the US that American lives in the modern era were difficult to squander, especially on TV. Norman Schwarzkopf's cautious approach, his emphasis on being visible to his men, his larger-than-life demeanour, his press conferences . . . I'm not saying anything. I'll leave that to better-qualified armchair generals.

5. Paintballing

. . . AND YOU SHALL KNOW THEM
BY THE TRAIL OF EMULSION

On occasion, I go paintballing. There – I've said it. If you've stuck with me this far you probably suspected that at some point I might have at least tried it. Those of you who've tried it will know: paintballing might best be described as playing at soldiers and getting home in time for your tea. I should like to point out that I've done it for fun too, not to research the inevitable sitcom episode in which everyone goes paintballing with hilarious consequences.

When I was a boy my dad would disappear for one of his frequent weekends of Territorial soldiering. He'd be off on Salisbury Plain somewhere, practising repelling the Soviet hordes. I thought it sounded incredibly exciting: he'd put on his uniform and put his bergen in the boot of the Maxi, the dog would jump onto the passenger seat and off he'd go. For this reason for me Salisbury Plain has never been somewhere full of mystic ancient Stonehenge-type vibes, it's somewhere I used to look for tank tracks as a lad.

For all its glamour mum would call it 'playing soldiers'. Seeing as her favourite story about the TA when we were kids was the one where they'd let her fire the Bren gun (that's the one with the curved magazine sticking out of the top of the gun – but you knew that) and not told her it was on automatic. Once she'd finished firing they waved a white flag from the butts – so it sounds like they did spend a fair chunk of their time playing. One of my earliest definite memories is going to see my father jumping out of the basket underneath a barrage balloon; he had to do so many jumps a year to stay qualified and keep his 'wings', and jumping from the balloon served as practice. We'd watch them get winched up in the basket and then jump out. I've a clear memory of him very urgently telling me not to pick up his reserve 'chute by its red handle (the one you pull when you need the thing to deploy). There's a great big compressed spring inside a reserve 'chute, it would've taken my head off and got him into trouble too. But no one jumps out of balloons and planes unless they enjoy it. Playing. In an event wreathed in family mystery and obfuscation dad once broke his leg playing leapfrog or rugby with a beret or something. Playing.

And paintballing is playing, plain and simple, you play games, they call them games, there's a score, your opposing teams play to win, they hand out certificates at the end (best shooter, best heroic dash etc.). You win, as often as not, by shooting more of the other team than they shoot of yours. But, of course, the games involve shooting at each other, and at the site I regularly play at the scenarios are unabashedly based around various war scenarios. There's a game called *Band of Brothers*. Tastefully, there's an Omaha Beach as well, where they stuff you into a plywood landing craft at the bottom of a slope and you have to fight your way uphill and place an (American) flag on one of three points on the hill. The opposing team are the Germans, etc. We've done a fair deal of grumbling about the flag being the Stars and Stripes. When you're hit by a paintball you head for the dead area where you wait out the rest of the game and watch how it's going for the rest of your team. It's a tricky arena to play in – the higher ground gives the 'Germans' a real command of the place. The people I play with have perfected tactics for this game – you bung in loads of smoke to obscure your movements, a few of you go up the right hand-side to draw the other side's fire/paint and the rest go left. You get the flag in if you're quick. It's all great fun and you're home in time for tea.

Further confessions, then. Not only do I go paintballing, I own a paintballing gun. Not a flashy one, not one of those paintball guns customised to look like a Kalashnikov or an Armalite, but one that can rapid fire (I'm a lousy shot so I'm more likely to hit someone if I can fire more paint in their direction). It also has its own rapid-feeding hopper, or magazine. It has a motor that feeds its supply of balls (ahem) into the breech of the gun faster than if left to gravity. Hey: I'm not that into it, but I do own my own mask, purely because the masks they hand you on arrival may well have been worn by a hundred others, sweated and snotted into in the heat of mock battle. I also have some Gore-Tex camouflage trousers for when it's wet, but I haven't worn them in ages. I had the boots anyway. Like I said, I'm not that into it, but I can see how easy it might be to get hooked. I haven't bought any knee pads or anything.

I've been possibly a dozen times now, and it takes on a familiar pattern as I tend to go to the same site with the same people. My proper introduction to paintball, though, was in Canada, when I was playing the Montreal Comedy Festival. I've only been once but it was great fun and odd – the few days before the American comics arrived we British comics were lauded and treated like comedy royalty. After that we seemed mainly to take on the role of flies in the ointment who weren't that punctual with the lengths of our sets. But whatever, in

95

Montreal I got my first taste of paintball. Not of the paint of course, no, you DON'T REMOVE THE MASK UNDER ANY CIRCUMSTANCES.

My manager had come along to Montreal, doubtless to protect me from the possibility of a Pub Landlord remark about the French going awry[42] or my accepting a part in an American sitcom at a bargain rate, and was looking for things to do with our days off: Montreal at the time seemed to consist chiefly of strip bars – I'm surely exaggerating but there were parts of the town where it seemed like one in three shops was a strip joint – and neither of us were all that interested. He'd braved the dial-up internet in the hotel, found us a paintball site to go to, and our party grew to four as another comic and his manager joined us. We got in the cab and left the centre of Montreal – which has been described as Parisian by someone who has either never been to Paris or has a twisted sense of geographical humour. It really isn't like Paris, and try as I might to let go of the fact that I was in North America and convince myself I was actually somewhere around the corner from the Bastille it just didn't happen (there are road signs to New York, for Pete's sake). Paris is more than three blocks of four-storey buildings that have a kind of greying belle-époque look, it's an entire sodding city of it. With an Eiffel Tower and everything.

Our cab driver for some reason couldn't understand why we might turn our back on such Parisian delights and head for the suburbs. However: he didn't shrug like a Parisian, he didn't

---

[42] As it was I got the devil in me and blew my nose on a hanky of the Canadian flag. Up to that point it'd gone well, being rude about the Americans which seemed to be something that couldn't fail. I was followed by Bill Maher who, for all his alternative point-of-view chops, fumed and fulminated about saving the Brits in two world wars. Etc. Still, I started it.

treat us like dirt like a Parisian might, so we definitely weren't in Paris. We pulled up at an industrial unit. My manager, the only old paintball hand amongst us, made it clear what our principal tactic was. Spending and volume. In the manner of US military doctrine the big idea was to smother the other side in fire/paint. We bought 1,000 paintballs each and suited up in the grimy overalls we'd been issued with. There were just the four of us there at this point, and the guy on the counter told us not to worry and that the other party would be arriving soon. Given that it was midweek that could have meant anyone. We didn't have to wait too long to find out, as in dribs and drabs the enemy, I mean the opposing team, presented itself. They were on average about 12 years old, they were French Canadian and all of them were boys. They went to the counter and looked carefully at their pocket money and spent it all in one go on probably a maximum of 150 paintballs each. We were then divided into two teams, the four of us with something like a dozen adolescent Quebecois.

Despite the obvious language barrier – I speak good enough French to order drinks, this French then improves with consumption of said drinks – our teaming-up worked fairly well. Actually, that's an understatement. It worked incredibly well. The other team seemed to think that taking the odd (carefully rationed) potshot would somehow hold off our team, loads of cannon-fodder kids bolstered by adults with an almost unending supply of paintballs. We got organised and discussed how best to make the most of the terrain. Terrain isn't the right word, though. This indoor 'arena' (not the right word either) had a sandy floor. Though it seemed rock hard. You'd hurl yourself onto the floor, taking cover behind a barricade, thinking that looks nice and sandy and soft and knock the wind out of yourself, jar your elbows, bruise your knees. But mainly we made the most of our chief tactical advantage – almost infinite firepower, thousands of paintballs. Around the sides, and through the centre of the arena (I'll stick with that word) were wooden structures, shacks, sheds, with doors, windows, walls that you could take cover in, or barge through looking for any French-Canadian kids hiding. At the far end was a fort. The games we played were pretty standard, you'd have to capture the flag in the middle of the arena, or take control of the other side's fort. We were thrashing the other side. Demolishing them. Pulling them to pieces. Crushing them. We'd pour endless paint onto the other side, and between games, while our guns were being recharged with gas, we went to the counter and bought even more paint, whole boxes of paintballs, copping envious looks from the opposition as they counted out their remaining paint supplies. I'm sorry to say we found this hilarious. Not very sorry, though.

The emulsified carnage came to a climax during a fort game. The two teams took turns to hold or capture the fort. We held the fort, losing hardly a man. Well, kid. I'm fairly sure that at no point were any of us shot, even though, being grown-ups, we were much larger and more obvious (not to mention slower) targets. We never even let them get near the fort, defending in depth, making sure they had to get through loads of us before they even got close. When it came our turn to capture the fort we were totally ruthless. Weaving our way through the buildings along the sides of the arena we started flushing out their defenders. Easily. Really easily. Thinking about it, these lads are all in their early twenties now and if we go back to Montreal there's every chance someone will step out of the crowd and lamp one of us. Though we were wearing masks most of the time, I expect seeing us at the counter buying up more and more paint is indelibly etched in their memories. Perhaps one of them has written a traumatised memoir about shattered teenage dreams while growing up in suburban Montreal. As we pushed further into the fort panic began to spread. Two of us reached the inside of the fort and the distressed defenders came running wildly out of the door on the other side, which we'd got covered with a couple of guns. The kids started screaming 'Ils sont fous, ces Anglais!'[43] Dark English laughter coming from inside the fort accompanied the French screaming. We were winning and we were in the grip of some strange bloodlust. And I'm sorry to say, again, that we found it hilarious.

Paintball hasn't been around that long, being invented in the 1970s by a couple of Americans who liked the idea of hunting humans as if they were big game. (At this point I could bung in an 'only in America' gibe, but in all honesty I'm amazed it didn't start here, you'd think there might be some twitchy toffs in mid-July desperate to shoot something, anything in the run-up to the Glorious Twelfth. Perhaps the notion of shooting people, albeit safely, was the taboo that had to be broken. Perhaps they wanted to shoot people and get away with it. Hmm. Anyway.)

It's everywhere now, a regular stag-do thirst generator. I've been at paintball sites at the same time as stag parties: outrageous, 'hilarious' costumes abound, the stag can be dressed as a stag, a bunny, a man-sized baby in a nappy or, as we saw once one November, in a mankini. Given that a paintball hitting you can leave quite a welt under your overalls – the paintballs go at something like 300 feet per second, and

---

[43] 'These English are crazy!' I know this not because of the tattered remains of my A-level French but because it's what Obélix says about Romans in Astérix books. My dad's job took him to France regularly at one point, and he'd always bring back an Astérix book, in French. I'd read the English translation, learn it up, and then try to impress my dad with my French skills – I'm not sure he was fooled by my curiously precocious command of idiom.

if you're lucky expend some of their energy bursting, the ones that don't burst are the ones that really hurt – this particular stag must have been well loathed by his compadrés: by the end of the day his bare skin was mottled like a black and blue Dalmatian. Maybe the bloodlust had got to them too, but he was in for an awkward wedding night.

In its favour paintball is a great way to fill your lungs with outdoor air and run around in nature, a great day's exercise that simply creeps up on you. It also involves not killing any wildlife, something I did do in my youth. I'm not so keen on that any more, what with being a lousy shot and guns being incredibly dangerous. Though as long as you're going to eat whatever it is you shoot, then really that's fine by me. But underlying paintball is the actual business of shooting at people. If and when you do go shooting for sport – game or clay pigeon – the fundamental rule about gun safety that's drummed into you right from the start is that you never, ever point your gun at anyone, even if it's not loaded or you've fired both barrels, or you've got the safety catch on, no matter what: you never point the gun at anyone. Ever. If you do, everyone freaks out, understandably. So pointing a gun at someone is full of taboo, obviously, but once you start paintballing you get used to it instantly. In fact, it's not a big deal at all. Which in itself should probably make you stop and wonder but in my case it simply didn't happen. No one else mentioned it, either – they just got on with trying to inflict grim welts on each other.

But the most important part of the appeal of paintball is that you get to go home. At the end of the day's ritualised firefighting you take off the overalls, bung them in the laundry bin, hand over your mask and bugger off. And it's here, maybe even more than the qualms about shooting at people, that it truly, definitely is playing. Aside from risking their lives, the men who took the beaches on D-Day or at Anzio, or who fought at El Alamein, or the Admin Box or Kohima in Burma, didn't break for lunch, and certainly didn't head home. Soaked through, seasick, deafened and dizzied by the noise, the men who landed at Gold beach in Normandy fought their way through the seaside town's defences and pushed as hard and as far inland as they could, leaving behind any casualties so as not to hold themselves up. They didn't then jump in the all too ironic VW and head home, stopping at the offie to pick up some cans for their passengers. They camped down that night, their kit wet through, mounting 'stag parties' to keep an eye on the Germans in case they counter-attacked at night.[44] No mankinis with these stags. The fighting in Normandy continued in this vein, living in the hedgerows, sleeping in ditches, in the open, through a stormy summer until the German army was encircled and broken near Falaise (William the Conqueror's home town) in the third week of August, and then on into Belgium, Holland and Germany, through the winter, finishing up in the Baltic in the early summer of the following year. These days, with camping having mutated into the hideously named 'glamping', waterproofs being actually waterproof, even the living-outdoors part would be hard to replicate without the being shelled, counter-attacked, etc., etc. that you'd need to experience to even get close to what men went through simply living in the field in Western Europe.

In the desert, the heat was oppressive during the day, the nights bitterly cold, the flies omnipresent. The truly wonderful

---

[44] For all their fabled prowess as soldiers, the Germans really didn't like to fight at night, something that became a British speciality and a German vulnerability, but they could always be relied on to counterattack.

desert-war drama *Ice Cold In Alex* is all very well but it's short on flies. Corned beef would cook in the can, you really could fry eggs on the bonnet of a vehicle. Cuts would easily become septic, water had to be purified and tea – essential for the British army to keep going – was disgusting as a result, and most likely with flies in it. Yet a friend of mine's grandfather, who spent the whole war in the Eighth Army, said that for him the war was in Technicolor and the rest of real life was black and white by comparison.[45] The desert war ran backwards and forwards along the roads on the North African coast – often in swooping tank/cavalry charges – the British based in Egypt, protecting the Middle East oilfields and the Suez Canal, both sides wrestling with the problem that whenever they had the enemy on the back foot they would find themselves at the end of their own supply lines and therefore vulnerable in turn. It was in the desert that the British Army finally regained its self-confidence and started to learn how to beat the Germans, who also had to deal with the heat, the implacable landscape and the flies as well as their not altogether reliable Italian allies. The 8th Army gained the upper hand by making the most of Rommel's momentum, which during 1942 had seemed irresistible, but in forcing the British back he had of course ended up taking himself to the full extent of his supply lines and then, with deciphered German codes, the British were able to destroy his resupply convoys. Until El Alamein the campaign ebbed and flowed (and to Churchill's frustration it did a great deal of ebbing), all the while the men coping with searing heat, freezing cold nights, a place where every drop of water and petrol was precious, in a landscape with little or no cover. And did I mention the flies? But while it's not really that

---

[45] Another veteran I spoke to said that Montgomery was a pain in the arse because he'd cancelled the beer ration and made them get fit.

sensible to judge any of these things, the jungle sounds worst of all.

The jungle – especially during the monsoon season – hardly bears thinking about. For flies think mosquitos. For the first two years of the war in the East, the British and Imperial armies found the jungle almost impossible to cope with. The Japanese had gone to great pains to get used to the jungle, and their way of fighting had the British armies in the Far East outwitted, out-fought and overwhelmed. The ignominy of the defeat in Singapore had elevated the Japanese soldier to some kind of Oriental jungle superman. The British were caught out culturally as well as militarily: for all their racist attitudes about the Japanese being inferior to Westerners, to get beaten comprehensively by the Japanese must have been akin to having a cultural nervous breakdown. The British had regarded the jungle as impassable and uninhabitable, relying on road transport for resupply, therefore they tended to fight in the jungle by setting up roadblocks. The Japanese would circumvent the roadblocks, stealing through the jungle, and attack the British from behind – a recipe for panic and collapse. In Burma, the campaign began with the British caught out and out-fought (this was the pattern for a great deal of World War Two, except when fighting the Italians).[46] The chaos and panic that Japanese infiltration had caused in Burma during their invasion in February of 1942 had meant that the British blew the crucial bridge on the Sittang river before everyone had got back across it. But it's little wonder that the jungle had so frustrated the temperate-zone British. It wasn't until the first of the (arguably completely disastrous) Chindit campaigns in 1943, led by a hare-brained/

---

[46] I know, that seems like a clichéd, hackneyed, exhausted thing to say, but it happens to be the case.

maverick, lunatic/genius, visionary/crazy-man, take your pick,[47] called Orde Wingate that the British began to get to grips with the jungle, and consequently with the Japanese.

Heat, humidity, rain and disease. Over a hundred species of poisonous snakes. Malaria in particular made up a staggering amount of the casualties – in October 1944 hospital admissions for the British in Burma broke down as follows: 49,195 admitted for disease, excluding venereal disease, compared to only 602 battle casualties (yeah, that one made me drop my digestive). No one was safe – in June 1944 the Fourteenth Army's boss General Slim had contracted malaria after taking an evening bath despite his personal rule of not having a bath after dusk. If ever there's an argument in favour of sousing entire countries in DDT that's it right there. Interestingly, although it still wasn't certain at the time how malaria was transmitted, seeing as in the heat and humidity men who suffered mosquito bites ran the risk of infected wounds precautions were taken to avoid getting bitten; men rolled their sleeves down and tucked their shirts in at night. Treatment at the time was quinine, which brought down your fever, and was also in gin and tonic. I don't like gin, but it seems this version has something to recommend it after all. Used since the seventeenth century as a remedy for malaria, quinine still had its bit to do in the middle of the twentieth, but because the Japanese had occupied Java – where quinine came from – British soldiers had to take a drug called Mepacrine, which amongst its side effects turned your face yellow. To be honest, if it helped with your malaria I can't imagine what colour your face might be would be that much of an issue. Especially if your face was covered in feasting

---

[47] To be frank I think I'm going easy on him there.

mosquitoes. This sort of thing, quinine in Java, was exactly what the war in the Far East was being fought over: the central reason for Japanese expansion and aggression was to get their hands on raw materials like quinine and oil and rubber so they could act like a proper Imperial power. Like Britain. Britain was acting like a proper old-school Imperial power and defending its right to control the stuff that there was in that part of the world.

So paintball is unrealistic in its core aim to replicate what combat might be like, if only because you don't live outdoors, fight all day and night, sleep in a ditch, dodge disease, have people trying to kill you, huge industrial build-up behind you, newspapers analysing your every move, nor do you have the machinations of post-Imperial politics to consider. But the business of crawling around on your belly behind bushes, working in pairs, laying down suppressing, um, paint on the enemy, that all seems pretty realistic, surely? Aside from the fact that there are no minefields or IEDs, no artillery or air strikes, and that the grenades make a lot of noise but do little else – the smoke is pretty reliable, though, surely it's a pretty good facsimile of the real thing. Apart from the not being injured or killed when shot part, that is. In some ways it's reminiscent of the Aztecs preferring simply to capture their enemies rather than kill them (though they were capturing them with a view to sacrificing them later). This possibly made things a lot easier for the Spanish when they first turned up in Mexico in the 1500s.

But paintballing is mainly fun. It involves hilarity and fantasy, I suppose. One Christmas we organised a big paintballing party, 'we' being the people I usually play with and a selection of playground dads. My brother-in-law joined us. He's very successful, and could have bought out everyone on both teams, and the site itself, but again and again he ran out of ammunition like a twelve-year-old French Canadian. To make things seasonal – and I am a sucker for a Santa hat – one team had to wear Santa hats and the other wore antlers. Right from the start the Reindeer suffered from a pretty basic level of disorganisation and we could hear they weren't talking to each other at all (a big part of paintball is communication, letting everyone know what they can see and where they think the other side are is very important, we get so organised that we even have a clock system when we're defending the fort – 'Two of them at three o'clock!', that sort of stuff). After the first couple of games the Reindeer returned to the safe area dejected, whilst we Santas were buoyant, terribly pleased with ourselves. We'd won two games hands down. A cup of coffee and a fag break later and we went back out. Again, the Santas had the upper hand. After the first two games the Reindeer returned to base, muttering about the (brown) antlers making them obvious and visible. They were saying this to people wearing red and white Santa hats. One or two of the Reindeer took off their antlers in defiance, as if the seasonal novelty-costume items were somehow bringing them bad luck. The Santas – some of them veterans of the Montreal campaign – ho-ho-hoed their way back to the counter and bought tons more paint. By the afternoon the Santas were overwhelmingly dominant, the Reindeer were ruined. And our hats had progressed from being a silly Christmas-party novelty to being a totem of our team's dominance. They also meant we could all see where the rest of our team was – like the Redcoats of old. As the red and white bobble hats pressed on towards the other side's barricades we felt invincible and, like Santa, capable of being everywhere at once somehow. As it got dark around four o'clock our red and white bonnets seemed to glow in the gloom. We didn't care if the other team were naughty or nice, we were coming to get them. The day ended with the Reindeer aggrieved, defeated, humiliated. While this may not have been in the Christmas spirit, it was, I'm sorry to say yet again, hilarious. And this is where it differs fundamentally from war – it's funny, and war definitely isn't a subject for humour.

6. Plastic scale-model kits

FOR WHEN REAL LIFE IS JUST TOO BIG

So much for running around in a wood in East Sussex. There's also the *stuff*: the planes, the tanks, the gear. And growing up in the 1970s being into the stuff was easy – in fact it was child's play, literally.[48] All thanks to Airfix. I'm pretty sure if it hadn't been for Airfix the national idolisation of the Spitfire could have turned out differently, but the curve of its elliptical wing is surely heavily imprinted on most men of my generation, whether they like it or not. I was in model making's thrall for at least ten years, and found myself almost completely distracted by it.

Airfix, and model making in general, is the reason I'm not very well read – this is why Dickens, Trollope, Tolstoy, Austen, and all other sundry indispensable greats of literature are just names to me. I was much more interested in trying to get the transfers onto the model in the right place without spoiling the paint-job I'd done. I should point out that even though I stopped

---

[48] It's nice to have been able to use a literally there, literally.

making models long ago, for some reason I don't have a burning urge to pick up any of these mega-tomes. Model making obligingly chewed up hours of my boyhood – these miniature weapons were designed to kill time. It's the reason more than any other why I don't suffer from the clearly divine agonies of supporting a football team; it's why I can't name a Liverpool or Arsenal squad from the 1970s, why I don't have a stack of Panini sticker-books somewhere in a loft, why old footballers can pop up on TV and I have no idea whatsoever who they are. It may be true that you can't trust a man who doesn't like football: but you can't fault me for being upfront about it. But even though it left me uncultured and dully senseless about the FA Cup, model making did me a huge favour in that it ate up vast chunks of that time that is hardest of all to overcome – Sunday afternoons.

Sunday afternoons hang heavy at the end of a week like a bloated appendix, a vestigial remains of the week that once was, a day of rest to be enhanced by Bible contemplation or hewing wood. Now that no one goes to church and everyone has central heating these two options are pretty much redundant. At school we did go to chapel an alarming amount – if you want to put young people off religion make it compulsory and not particularly gripping, backed up with a diet of wildly contradictory sermons, that's my tip for those of you out there wanting to bring down the Church.

Now that you can shop and watch football on a Sunday[49] this long empty temporal tundra has at least been colonised by things to do. Sometimes I think Sundays groan under the strain of being a sort of ersatz family weekday into which you're meant to cram family Sunday lunch as well as some meaningful

---

[49] Not that this once hugely controversial change really troubles me. 'Not really being bothered about football allows a man to travel light in life.' Me, 2013.

shopping. But in the empty arid plains of a 1980s Sunday afternoon I'd spend the time at my desk, making models. It was good for holidays, too – four weeks over Easter is something pretty close to an eternity; there used to be no daytime telly back then. A world without Richard and Judy, Holly and Phil, *Cash in the Attic*. I'd keep myself to myself, assembling and painting, in the end modifying and customising. It was solitary, yes, time on my own, space away from the continual low-level pecking-order jostle of boarding-school life, but above all it was a gripping, hands-on hobby – tactile, imaginative and historical, bringing dumb plastic to life. Nerdy, yes, but ask any nerd why he's a nerd and he doesn't know what you're on about – he's simply interested in what he's doing. Back off.

Looking back at it now I marvel at my powers of concentration – it was rock solid, I'd be there for hours, no distractions. Now I've been a comic for something like 20 years I find a vast part of my writing life is spent trying to do anything other than write. The last few years have got progressively worse with the internet and of course its distilled, pure crack-like[50] form, Twitter. But back then the closest thing to a distraction was the dog, which dad was walking anyway, my sisters with whom I lived in a state of mutual non-interest, and the radio. I can't see how I'd be able to make a model these days (though I don't really want to, in all honesty); the phone would ring, there'd be an email to reply to, the news to peek at, something on YouTube I'd been sent to look at or bloody Twitter to update – I've done it just now. Unimaginable as it is to everyone's kids there was none of this back then (you know this, they know this, but sometimes

---

[50] I've no idea if it's like crack, don't be silly, like most people who refer to crack, especially when they use the expression 'crack-like'.

it's simply worth saying). With boxes full of paints, a set of brushes, with one or two trusty and reliable favourites amongst them, I'd make the kits I'd saved up my pocket money for, often building them too quickly, trying to make the most of the time I had, not waiting for the paint to quite dry or the glue to set properly. But I could be meticulous too, a word I only know the meaning of because that was how my dad had described me obsessing over making a jeep look properly muddy or getting a 1/35 scale boot's laces to look right.

What this hobby did mean was that the teenaged me might not have known all that much about the outside world – boarding school and modelling, not really a recipe for street smarts – but what I did know was which mark of Spitfire had which canopy and on and on and on. This wasn't via books, or history TV – something no one had even dreamed of in the era of three channels at most and no videotape – it mainly came from the fact-packed notes on the instruction guide that you found at the bottom of the box along with the water-based transfers. These terse but dense histories in their tiny font told you everything you needed to know about the aircraft you were making, and pulled no punches if the type you'd chosen had been a failure (like the sad, benighted Westland Whirlwind heavy fighter.[51] It never felt that good to make a model of a plane type that had stiffed, you felt faintly like you were an Air Ministry mandarin wasting your time with a dud tendering specification). A lot of this stuff has pretty much stayed with me. It's thanks to Airfix producing a Spitfire Mark Vb with

---

[51] I always loved the look of the Lightning – it had two engines and looked sort of rangy. Unfortunately the engines weren't all that reliable. Its main advantage as the pilots saw it, was that you could crash land it and walk away: damning with faint praise or what?

Polish squadron markings that I knew about Poles[52] fighting in the Battle of Britain long before I'd been near a history book.

Modelling is, of course, a deadly serious pursuit, and like most deadly serious pursuits it's a game, it's the upgraded plastic-age inheritor of playing with lead soldiers. Churchill was a big fan of playing with lead soldiers: his nursery floor would be the scene of huge battles, strewn with platoons of toxic troops. Those of us living in the era that followed in the wake of Churchill's real war were living in a plastics boom and we had had war toys galore, war toys of new and exciting glamour, and dripping with recent history. The possibility was there in a multitude of scales to re-enact on your bedroom floor, or dangle on a thread from your ceiling virtually every moment of the titanic struggle that had gripped the world. You could create dogfights real and imaginary, make up improbable mismatched squadrons. The added bonus was that none of these toys were made of lead (though the ones that had been didn't seem to stop Churchill getting to ninety). The glue smelt good, though . . .

In this it was Airfix that led the way – the first model I made was one of theirs and I'm pretty sure it was their Mark IX Spitfire JE-J as flown by Johnny Johnson DSO and two bars, DFC and bar. He was the closest thing the RAF had to a major ace with 21 kills. However, the RAF liked to play down the whole business of aces during WW2, determined as it was to emphasise how theirs was a team effort, but the glamour is undeniable and Airfix didn't have to abide by RAF policy and seemingly could not resist.[53] Aircraft-model snobs don't rate this

---

[52] Coming over here, shooting down our Germans.

[53] Another big ace was 'Sailor' Malan, a South African pilot with 27 kills, 7 shared, 3 probables, 16 damaged. He was known as 'Sailor' because he'd been in the Merchant Navy, but maybe also because his first name was Adolph, which wouldn't

old kit, it was very simple to assemble and a possibly crude model in itself, but that shouldn't matter – your first kiss is doubtless simple and crude yet it leads (with any luck) to more fabulous kissing; you'd hardly look back at your first kiss and critique it: 'sloppy and above all a complete surprise, the kiss defied and redefined all expectations.'

So the Airfix JE-J Spitfire is a glorious kit – they still make it – and if you feel the need to get a kid bitten by the modelling bug I'd say it's still the way to go. Or if you're an adult and fancy feeling ancient and clumsy you could buy one: your fat old fingers will defeat you. If the kid gets bitten properly it'll keep them occupied and off the streets if my experience is anything to go by – this tip could save your family an ASBO somewhere down the line. With this classic kit you end up not necessarily with a precise model of what a Spitfire Mk IX looked like but with a fair impressionistic memory of one, in plastic, a fair distance away. You could say it's as roughly accurate as the Mark IX Spitfires that turn up a couple of years 'too early' in the *Battle of Britain* movie.

The Mark IX in itself was a brilliant aircraft, being a response to the arrival on the scene of the Focke-Wulf Fw 190 in August 1941. Go on, make your priceless Focke jokes now – ah, they never get old. The Fw 190 appeared and outclassed the Spitfire Vb in almost every aspect. Faster than the Mark Vb Spitfire, and more manoeuvrable, the Fw 190 meant that the RAF lost air superiority over France. Given that 'flying fighter sweeps over the French coast' was all the RAF could do in the way of taking the fight to the enemy at the time – the bombing campaign at this point was having

---

have had quite so much zing in 1941. He came up with ten rules for air combat that were then used throughout the RAF – rule 10 'Go in quickly – Punch hard – Get out!'

problems finding towns in Germany and often Germany itself – this was a tactical shock that undermined overall RAF strategy, the kind of technological surprise that the Germans often sprang during the war. At lower altitudes the Spitfire Vb was at a proper disadvantage, and before the Mark IX was introduced the RAF experimented with removing the Spitfires' wing tips, reducing drag and speeding them up, allowing them to turn tighter circles. It was decided to take the airframes of the scheduled Spitfire Vc and stick on a more powerful engine, the Rolls-Royce Merlin 61 – engines left over from an abandoned high-altitude-bomber project. This engine was much more powerful than the old Vb – you can spot a Mark IX because it has a longer, straighter nose than the previous marks of Spitfire, and the exhaust has six smaller flues, not three larger ones. The larger ones look like flared fins. This new stopgap hybrid proved to be far superior to the old Spitfire Vb and, more importantly, the Fw 190. The Spitfire Mark IX was the most successful of the Spitfire types – over 4,000 were made and flew in all theatres and even ended up dogfighting each other in the Egyptian and Israeli air forces during 1948.

Who knows how many model Mark IXs Airfix made. These kits were affordable and, elegantly, as difficult as you wanted them to be – you could paint the pilot's goggles if you wanted to, painstakingly marking out the tiniest details or not. Everyone was free to cloud the canopy with 'cement' if they wanted, and if you did, everyone understood, everyone else had been there. I got better and better at modelling, though I developed my own techniques and refused to read about how the 'pros' did it. (How could they be professional modellers? I thought, even aged 9, who pays for someone to make them models of 1/72 Mark Vb Spitfires? *The point is you do it yourself*.) As I got older I shifted from planes mainly because I'd made all of the planes I was interested in too many times – I found myself losing interest as I cracked open yet another Spitfire Vb (the box with a Polish squadron Spitfire with Donald Duck and the red chequer pattern painted beside the cockpit). Even ingeniously manipulating the decals so the planes were all different members of the same squadron had lost its appeal. I had a piece of plywood painted green with a grey strip of runway on it on which the planes would line up on the top shelf in my bedroom. It claimed to be the airfield that lay at the end of the village I grew up in, though I'd taken some liberties there as that airfield had been a bomber-training conversion base.

I got properly into making model kits. Maybe because boarding school was all pecking order, on a Sunday I would make kits pretty much all day, on my own. It offered me space and solitude, but space and solitude put to use; from this time squadrons of Spitfires were born. And Hurricanes too. Given its association with its better-known cousin the Spitfire you'd be forgiven for thinking the Hurricane's proper name was the '. . . and Hurricanes'. I'm slightly ashamed to say that even though I knew all the mitigating Hurricane facts they never quite held the same appeal. The mitigating Hurricane facts (and forgive me if you know these) are that compared to the Spitfire (a) there were more of them during the Battle of Britain, (b) they were a more stable gun platform (c) they could take more damage and (d) they were easier to repair. A Hurricane's fuselage was a frame coated in Irish linen – a tea-towel fighter plane. When it was damaged the aircrew would simply patch it with more linen – the Spitfire with its metal fuselage wasn't quite so simple. Sadly for the Hurricane, for some reason they didn't capture the public imagination in the same way, and by the time I was making kits they were like the slightly fatter and slower and uncooler cousin. Apart from the Mark II with a great big tank-busting cannon underneath it, which was what you'd call badass if anyone in the Home Counties in the 1970s and 1980s had ever heard the term. The Hurricane's disadvantage compared with the Spitfire was that its airframe wasn't anything like as open-ended a design, and the Spitfire's development potential quickly outstripped the Hurricane's.

I like to think I built everything Airfix made, certainly everything that the RAF would have flown. One kit that sticks in the mind as an awkward bastard was the de Havilland Mosquito, with fiendishly fiddly cannon that had to go through the nose cone – sometimes the holes in the nose cone needed cutting as the moulding wasn't too accurate. The Mosquito kit had (and indeed still has, judging by the last trip I made to a model shop for research and nostalgia purposes) lots of options: just like the real thing you could have it as a bomber, night fighter, fighter-bomber and maritime strike aircraft – if nothing else Airfix were educational and wanted you to know about the sheer ingenuity of the British aircraft industry during the war. Or maybe they were not sure they'd be able to sell me two essentially identical kits so decided to spread bet on the Mosquito types.

The Mosquito has a fascinating story. Like the Spitfire and Hurricane before it, it had been a private venture by a British aircraft manufacturer in anticipation of the war – both Hawker and Supermarine had taken a punt on their planes being accepted by the Air Ministry, which had issued a spec for a 'modern' fighter plane. De Havilland took this one stage further by offering a plane that the Ministry hadn't asked for. Like many of the aircraft manufacturers in Britain de Havilland was a family firm – a business taken so seriously by Geoffrey de Havilland that two of his sons were killed testing aircraft. De Havilland was a tough man, ruthless. Progressing from biplane trainers such as the Gypsy Moth to airliners like the Dragon Rapide, his company had great experience in making fast twin engine aircraft: his DH.88 mail plane set records wherever it flew, capable of making the Croydon-to-Paris run in 52 minutes and flying to Melbourne in a then-gobsmacking 70 hours and 55 minutes. He'd built it for one of the many aircraft competitions and races that had kept innovation going during the disarmed interwar years.

When de Havilland submitted his design for the Mosquito it was too radical for the Air Ministry – the company had designed a plane that would fly faster than any enemy fighter so it wouldn't need any of the defensive armaments, gun turrets, guns, etc. – and the Air Ministry went ahead and turned it down. De Havilland carried on with the Mosquito, but in the meantime to shut the Ministry up built some mock-ups with turrets. A tortuous year and a half of personal lobbying, as well as de Havilland hedging his bets by offering a fighter variant, saved the project and the 'fastest bomber in the world' went ahead. The boast was true. The other thing everyone knows – well, I say everyone, but I wouldn't count on the cast of *TOWIE* knowing it – about the Mosquito is it was made of wood: balsa wood, birch and plywood. The fuselages – the bodies of the aircraft – were built in furniture factories. It's often worth finding out what the enemy thought about things – what Wellington called knowing what was happening 'on the other side of the hill'. Hermann Goering – head of the Luftwaffe and responsible for defending Germany from air attack – had something to say about the Mosquito, which could bomb Germany unarmed, outrunning his fighters:

'It makes me furious when I see the Mosquito. I turn green and yellow with envy. The British, who can afford aluminium better than we can, knock together a beautiful wooden aircraft that every piano factory over there is building, and they give it a speed which they have now increased yet again. What do you make of that? There is nothing the British do not have. They have the geniuses and we have the nincompoops. After the war is over I'm going to buy a British radio set – then at least I'll own something that has always worked.'

He didn't get the chance, thank God. And interesting to hear one of Hitler's number twos (pun intended) saying that the Allies had better stuff than the Germans . . .

One thing I didn't do with my model planes was get an airgun and shoot at them, like apparently all my generation is meant to have done. They were too precious and too big a draw on my pocket money for me to simply trash. I perfected making these aircraft, and the greens and browns and greys and duck-egg colours the RAF used to have had become a sort of reflexive mental palate – trips to aircraft museums were a chance to mentally tick off the paint colours and the look of the things. This will sound stupid, but the aircraft were always surprisingly big, a side effect of working in 1/72nd scale most of the time. The Lancaster bomber at Hendon, for instance, is particularly enormous if you're used to looking at it in 1/72nd. The rare times I'd build a plane in Airfix's next scale up, 1/48th, the kit would seem huge, unwieldy, its pilot like some bloated giant. But thanks to this hobby I am pretty sure the lines of the Spitfire and its famous, over-rhapsodised elliptical wing are burnished in my memory indelibly, the way some people can recite football scores.

So when the moment actually came, it made flying in a Spitfire most peculiar. Last year the chance came up, after endless successful nagging and needling, to fly in a twin-seat Mark IX Spitfire. It was the strangest experience. Yes, it was amazing, yes, it was dreams coming true and all that, but chiefly it was odd. Maybe part of the reason it was odd was the circumstances: in order to get the flight I'd agreed to do a whole load of press to publicise the Imperial War Museum at Duxford near Cambridge. This museum is simply wonderful, and somewhere anyone with kids should go: it has an amazing array of exhibits, lots of aircraft that are flying, hangars where you can look at the work of restoration going on – ancient engines in pieces being lovingly restored. When I'm touring, if we're anywhere in East Anglia we'll drop in. Duxford was a famous fighter station during the war, and the home of the renowned wooden-legged fighter ace Douglas Bader.

Bader is one of those people you can do in a sentence or a whole book. Guess which I'm going for. By all accounts he was a colossal pain in the arse and a massively inspirational figure – in my view these things aren't a question of either/or. In fact, I think the more you try to apply an either/or way of looking at people like Bader, the mightier they become and the more the argument diminishes you: though like Montgomery his views on race and apartheid were hair-raising, and of their time. Why anyone ever needed to invent the anti-hero beats me. Anyway, during the summer Duxford hosts air shows and the sky teems with aircraft from every era. Last summer we were passing through on our way to a gig in East Anglia and an F-16 from a nearby American base came in to practise his display. The noise a plane like an F-16 throwing on its twin afterburners as it turns its back on you to power away isn't so much a noise as the sky itself being torn apart and squashed into your face through a narrow funnel. Your head feels it, your stomach feels it, your arse feels it: you don't hear it as such. The sound goes right through you.

When we went to the display that weekend my daughters were largely uninterested (except when it came to the gift shop). I did what I could to hype the afternoon's display and made all sorts of wild promises that the F-16 would blow their minds. As it had been raining things were getting pretty miserable, and we'd been fortunate enough to be rescued by Esther, who is in charge of publicity at the airfield, and whisked away to the corporate area, where we found ourselves drinking coffee with Air Marshals and the great and good of military aviation. I'd got stuck into a conversation with the head of the RAF that I can't relate in any way whatsoever. Boredom was creeping back in, the kids were giving off telltale fidgety signs of wandering attention, and I began to watch the timetable anxiously – tricky to do whilst making small talk with an Air Marshal.

Then, exactly on time, as far away as I could see, I spotted a tiny grey dot, approaching rapidly. Eight-year-old girls aren't much excited about tiny grey dots, but it was going at such a speed that she found she couldn't look away. The F-16 slowed as it neared the airstrip, got two-thirds of the way down the runway and then turned hard right, its afterburners facing us and glowing a fierce, fiery orange. Afterburners are well named – fuel is pumped into the extremely hot air exiting a jet engine, catches fire and delivers loads of extra thrust (basically). They're not very fuel-efficient: Concorde had afterburners. Concorde used to fly right over the end of my garden – or at least it felt like it, it was so bloody noisy. Around five o'clock the New York Concorde would come in, mildly pulling the sky apart as if to remind everyone that the millionaires who simply couldn't waste an extra couple of hours flying in from New York and possibly Joan Collins were back in town. When they retired the remaining Concordes for being old, expensive and unrepairable, all three flew in over the end of the garden: it was spectacular, funny-looking and, for me, strangely unsentimental. The F-16's afterburners made a noise like the sky falling in and he set off dozens of car alarms in the museum car park with his downdraught when he flicked the plane to its right and zoomed up and away from us. From then on he had everyone's attention, including that of any eight-year-old girls.

When the day came for the Spitfire flight I was doing everything I could to be cool about it. Everything. I'd tried to lie in. I'd tried to go to bed early as well. I did what I could not to get there stupidly early. Looking back at it, it's one of those times where I wish I'd allowed myself to be a little less cool about it, but a babbling, gushing overexcited me isn't something I'd want to inflict on anyone, especially not when there are journalists about. We arrived at Duxford and the day couldn't have been more perfect – a bright blue summer sky with little white fluffy clouds. The people from Duxford made a tremendous fuss of me. (Have I mentioned what a great museum it is yet?) I'd attracted the museum's attention when I'd been asked to write about one of my tours for the *Sun* newspaper. I'd used some of the pictures you'll run into later of my Monty doll posing with various aircraft at Duxford. The museum had got wind of this and invited me and my tour manager, Adam, to pop in again sometime and have a look inside the aircraft. 'How about the B 52, or the Flying Fortress, what do you reckon?' This was an offer we couldn't refuse. It also meant we had to sign a health-and-safety waiver – the instruments in the Flying Fortress are all painted with radioactive luminous paint and we were exposing ourselves to (very) low-level radiation. Compared with the danger these young crews were exposed to while flying on raids over Germany in broad daylight, signing it seemed both easy and faintly feeble. This visit marked the start of a beautiful relationship – for me, at least. Heaven knows what they get out of it. Did I mention what a great museum it is?

The Spitfire I flew in was operated by the Aircraft Restoration Company, flown by the MD and Chief Test Pilot John Romain. John's love of Spitfires came from watching *The Battle of Britain* movie – it seems that the wrong aircraft types didn't put him off. Weird. The people at ARCo are dedicated to making old aircraft of all sorts fly but on this visit their pride and joy was the Spitfire they were about to finish and test fly – a Mark I that had crashed on the beach at Dunkirk and been recovered, and restored to exactly how it would have been in 1940. Exactly how it was. Some restored planes will have a Garmin satnav in the cockpit to help out with the tricky business of where you are, but not this Mark I, it was a pristine true-to-1940 type. The plane I flew in had been converted to a two-seater trainer in 1950. Seeing it parked outside the hangar had a strange numbing effect on me: it was painted in the green and brown colours used by the RAF during the first part of the war – the green and brown were familiar like an ancient rug or an old friend's face, my reflexive mental palette.

ARCo take people up in this Spitfire fairly regularly, so they're super-cool about the whole business. Needless to say, they're quite used to people being stuffed into a one-size-fits-all flying suit, asking daft questions, saying 'Oh my God, I don't believe this is really happening' and taking endless pictures. We wandered out of the hangar and towards the Spitfire as John explained the aircraft's history. Various hacks and photographers were there, and a camera crew. I was shown to the plane, then climbed into the rear cockpit and sat on the parachute. There then followed a health-and-safety briefing. There being no aisle and no fire exits and no safety-slide-cum-raft thing on the doors over the wing and no oxygen masks that drop down and no emergency-exit doors to open, this wasn't the average aeroplane-safety briefing. The press were asked to clear off – they'd been taking a load of anticipatory pictures in which I look mainly like an ecstatic ten-year-old. The briefing soon wiped the smile off my face. It went a bit like this:

'Right, if there's a problem during take-off, it's most likely John will simply put the plane down in a field, so hold tight and once the plane has stopped get the canopy open – by winding that handle on your right there.'

'Er, right, OK.'

'The only time you might have to bail out other than that is if there's an engine fire, for instance, and John has lost control of the aircraft. If this happens John will tell you to bale out of the aircraft. Open the canopy . . .'

'With the handle?' That handle again. It's tiny, smaller than the handle you wind on a fishing rod. You wind it (frantically, no doubt) to open the canopy. It's one of those things you'd have to do quicker than the explanation if you want to survive.

'With the handle, yes, undo your harness, stand up, step onto the canopy door to your left and then jump forwards towards the wing.'

'Towards the wing?'

'Yes, towards the wing or you'll hit the tail.'

'I'll hit the tail.'

'Then pull your ripcord and down you go.'

124

'OK.'

'You'll have to be quite quick as you're not going to be flying much above four thousand feet.'

'Yeah.'

'Great. So are you comfortable with the harness?' I snapped out of the moment I'd found myself in, the moment being the plane on fire, winding the handle frantically, standing on the edge of the door reminding myself to jump towards – no, wait, was it away? – from the wing and the ground being not all that far away. The harness was comfortable, yes.

Then John got in the plane and we were left alone. On went the headset, he explained how the flight would go, we'd make sure we swung past the hangar so the cameramen could get a picture, then do a few circuits – if I had a problem I was to waggle the controls – and he started the engine. He'd warned me it would belch fumes through the cockpit, but I wasn't too bothered when it did – the noise and the smell had completely snapped me out of my I'm-not-going-to-get-overexcited mood. Suddenly I had to try to take in this experience I'd been trying my damnedest to be blasé about, that I'd erected defences around. The engine was roaring, the familiar low growl of the Merlin that air shows know draw definite crowds and that has become part of aviation legend. And I was sat behind someone sat behind one. It was like being inside the sound. The noise was fabulous, intoxicating. We taxied along the grass – Spitfires were designed for grass airstrips – and we made our faintly sideways progress to the end of the runway. Spitfires have such long noses that for a pilot to see where he's going he needs to crab along slightly sideways. Was John explaining this to me or was I reciting these Spitfire-facts to myself? We turned into the wind (and towards the M11 which is at the end of the runway) and off we went.

That's me in the back, honest.

In 1938 Duxford was home to 19 Squadron, the first squadron in the RAF to take delivery of Spitfires – the first one was delivered by Supermarine's chief test pilot Jeffery Quill. During the Battle of Britain the airfield was home to aircraft in No. 12 Group. At Duxford, as the battle raged, Douglas Bader was busy being a colossal pain in the arse/inspirational leader. He was an advocate of something called the Big Wing – the idea of amassing loads of fighter planes to attack German bomber formations. Big Wings were hugely controversial; No. 11 Group to the south – covering the Channel, Kent and London, dealing with the brunt of the German air offensive – favoured sending single squadrons up as and when they were needed to meet the German bombers and fighters coming from France and the Low Countries.[54] Big Wings seemed to belong to a plain and simple 'big is better' attitude, the big idea (sorry) being that they would deliver a 'knockout' blow to an enemy bomber formation: three to five squadrons would form up,

---

[54] No one says the Low Countries any more. And the Low Countries being Belgium and Holland, one of them at least is a High Country (obligatory Dutch dope joke).

something like thirty or forty fighters in all. I know, it sounds great, doesn't it?!

The only problem was that Big Wings used up crucial time (and fuel) to form up, and took more effort to coordinate, unlike a squadron being scrambled and sent to intercept. Also, as the Duxford squadrons were flying both Spitfires and Hurricanes, they could only go as fast as the slower Hurricanes. Oops. Keith Park who commanded 11 Group had tried Big Wings for himself and was not convinced – they lacked the flexibility needed to deal with the Luftwaffe, in fact they cancelled out one of Fighter Command's big advantages which was, above all else, flexibility. When the Battle of Britain had ended, this being Britain, those who'd opposed the Big Wing, which didn't suit the situation or work at all well, found themselves sacked for having mismanaged the Battle. The Battle of Britain also presents an interesting conundrum for national stereotyping. The British, whose self-image was (still is?) one of plucky improvisation and making do, were in fact very well-organised and had prepared for this exact kind of fighter defence of the UK, whereas the Germans – who even now are meant to be super-efficient and ruthless – were making it up as they went along and couldn't decide what it was they were trying to do, switching from attacking airfields and radar installations to bombing cities at precisely the moment when they were beginning to seriously damage the RAF's ability to defend itself. The RAF was ruthlessly efficient and achieved what it set out to do, the Luftwaffe – conceived principally as air support for ground forces, not for bombing cities strategically – pluckily improvised and made do and lost. So much for cliché. Perhaps the cliché has stuck because we prefer to see ourselves that way.

As we started to pick up speed I was mesmerised by the shape and colour of the Spitfire's wing: the brown felt so familiar, the blue of the roundel like the face of an old friend I'd just pulled up a chair for a chat with. Then, almost imperceptibly, we were airborne. Flying. Flying, in a Spitfire. My emotional register didn't really have a response ready – it was really happening, to me, it hadn't really involved much hoo-ha, we were flying in a Spitfire! A Spitfire!!!! . . . ooh, look there's all the hacks down next to the hangar . . . We zoomed over the journalists below and as we did I didn't know whether to wave or flick cocky V-signs – I settled for a wave but even then didn't know what I was doing or why, the irresistible noise and power of the aircraft as we pulled up and away could have been powered by my bewildered ecstatic grin. I looked up through the canopy; it gleamed, it sparkled in the sunshine, its curve studded with perfect little white fluffy clouds. At this point, dear reader, I was speechless. Some might say this is a great tragedy that there was only one person there to experience this choice and rare moment. I'd been speechless before in a plane, but in very different circumstances, circumstances that related to another Spitfire flight.

When we were making *Road to Berlin* in 2004 there was a grand plan to fly in a two-seater Spitfire. Needless to say, I was all for it. The episode was about V-bombs; the V stands for *Vergeltungswaffen* which translates as 'Vengeance Weapons',[55] another lovely, cuddly Nazi idea. Spitfires were used to attack

---

[55] Vengeance for what, you might ask, seeing as they started it? Well, vengeance for the bombing campaign on Germany, which the Nazi government had successfully, and without much difficulty, portrayed as terror-bombing – bomber crews were *Terrorflieger*. German soldiers were said to be motivated by the destruction of their home towns by the bombing offensive – well, who wouldn't be? After all, Coventry had galvanised Britain's response to the Blitz and become emblematic of resistance. It's always struck me as odd that seeing as we weren't bombed into submission, and like to say how proud we are of how we weren't, that we expect anyone else to be.

the V1 and V2 launch sites – the crude V1 cruise missiles took off by being fired up a ramp. I interviewed a veteran who had flown Spitfires on these sorties: he told us about dive-bombing mobile V2 rocket launchers, how dangerous these sorties were – he described how he had seen a missile climb away as he came in to attack. Sat in the cockpit of a Spitfire for us at Duxford he waxed eloquent about how the Spitfire was the perfect combination of form and function, a truly wonderful aircraft to fly, and said with a deliciously sly smile that if we gave him fifteen minutes he reckoned he'd remember how to fly it: 'It's all coming back to me, yes.' In addition, for this programme we'd decided that I would fly in a twin-seater Spitfire. Hiring a Spitfire isn't cheap: buying one is for Euro-lottery-winner types only, they cost at least one million pounds, and three to four thousand quid an hour to run. (Little wonder as each hour in the air requires twenty-four hours' maintenance.) Our meagre budget couldn't really cover it, but the footage would be brilliant (I was very keen on getting brilliant footage, obviously, not just flying in the legendary fighter). To ease the cost I'd suggested my brother-in-law join us, he has a pilot's licence and was keen to get a go in a Spitfire. (Who isn't? If you're reading this book I'd say it was a safe bet.) To take this flight we'd had to go to Shropshire. We spent all day sitting on an aerodrome near Shrewsbury, waiting for the Spitfire to arrive. It didn't, the weather had let us down. Low cloud. Not where we were but at the airstrip where the Spitfire was: doubly frustrating. While we waited we shot some pieces to camera, some to fill the gap that the weather and Spitfire no-show had made for us and some that would save us another afternoon's filming. The time hung heavy until we knew there was no chance of the Spitfire coming to play.

My brother-in-law, who had flown up that morning, offered

to fly me back to London. Tom, our brilliant and thoughtful director, asked if he could cadge a lift too. Once we'd made ourselves comfortable, I sat in the front in the co-pilot's chair and Tom took the back seat. My brother-in-law took us through the rules of flying in a small aircraft (well, his, anyway). If you don't mind, look out of the windows, keep your eyes peeled, and if you see anyone else up here let me know, point them out to me. Fine, we said, no problem. We took off and flew right into the low cloud, which all of a sudden did seem really very low. At least we'd got to it a lot quicker than I'd expected. For five entire minutes, maybe longer (it certainly seemed it) as we climbed to get clear of the cloud, we were completely whited out. You couldn't see beyond the canopy. The view was of glass on nothingness. Blank. White. I was transfixed, looking out of my side for anyone else 'up here with us'.

Well, I couldn't see anything but white cloud, couldn't judge distances, the whiteness of the cloud was almost dazzling, as if my optic nerve was overwhelmed by having no colour to work with. It slowly crept up on me: if I did see anyone 'up here with us' it would be as we were hitting them. The exact moment we crashed. Not just before, not just after, but as it happened. Up we went, still climbing. I sat, gripping my seat, anticipating the worst, utterly speechless and paralysed by fear, telling myself it would at least be instant but wasn't going to happen anyway. The engine buzzed away, in a monotone, though its sound was drowned out by the fear running around inside my head. My balls began making the apologetic return journey to the protection of inside my body – though a fat lot of good that'd do if we clunked into a passing Airbus and made the return journey to earth *sans* light aeroplane. If there'd been a handle by the canopy to wind down, there wouldn't have been time to wind it down. Then, without fanfare, announcement or any kind of warning, the engine still buzzing its lone note, we cleared the cloud and suddenly there was blue sky, fields, a helicopter several thousand feet below us whizzing from left to right, the M4 traffic crawling beneath us . . . The rest of the flight was uneventful if not actually boring. The sweat cooled as it pooled in my underpants. Once we'd landed at Denham outside West London, Tom and I said our goodbyes to my brother-in-law, who seemed unaware of the flight of terror he's subjected us to and jumped in the car that was waiting for us (telly, don't you know). I said to him, 'I know this sounds stupid, but . . .' and explained the sheer, blind, white-out terror I'd experienced.

'Me too,' Tom replied. We left it there.

'OK, we're going to do a couple of barrel rolls now,' said John. I'd already had a go at flying the Spitfire myself, taking the stick and gingerly moving the plane around. It was light, delicate, handling exactly as all the legends tell you, responsive, kind to the pilot. But don't ask me, I'm not a pilot, I'm a comic who blagged a flight, I don't really know what I'm talking about. What I can tell you is that this memory is one I'm saving loads of brain space for so it can remain in HD. As we turned upside down and the ground swung round over my head, I felt what's best described as long, slow surprise. This was really, really, really happening. And it was happening quickly, and was over all too soon. We came in over the airfield again, and then came in to land. We pulled up outside the hangar, and once the engine had stopped we got out. I stumbled on the steps getting out and immediately microphones were shoved in my face and I was asked how it felt. I didn't really know, I hadn't had time to think about it, let alone address the creeping melancholy that it was over already. I'd been in a Spitfire. A real one. My main feeling was that compared with the models it was enormous.

But I did reach a point where the modelling challenges and the variety of the kits ran out, and I turned to bigger kits. There is a Japanese model firm called Tamiya, who make amazing model kits, but when I was a lad there was a snag. They made amazing model kits and the amazing model kits were of German tanks. It is true that the German armoured tech of the Second World War is still regarded as superior (for all its shortcomings the Tiger tank is still regarded by many as the greatest tank of the Second World War, a spell cast when it first appeared on the battlefield in North Africa and one that endures to this day – I touched on this above). But luckily for the model manufacturer and the model maker the Germans developed a plethora of types, variations and customisations and Tamiya were able to oblige the keen modeller with endless kits to make. Every mark of German tank from the titchy *Panzerkampfwagen* Mark I through to the King Tiger via the Panther could be built. The Mark I Panzer was the tank that swept the German Blitzkrieg into Poland and France in the opening stages of the war. The best way to describe it is titchy. Each time I see one in the flesh it makes me jump it's so small. The French might have crumbled in the face of the Germans in May 1940 but they never sported as titchy and frankly preposterously tiny a tank as the Mark I Panzer. (It's worth pointing out that the Blitzkrieg didn't really exist – it's a classic example of something being named, 'dubbed'[56] as the tabloids would have it, and the name sticking – meaning 'lightning war' it sounds great, it's the kind of name that once you've been

---

[56] I don't know why but whenever I see the expression 'dubbed' I am always reminded of Lady Helen Windsor, dubbed 'Melons'. That's what the papers always used to say about her. By whom? We'll never know.

given you wouldn't want to play down. Like Goldenballs, I suppose.)[57]

The Germans had perfected combined operations, integrating armour (tanks), artillery, 'storm troopers' and air cover. The chief proponent of using tanks so aggressively was called Heinz Guderian. He'd got a great deal of inspiration from the last army to perfect combined operations, the British Army. Towards the end of World War One the British army had got very good at coordinating its different component parts – and it had been the British, after all, who had been first in with the idea of the tank. British generals like the meticulous Herbert 'Old Plum' Plumer and Edmund Allenby had become adept at combining all elements tactically, and Guderian knew it – Allenby's conduct of the Battle of Megiddo[58] is pretty much Blitzkrieg in embryo. Guderian, who also knew perfectly well that the Germans had been beaten in 1918, as well as how, went about studying British military theory. He even checked out the radical tank theories of a little-known French armour enthusiast called Charles de Gaulle. In Poland and in France the Germans got 'inside the decision loop' of their opponents. Basically, this means they had the initiative and didn't let go of it. The Germans had learned the lessons of the First World War and how to win it, the French and the British perhaps hadn't spotted what those lessons were. The Germans were also prepared to take casualties of the kind we wouldn't even begin to tolerate nowadays – something like 150,000 in total, with maybe 40,000 of them being killed. These kind of figures make you wonder exactly how miraculous Blitzkrieg (no such thing!) really was. But at the front of Guderian's offensive was the Mark I Panzer.

---

[57] I'm not really comparing David Beckham to Blitzkrieg there.
[58] Armageddon!

One word, titchy: how does he even sit down in that thing?
Where do his legs go?

Just look at the size of these King Tigers (I expect that's what
they said at the time).

That this midget machine's lineage led to the King Tiger seems entirely unlikely at a glance. I'm not sure I ever made the Mark I, despite its cataclysmic role in world history. The King Tiger (the Tiger II) was offered with either turret type – the 'production' or the 'Porsche' (oh yes). The types had exotic names, exotic weaponry, and there were lot and lots of them. Maybe Tamiya had taken a leaf out of the Germans' book and used the same chassis for lots of different types, but the choices were overwhelming. There were the straight-up Mark IVs – a tank that had a similar profile to the Tiger and might have been responsible for what the Allied armies called 'Tiger Fever' in Normandy; Allied tank crews were seeing Tigers in every hedgerow, around every corner, though, fair enough, an encounter with a Tiger was likely to go very badly. There were the original Mark IVs, then there were up-gunned Mark IVs with a more powerful main weapon; the self-propelled-gun version without a turret – the *Jagdpanzer* IV – Hunting-panzer; the *Wirbelwind* anti-aircraft Mark IV boasting four 20mm cannon; the *Brummbär* self-propelled gun with a large-calibre 15-centimetre gun for close support of infantry in urban fighting, e.g. knocking over buildings. The British and American armoured fighting vehicles lacked the German tanks' glamour, and the notes on Tamiya's boxes, terse and written in the translated English peculiar to Japanese imports at that time, also let you know exactly how the British types were inferior.

And the thing is, despite being on the losing side, the German stuff was undeniably better, certainly from a 12-year-old model maker's perspective. The British never got their act together with tank types – the Churchill[59] tank by comparison looked

---

[59] Churchill himself said 'they named it after me when they realised it was no bloody good.' The Churchill, for all its ponderous and dated looks, had very thick armour that its crews appreciated. In the desert one Churchill was said to have been hit 80

135

lumpy and slow, even the model with the flame-thrower trailer seemed lacklustre. Yes, the Allies had manufactured all manner of specialist tanks, particularly with D-Day in mind – floating DD tanks, minefield-clearing 'flail' tanks, bridging tanks, Major General Hobart's 'Funnies', etc. – but they didn't seem to have the air of technical innovation and superiority that the seemingly endless German marks had. Allied tanks tended to be painted one colour, a drab olive green, rather than the mottled camouflage and anti-magnetic stippling called *Zimmerit* that the Germans would use. And because Allied tank production centred around fewer types produced in larger quantities, there wasn't much difference between all the Grants and the Shermans. It was the same for Soviet tank types: the multiple German types (no matter how advanced they might be) were overwhelmed by legions of identical T-34s. In fact, one of the Germans' war problems was the ingenuity and complex thinking of their engineers – they were too clever by half. This increasing complexity was also ill-timed because as German industry came under more and more pressure from the bomber offensive, turning out more complex, expensive types of weaponry required all the more effort. It could and has been said that the Germans became fixated on designing the weapons of the 1950s – modern tanks, jet planes, cruise missiles and rockets – which they could ill afford, while the Allies perfected the weapons of the 1930s and beat them. But the German modern-technical-marvel tanks made for better model kits.

So, thanks to Tamiya, I became well acquainted with German tanks and tank design, and its innate and undeniable superiority over Allied technology. But still, they lost. Even though they

times by anti-tank fire! The Churchill could take several hits from Panzer IIIs and IVs, and even from a Tiger, which was just as well as its own gun meant it had to get good and close to the German tanks to knock them out.

had snazzier gear: because they had snazzier gear. Another one of those stereotypes that doesn't quite deliver, and certainly one you don't think about when you're painting yet another self-propelled gun. But before there was Airfix, before there was Tamiya, there was Action Man.

7. Action Man
THE MOVABLE FIGHTING MAN

And so we come to Action Man, my (male) generation's little secret. Before *Star Wars* came along and forced us into nostalgic conformity – and I think *Star Wars* is a good enough kids' film, and that's that, I'm not eight any more, don't expect me to remember stuff about it, please, Boba Who? – we were making our own adventures, with near-infinite variation in our bedrooms, gardens, wherever.

But why did I call it our little secret? Because the thing is that Action Man – and I am breaking no new ground in saying this, in fact saying this has more of the character of an alcoholic hauling himself to his feet clutching a half-drunk bottle of whisky and declaring his alcoholism – Action Man was a doll. For boys. A doll that we, boys, would dress up. For all the on-the-nose gender stereotyping of a boy playing with a 'war toy', Action Man was a boy's doll. We'd change his costumes, decide on what looked good and dress him up in that stuff. As well as being a doll, he had accessories. Different boots. Hats. Trousers. Guns. Lots of guns, which were often painted brown. We'd dress him up in different outfits with different accessories depending on where he was off out to, I mean, which mission

139

he was embarking on. And while Action Man was a hugely successful toy, a mainstay of my generation, a boys' doll – one thing has always baffled me: my God, it must have been a hard sell for whoever came up with it. Sisters had Sindy – this was before Barbie had forced her way absurd-tits-first into girls' toy collections – and Sindy was a doll you dressed up. In costumes, with accessories. So was Action Man. But Action Man had gripping hands, realistic hair (at least the later ones did – purists hate him, apparently, much preferring the smooth black or lemon-coloured painted hair), loads of guns and, if you were lucky, Eagle Eyes.

Whoever had come up with Action Man was without a doubt a genius: it had us hooked, and we were having all our buttons pressed, all our strings pulled. Not unlike the talking Action Man whose string you'd pull and he'd say stuff from under his coat in a strangled voice.

'Enemy tanks approaching!'

'What's the password?'

'Send out the patrol!'

'Advance in single file!'

'Give me some cover!'

Which, when put together like that, sounds all too much like a British military operation unravelling in five easy commands.

Palitoy, who made Action Man, had us all trapped like dying flies on flypaper with a scheme for collecting stars on the packaging. Everything you bought came with stars and if you saved them as you built up your wardrobe – sorry, Quartermaster's Store – you could cash in the stars for the top-of-the-shop item which was a Mountie uniform complete with guard dog. The guard dog didn't have an articulated body like Action Man – he stood stock-still, straining at the lead, jowls out – but for all his limits he was the pinnacle of Action Man collectability. You simply couldn't buy the Mountie outfit in the UK, you had to collect the stars, so if you ran into a playmate who had the Mountie outfit you knew what you were up against. Most likely an only child with multiple uncles and aunts. Envy is a bastard when you're six. I never had either the patience or the turnover of stars to collect a Mountie outfit, and I'm fairly sure – though I'd never have said it like this – I thought that the Mountie uniform was ever so slightly camp. Too camp for my boys' doll. My doll.

My Action Men lived with all their uniforms and weapons in an old ammunition box that my father had purloined from somewhere and were my pride and joy as a kid. When *Blue Peter* got in on the act by devising home-made mountaineering costumes for them,[60] with a ping-pong ball as a helmet, my grandmother bought a place in grandson heaven by knocking out several outfits at the cost of a couple of my dad's socks. Action Man was the absolute go-to toy for me before I was nine – he had the lot: guns, a dashing scar, green jumpers with patches on the shoulders. Dammit, he was the real thing.

Also, crucially, he was British. Because I would occasionally read Marvel comics, I was dimly aware of what seemed to be some pale American echo, GI Joe. There were ads in the comics for GI Joe. GI Joe had many weaknesses, but the most obvious was that he was called GI Joe. He had a name. Action Man didn't, so he could be anybody. GI Joe had a name and also the faint whiff of defeat in Vietnam about him. (Is this hindsight? I don't know, but the uniforms, the weapons, something about him didn't smell right. I knew about Vietnam pretty much because I remember helicopters on a roof on the telly and the

---

[60] *Blue Peter* always coyly referred to them as anything but Action Men: this was the golden age of covered-up cornflakes' labels, John Noakes, Peter Purves, Leslie Judd, etc. They'll never replace the old stars, will they?

all too clear implication that something had gone wrong, and had been going wrong for ages.)[61] Action Man was British, he wasn't a GI, he could be any rank you liked, though the officers' uniforms must have been a bit pricey because I never had an officer. He generally hung out in his olive-green trousers, with jumper, khaki belt, inexplicable Royal Tank Regiment beret (everything about Action Man when your parents couldn't afford a tank for him suggested he was an infantryman), one-size-fits-all black boots and his clunky unglamorous (chiefly brown and, I was shocked to discover, Belgian) FN rifle, also known as an SLR. In other words he looked about as glamorous as real 1970s British soldiers, so he was a proper true-to-life toy and no mistake. At a distance – a hundred yards, perhaps? – he could easily be mistaken for the men I'd seen at Salisbury Plain when visiting dad parachuting (wrong colour beret, though). If you need to picture what he looked like with his rifle, he looked a lot like the soldiers you see on old footage of Northern Ireland.

Using my stars I saved up and got an Action Man with Eagle Eyes and gripping hands. The previous Action Man had gripping hands, and these had perished, so we sent him back to Palitoy in Leicester and, lo and behold, he came back with fresh hands. (I'm still amazed by this – would this happen nowadays? Probably not without resorting to a whiny letter to *Watchdog* shaming them into doing it.) Eagle Eyes were a work of genius – and, like the realistic hair, an innovation made by British Palitoy who were making GI Joes under licence from Hasbro. A slit in the back of his astroturfed head ('Realistic hair' – another British Palitoy innovation) had a small black lever, which enabled you to move Action Man's eyes from side to

---

[61] You can say what you like about the Suez Crisis, and people very much do, but at least we got our moment of international military humiliation over with pronto rather than drawing it out over a decade like the Americans did in Vietnam.

side. This shifty, stuttering glance made him unspeakably superior to the other Action Men – he was instantly elevated to marksman. His eyes, like his rifle, never jammed. If memory serves – and I may be very wrong – because he'd been acquired with stars, he came stark naked in a box and had to be dressed with the first stuff that came to hand. From then on he was the favourite Action Man in the box, and often got to dress up in my grandmother's home-made outfits and go on special missions.

We had had a fatality, though. Early on in my time of Action Man service at my grandparents' place in Bath I remember distinctly – and sitting here recalling it is bringing it into sharper and more traumatic[62] focus – my uncle taking one of my Action Men out into their garden and killing it. OK, perhaps that isn't how it happened but that's what the end result was. This was when I was about three, at a guess. Maybe four. My grandparents' house was unspeakably exotic to me at the time: it was three storeys tall and they had a long staircase with a broad curve that was laid with a dark blue carpet. Naturally, this staircase was a waterfall that Action Man had to climb up, or surf down, depending on the mission he had been assigned. One summer while staying with my grandparents, somewhat inevitably I'd been given an Action Man with a parachute, and these parachutes with some coaxing do actually work. Not unlike the real thing (given that they're actually some brown string and a khaki hanky), if they're packed properly they will open as they ought to and bring their cargo sailing down to earth fairly safely. The Action Man parachute is packed into a green plastic box with

[62] Please note, I am aware of my misuse of the word 'traumatic'. 'Traumatic' has come to mean pretty much anything disagreeable, and I feel, for reasons of hyperbole, forced into using the word. There might be people reading this who only know 'trauma' in its modern debased sense and wonder why it gets used when referring to missing limbs, etc. But it's OK, I know what I'm doing, don't panic.

a lid that is flipped open by a ring-pulled 'ripcord' as you throw it. Obviously, it couldn't be left to Action Man to open his own parachute.

(In this it's not unlike a static-line-release parachute. Static-line-release parachutes open for you automatically – they're clipped to a steel wire in the aircraft and pay out of the 'chute as you fall from the plane before pulling the parachute clear and opening it. They're used in combat because getting lots of men out of a plane quickly at low level doesn't give anyone the time to choose for themselves when they should open their 'chute. They open like clockwork, the men land like clockwork. The British one used in the war was very smooth, having a series of ties that would break as they fed out the canopy's lines. The American parachute cracked itself open in one go and sent a great jolt through your goolies; no wonder American airborne soldiers were so aggressive.)

I know the details of this toy 'chute because (a) I have clear recall of it, recall doused in and heightened by trauma[63] and (b) I bought a new one when the year before last someone reissued all the Action Men – and I mean all – for anniversary cash-in purposes. The reissue was amazing – they printed the catalogues, the booklets, his secret maps, every detail lovingly recreated. Opening the boxes released the same heady new Action Man smell – instantly transporting me back to being five. And they'd gone the distance with nostalgic gratification: you could *buy* the Mountie suit and accompanying bloody dog. But the parachute works fairly well, although you need to be careful. What you don't need to do is let it be snatched by your cackling, burbling uncle (he was a medical student at the time, perhaps it was research) who goes to the top of a three-storey house

---

[63] There I go again. Sorry.

and then hurls the Action Man out of the window with little regard for the correct packing of the 'chute or its operation. Action Man went up some way, the 'chute didn't open, and he plummeted – not like a rock, but like a falling doomed beloved toy – onto the limestone steps outside my grandparents' back door. He landed with a great crack and a leg was permanently broken; I think the mounting of one of the pins attached to the elastic inside him that held him together was shattered. I know I bawled about it. My memory – probably organising events for future anecdotal purposes – has my uncle leaping into a Mini or an MG and driving off, still chuckling. He simply went back to medical school and pleaded poverty: he couldn't afford to replace my downed comrade in play nor, for all his medical training, was he able to fix Action Man's shattered leg. This black-haired Action Man returned to the ammo box broken but unbowed. He became the man back at base, the I'd-go-if-I-could-chaps member of the team – for all the Action Men with scars on their faces he was the only one I'd ever seen actually injured.

I grew out of Action Man, or rather found myself grown out of Action Man when I got to boarding school when I was nine. God knows what I thought it was going to be like, but I'd been given a wooden tuck-box – I've still got it, and I still call it a tuck-box though now it's full of grown-up male electrical gubbins – and I discovered to my delight that an Action Man would fit in the internal compartment in the top-left of the box. Popping him into the tuck-box as I packed and prepared for my first day, he took pride of place with all the ginger nuts and maybe a penknife.[64] I'm not sure. I imagine that in my naivety I'd thought everyone else would bring their Action Man too,

---

[64] Yes – knives at school! Late 1970s chaos!

and bonding through the greatest toy the world had known would occur. Hooray! What larks! This didn't work out. Boarding school – long before you factor in teachers – can be a brutal environment. Boys between, say, 9 and 12 are chiefly concerned with the pecking order and their place in it. (I don't really know why I just put an age limit on that: it's all males, surely? People, even.) So turning up with what was – of course – a doll wasn't the smartest move. Oh yes, it might well have been a boys' doll, but it was a doll nevertheless. Lacking the marketing skills of the man who pitched the first Action Man, and with no one else having brought theirs in with them, he found himself back in his compartment instantly. We were weekly boarders and that first weekend Action Man took the first troop transport home. He and I never recovered from this body blow to our partnership, but fair enough, I was nine and getting on a bit. And at this point the model kits were waiting in the wings ready to exploit Action Man's moment of weakness.

I had at one point been Action Man myself, with realistic hair, a beret, a green jumper, belt, ill-fitting boots and camouflage trousers. The school I went to had, not to put too fine a point on it, its own army. Yes, the only man allowed a private army in the UK is the Earl of Athol (surname Murray, as it happens) but like many public schools we had a CCF, a Combined Cadet Force, our own army, our Captain-General as of 1953 the Queen herself. At the school we had an armoury, with Lee-Enfield .303 rifles (accurate to a mile!) and Bren light machine guns locked away in it.[65] Honest. I almost don't believe it myself. Teachers would double as captains and flight lieutenants and commodores on Wednesday afternoons (they got paid for it, don't panic). The CCF, I guess, though God knows how really, was designed

---

[65] See, the knives were the thin end of the wedge! By the 1980s, guns in school!!

to point any potential officers in the direction of fulfilling that potential and joining the army. I say 'God knows how' because we spent a lot of time doing school-boy-quality drill, taught by other schoolboys, marching up and down in hideously uncomfortable boots, never quite sure we were getting it right, wondering what else you could do on a Wednesday afternoon.

Needless to say, I wanted to love this, it seemed tailor-made for me, how could I not love this? I would put everything I could into the drill, trying to turn myself into a 14-year-old gangling mop-haired guardsman. But I'm getting ahead of myself – I should explain the CCF. There was a choice: you could join the Army, Navy or RAF. Activities fitted the beret and badge you chose. Sort of. The Navy lads actually went sailing, which as well as being something to do with them being sailors was easily the most realistic element of the CCF – but if push came to shove with the Eastern Bloc the Senior Service could launch a fleet of mighty Wayfarer dinghies as long as it wasn't too choppy. However, they did have to wear the most preposterous bell-bottoms and little sailor hats as if to restore balance. Sometimes the RAF lads went flying, or maybe gliding, I can't remember – there was talk of going up in a Chipmunk trainer and waggling the control stick. The Army, though, went on exercises. Sometimes. At least we didn't need to get in a boat or a plane on a strict rota basis to do army-like things (and doing bad drill over and over is certainly an army-like thing to do, and all you need for that is a nice stretch of tarmac). There was an alternative to all three of these crack units: the Community Service Unit, CSU. This was rumoured to consist of wiping old ladies' bums and/or having to talk to them (and for teenaged boys afflicted with those strange, crippling lightning strikes of shyness alternating with profound and unsettling ideas about what cool is that goes with that age, both were as bad as each other). So the CCF had plenty of takers.

147

Our enthusiastic Regimental Sergeant Major would yell and chide and bark and wave his stick at us – he was the very model of a short, shouting RSM, toecaps gleaming, tonsils vibrating with every holler. I'm sure he knew it. He'd acquired an old bus for moving us about in: it was very slow, the journeys we made in it defined interminable, you'd wonder if you'd ever get back in time for tea. Of an evening, walking back to the boarding house after tea, you'd see him sat with a paintbrush, tarting up the vehicle in a royal blue gloss. I felt a real warmth for the RSM, he was playing his part to perfection – he was one of my earliest encounters with what we might call an avatar nowadays. Who knows what he was really like – the turn he was doing was so perfect – he called cutlery 'gobbling rods' once: beautiful. One time at a rifle range, when we were getting to use our delicious antique .303s[66]– just like the ones in the WW2 movies, oh bliss, but also very noisy, and the recoil!!! if you didn't hold the rifle firmly into your shoulder it kicked like the proverbial stubborn animal – I miscounted the number of rounds I'd fired. Thought that maybe I'd had a misfire: 'And-if-you have-a-misfire-you-must-raise-your-hand-and-shout-misfire!!!!!!!' the RSM had hollered with the power of a small wind tunnel. After what I thought was ten rounds but might have been nine, I wasn't sure, I put my hand up and hollered 'Misfire!' with the confidence in hollering while wearing ear defenders of someone frightened of the RSM. Was it too soft? Too loud? I needn't have worried – he bounded over and made me open the rifle's breech to check for the misfired round. Lo and behold, I had miscounted and I received – even through the ear defenders – an exciting and invigorating lecture on how everything I did was a load of bollocks. These days I guess you'd call Childline.

---

[66] In service with the British Army in variations on its Short Magazine Lee-Enfield format from 1907 all the way to the 1990s.

CCF afternoons at school, when we weren't doing drill, might consist of some light manoeuvring. Seeing as there's no cover of any kind on rugby or cricket fields, this had an air of delicious pointlessness. The enemy would have been in the cricket pavilion and would have mown us down long before we got anywhere near them. Though they'd have mowed down the lads playing cricket, too. Another thing that only now occurs to me: I can't figure out why budding bank robbers didn't simply wander into the school grounds on a Wednesday afternoon and, with the judicious use of menaces and the odd punch in the face, help themselves to a couple of our antique Lee-Enfields and a Bren gun and do over the NatWest. Perhaps it's because you couldn't get the ammunition any more. Perhaps it's because we lived in pre-*Lock, Stock* Britain.

Attempts were made to broaden our fighting technique: one afternoon we crashed absurdly around one of the houses on the school site – I think it was where some of the school admin was done, judging by the bemused people doing their filing – learning how to do house-to-house urban fighting, but without blowing any holes in any walls or smashing any windows in, or tearing down curtains, or filling baths in case the enemy cut off the water supply or, frankly, a point. Thundering up the stairs while worrying about scuffing the toecaps we'd spent Tuesday night polishing to a mirrored gleam made me laugh. I didn't want to laugh; I wanted to take it seriously. Damn. The main skills I took away from my time in the CCF were how to polish toecaps so I could see my own face in them and iron razor-sharp creases in trousers. God, we were dangerous. I'm sure the Kremlin had us marked down for a pre-emptive strike in case we somehow ended up behind enemy lines and blundered around causing consternation and chaos.

To hone our combat skills we went on camp. Once to Penrith

– a place, if you're from Bedford, at the very end of the earth (or M6). We went up the motorway by coach, though the blue bus was already there, having surely left weeks in advance. We drilled, hung around a fair bit, went running and on assault courses, but the main event was going on exercise. Exercises, running around in the dark and stuff with our rifles, patrolling, attacking 'enemy' positions. Also important was avoiding the short straw of having to carry the Bren gun as it was improbably heavy. A subtle separation between the nerds, dweebs and wimps and the sporty lads enforced itself – those of us who'd gangled with the onset of puberty rarely did the attacks, the sportier lads, much fitter of course, got to have the fun with all the thunder-flashes and blanks going off. We would wait in reserve and get to watch the fireworks. I remember one night lying in the grass as the penny dropped that we weren't going to be a part of the attack – the bangs and thumps were coming from the other end of the heath we were on. The Lake District is incredibly beautiful whichever way you experience it, even if it's lying by a lake while the 16-year-old lance corporal babysitting you, sorry, 'in command', wanders off into the night trying to find the section we were meant to be patrolling behind. Or something. He was gone a fair while and returned with a heavy stage whisper because he couldn't find us. We'd been told to be as quiet as possible, so no one wanted to reply; he crashed around in the reeds cursing us until someone piped up. It would be too harsh to call it farcical. On reflection the whole thing feels like a scanned picture of an adventure when your printer has run out of one of the coloured ink cartridges.

A lot of what we did was orienteering dressed up as junior soldiering (though I suppose if you're lost you're not much good to anyone). This led to a particularly hilarious episode, sorry, exercise. We were driven in the very slow blue bus to a place the TA used for their own exercises somewhere north of Bedford. Though it can't have been uphill all the way that's how the very slow bus made it seem. I couldn't tell you how far from Bedford we were because the bus was so slow. Maybe we never left Bedford. We debussed – yes, that's an army word for getting off a bus – and were set our orienteering task. Put into groups of four or five, and again with some jock/nerd separatism in action, we were given a compass and a rudimentary map and told to find the waypoints and complete the course as quickly as possible. This rapidly descended into farce, as the first groups got their bearings and hared out across the heath (they were usually the jocks, hence the haring), everyone else simply followed, lumbering around after each other. Before we knew it the task that was meant to take all afternoon was over, and the very slow bus was heading back the way it had come, but seemingly and paradoxically uphill.

The climax, and for me the end of the affair with the CCF, was the trip we made to Germany. Something like 20 of us signed up for an Easter holiday jaunt to Osnabruck. We'd been promised exercises and everything – SLRs, Self-Loading Rifles, the one Action Man came in the box with, the works. No longer would we lie on a heath somewhere (not sure where) in the North-West, this time we were going to be on or somewhere near where the action wouldn't be either. But that wasn't the point. This was the real thing. We were going to be Action Men all right. However, this isn't really what sticks with me about the trip. Because this was my and everyone else's first encounter with Geordies. I'd never heard anything like it, it was beyond my wildest imaginings. At school I was studying German, an O level characterised by an endless desperate struggle with word order and, even more mind-bendingly, the three genders that inhabit German like a series of complex man-woman-neuter traps. If you don't learn a word's gender from the off, you're scuppered, and where they fall bears no resemblance to what you might think so there's no point guessing: get it wrong and your possessives and adjectives won't all add up. It's a nightmare. We'd been taught by a deeply patient German master that the very best way to start any O-level composition was with the words 'Eines Tages, bleibe ich zu hause.' 'One day, was staying I at home'. The point of this bland phrase was it got your composition off on a confident start, getting the genders right from the off.[67] After that you were on your own, though. Anyway, I was expecting maybe to try a tiny bit of O-level German at some point, what with us being in Germany, maybe ordering a coffee in a way designed to show off the tip of my non-existent linguistic iceberg. (Is there any more bone-chilling moment for middle-class British people than when they do, contrary to national type, use a foreign language – often burning up all the words at their disposal – and get a full and fluent reply that is utterly incomprehensible?) But Geordies – what was this? What were they saying?

I know that now that we live in the Ant & Dec era what I'm saying might seem odd. Geordies now are everywhere. But in the early 1980s the biggest Geordie star in the world was Sting, who'd done all he could to straighten out his accent. A big part of my incomprehension was a result of going to boarding school. ITV could show as many episodes of *Auf Wiedersehen, Pet* as they liked but we didn't watch it, because we were doing 'prep' (*trans.*: homework) for hours on end every night, so there was no way we'd ever see it. We were more into *The Professionals*, anyway. So Geordies were something we knew nothing about, and if we did they were on telly, and builders too. These lads were all huge, for a start – infantrymen, fit as fleas and very

---

[67] I used it in my exam.

thirsty with it. We settled into a state of mutual incomprehension and fascination. What must they have made of us? (I don't know, they never told us, and I'd have been loath to say 'What did you say?' again.) They were kind to us to a fault, and were very happy to buy beer from the NAAFI with our pocket money. One night we watched *Easy Rider*, though everyone fell asleep, worn out from the day's exercise and fresh air, and the beer from the NAAFI. Before I nodded off and joined in with the mild snoring I remember finding the film boring as well as improbable, us market-town public schoolboys watching a freak-out classic with our friendly Geordie squaddies. It was their ability to sleep that I marvelled at. That morning, heading in a bus to an exercise (a fast bus, a novel experience for us cadets) I was amazed at how all the squaddies were able to grab some sleep then and there. Instead of closing my eyes and trying to nod off, I'd simmer with envy. But it was this same exercise we were going to in the fast bus that provided the pinnacle of Geordie hilarity. It turned out that they were all soldiers who'd been left behind when the rest of their battalion went to Canada for training exercises: left behind because they were all naughty boys.

The regiment we'd been attached to was mechanised infantry. Mechanised infantry ride around in armoured personnel carriers – APCs. They look to you and me like tanks without turrets, but they're not tanks at all. They're light and fast, essentially armoured transit vans with tracks and a machine gun on top. The idea is that they ferry infantrymen safely to where they're meant to be, they then get out through the door at the back as quickly as possible, form up and fight where they're required (oh, it all sounds so simple!). APCs were invented in Normandy in 1944 by a Canadian general called Guy Simonds, one of the great tactical innovators of the war on the Allied side. He was concerned about infantry losses (nice to hear that about a general, isn't it?) and decided to adapt some of the existing vehicles he had for his infantry to arrive where they were needed in one piece. He took a vehicle called an M7 Priest – basically a Sherman tank's chassis without a turret but with an American 105mm howitzer in the back. The British and Canadian armies used these, but wanted something compatible with their existing artillery, so the Priests were being decommissioned ('defrocked') and replaced with a virtually identical vehicle with a 25-pounder gun instead. Simonds had 72 of these vehicles converted into armoured personnel carriers, removing the gun and having a steel plate welded in place over the gap the gun fired through – they were called Kangaroos. Twelve infantrymen could ride in the Kangaroo, and Simonds used them in a night offensive called Operation Totalize in August 1944, another offensive designed to put pressure on the German lines, make them crack and enable a breakout (or was it? Oh controversy). Totalize, like Operation Goodwood, was about seizing high ground held by the Germans south of Caen, but it was very different in execution to Goodwood: Simons wasn't going to make the same mistakes the British had made. Under cover of an artillery barrage, smoke and fog, as well as bombers attacking German positions, the Canadian infantry were able to ride in relative safety up to their objectives, and were able to get out within a couple of hundred yards of what they were attacking rather than having to make the journey on foot while under fire. Kangaroos were a huge breakthrough, affording the Canadian infantry an immediate advantage. They were pretty popular as a result and were used for the rest of the war. After the war APCs became standard all over the world.

In Germany in the 1980s, the British Army of the Rhine had undergone a big shake-up in how it planned to deal with a Soviet Invasion, and rather than defending statically it was going to try to fight a great big mobile swirling battle across Germany. Given that they were outnumbered something like three to one in tanks, and seven to one in aircraft I suppose a great big mobile swirling battle would have been worth a punt. Something of a forgotten history, Cold War battle plans make sobering reading. The RAF was expected to last something like 48 hours. NATO – providing it had held together politically in the event of hostilities breaking out – was going to fight its way back to the Rhine and try to hold the Soviet Army there while the politicians made up their minds about what to do next. Dad had war-gamed it in the TA in the 1970s, and they would rehearse what they thought might happen right up to the point where they'd go nuclear, at which point the politicians would get a phone call.

The nuclear options are worth a brief look. While in the UK we had visions of cities being immolated by great big nuclear bombs, the West Germans saw it slightly differently. Given that World War Three was most likely to kick off with great big Soviet shock armies thrusting up the autobahn into West Germany – supposedly, Eastern Bloc officers would often ride in lorries as drivers' mates to familiarise themselves with the routes into West Germany – West Germans were at best ambivalent about the whole business. They also had a keen and clear understanding of what being invaded by the Red Army entailed. To say the Soviets were expected to make rapid progress is putting it mildly. Certain formations in the Red Army were expected to be extremely well motivated politically and well trained, and while the NATO armies were well equipped and well trained they were going to be overwhelmed. But a huge Soviet surge like this would have a great big backlog of traffic behind it. NATO's air forces were expected to hit this hard, but if and when they ran out of planes or the land battle looked like it would be lost, there was the option of using battlefield (or tactical) nuclear weapons instead, amongst them the infamous Greenham Common cruise missiles. Tactical nukes have a grim history – in the 1950s the Americans had a jeep-launched battlefield nuke called the Davy Crockett that had a launch range of about a mile and a half, leaving the crew well within harm's way. Given that this huge backlog of Soviet traffic would be in West Germany, the West Germans were understandably edgy about the whole business. And using battlefield nuclear weapons marked an escalation that might lead to strategic nuclear weapons being dropped on cities. In all honesty it doesn't bear thinking about; thank God that time has passed.

As part of our schedule we were driven to the 'internal border' between East and West. Not the Berlin Wall, that would have been too good somehow. We didn't go in uniform. As part of our briefing we were told not to wave at the East German guards watching us over the minefield and through the razor wire because they would take our picture and doctor the photos to make it look like we were making obscene gestures: 'indoctrinated schoolkids' propaganda fodder. The odd thing about going to see the border was that it felt normal in the context of the Cold War. We lived in a world that was poised on the brink of nuclear extinction, so a country sliced in two and its population sundered seemed like a pretty small price to pay. Especially if you were on this side of it.

We had been taken out for an exercise with the APCs. The plan was that in the afternoon we'd do some driving-up-and-getting-out stuff. The morning was spent getting to know what it was like in the back of an APC. Cramped and bumpy. Noisy. Diesely. Rifles everywhere poking in people's faces. That pretty much covers it; there, I've saved you a bumpy morning. Cold War West Germany was routinely driven all over by British armoured vehicles, there seemed to be tank tracks everywhere we went. And – lucky us! – the Geordies had taken a shine to us, and were going to let us have a go at driving. There were several ponds on the scrubland we were tooling around on that looked like they had been scooped out of the landscape and filled with clay-coloured water. Maybe they were shell craters. I was terrified they were going to pick me (I've driven one since in Bosnia-Herzegovina, I'm so glad they didn't pick me or this would be an hilarious anecdote about me smashing my teeth in on the edge of the driver's hatch). One of the older boys was offered the driver's seat. He scrambled up front, sat down and was taken through the controls. He set off with jerky gusto, the rest of us rattled around on the benches in the back trying not to scream like girls as he lurched left, then right, then straight on.

You could feel our guy's confidence growing after a few minutes and the lurching decreased from all the sodding time to half the sodding time. We approached one of the ponds. There was no telling how deep it might be – the water was a flat tan colour. We pulled up about fifty yards from it, the engine idling. In the back we listened to the clear and precise instructions (in Geordie). It was like we were at the top of an odd, jerky, khaki roller coaster.

'Whatever you do, don't stop! Keep going! Keep your foot down!' hollered our impromptu instructor – I shan't attempt to relay this in Geordie. 'If you stop or slow down the water will come in the cab!! Don't stop!'

'OK!'

We started with a medium-sized lurch and bowled over the rim of the pond, powered down its side and into the brown water. At this point our cadet driver hesitated, stopped, and – exactly as he'd been told – the bow wave the APC had made as

157

it barged into the pond sloshed back into the cab, onto the engine and through into the back where the rest of us were sitting, soaking our boots. Steam billowed from under the hood of the APC. The engine gargled to a halt. Another vehicle pulled up on the rim of the pond, the boys and the crew scrambled out to have a look, laughing their heads off, pointing. The Geordie driver tried to restart the engine, but without luck. It was then that some truly immortal words were uttered. Brace yourself:

'Aw fuck, the fucking fucker's fucking fucked.'

We were going to have to wade out. The soldiers on the other APC started to piss in the pond even though they were doubled up with laughter. This never happened to Action Man.

What also didn't happen to Action Man was he didn't have to share a slit trench with an exchange teacher. We'd been promised a night exercise, going out into the woods and practising 'fighting' each other. We were given our SLR rifles – self-loading things that seemed beyond new-fangled compared with our old bolt-action .303s. They had yellow caps on the end that meant you could fire them with blanks and their gas-driven actions would work. We smeared camouflage cream on our faces: we'd been told it was edible so some of us tried it – we believed anything they told us at that point. We made our way into the woods next to the scrubland where one of our number had drowned the APC and formed a platoon triangle. This triangle had an impossibly heavy 'General Purpose[68] machine gun on every corner, a section on each side, a 'headquarters' in the middle. Fortunately we moved into an area where someone had already dug foxholes before – we soft-handed public schoolboys probably weren't up to the digging, to be honest. We bivouacked there and then. That always sounds great, dynamic, rugged, outdoorsy,

---

[68] General Purpose?? Try unblocking a sink with one.

but what it meant was stretching the olive-green tarpaulin we'd been given between some trees with bungees, putting some foliage on top for camouflage purposes and settling down for the night. It's a chore at best, something Ray Mears doesn't let on. And bungees like to ping off and make your bivvy collapse when you're attaching the bungee at the other end. We opened our ration packs, lit the burners and cooked the sausages in beans we'd been given. There were Rolos. Then, once the sporty lads had gone off to locate the other platoon, unsuccessfully, and returned, we settled in for the night, expecting an attack. I found myself in the dugout in the corner with an exchange teacher.

It was getting cold, and I was getting tired – I was paying the price for not being able to nod off like a squaddie and for being used to and quite liking the fact that at boarding school we had to be in bed nice and early. It was my turn to go on watch – I think it was two hours on, two hours off – and the other cadet, called Tim if memory serves, with me was curled up in the bottom of the trench, fast asleep. I'd decided that by far the best way to keep watch on this corner was to put my legs in my sleeping bag. The night wore on. I grew sleepier, and my companion – a captain, no less – was obviously as tired as me. Eyes strained into the darkness, wolves howled eerily in the distance. Yes, wolves. Actual wolves. Every sound in the wood – I've changed my mind, it was a forest – every sound in the forest became amplified, and every amplified sound seemed to be unmistakably a footstep, someone creeping up on us in the night. The captain – manning the incredibly heavy machine gun – spotted my sleeping-bag arrangement. He muttered something about how I wasn't supposed to really but not to worry. I suspect, with hindsight,[69] that he envied me.

---

[69] And I've made how I feel about hindsight clear at the start of this book.

We watched, we waited, I looked at my watch a lot. The forest continued its eerie soundtrack of noises. We'd been taught that movement would be the thing that caught your eye at night, but I had become transfixed by a utterly, eerily still silhouette of what I thought was a man, standing, looking right at us about fifteen metres away. I did what I could to point it out to Captain Exchange. He pooh-poohed it, there was nothing there. I looked right back at the silent figure for what felt like at least another ten minutes, straining my eyes – oh for Eagle Eyes right now. I asked the captain, my captain, who, by all accounts, was a decent bloke, to take another look. Again, nothing there, he whispered. If it *was* someone he knew exactly where we were, what with all the debate. We watched and waited some more. All of a sudden there was an almighty fucking BANG!!! from right inside the triangle – someone had thrown a thunderflash, a bloody great big banger, into the headquarters bivouac – and there was the pop-pop-pop of rifle fire. More bangs. The captain grabbed the incredibly heavy machine gun in a general-purpose way and opened up right next to me at nothing in particular, a magnificent racket. I fired my rifle once at where the man/bush had been and then it jammed, possibly because my mind had wandered during the weapons briefing about how to attach the yellow gas regulator for firing blanks. I couldn't chase after anyone, because I had a sleeping bag on. We'd been breached, ambushed, and had committed a textbook's worth of schoolboy errors (which on reflection seems fair enough).

In the morning at dawn there we were, stood in a desultory row, downcast and some of us – me – were really very, very sleepy. The RSM had appeared – I'm not sure where he'd been that night, the pub? Maybe he'd been the man/bush! – and had a few choice words to say to us.

'They came in by that bloody corner!' he yelped. 'Who was on that bloody corner?'

'Me, sir,' I could have said but for some reason didn't.

'Murray, sir,' said the captain.

'You useless bastard, Murray!' barked the RSM. 'Why weren't you looking out properly?'

'I was, sir, I thought I saw—'

'He had his sleeping bag on, sergeant major,' cut in the Captain.

'But you said . . .' I ventured, shooting a wounded look at him but realising that he was doing what any of us would do in a conflict situation when facing the RSM: sacrifice all around to save your own skin. I wish I'd known I was going to write about it 30 years later – I'd have congratulated myself on collecting a half-decent anecdote.

'You hopeless bastard, Murray!' the RSM hollered.

He was right, too. I *was* a hopeless bastard. The spell was broken. Maybe I wasn't cut out to be Action Man. I wasn't all that fit, I couldn't stay awake at night, my mind was prone to wandering off on flights of imaginative fancy, and I couldn't confidently tell the difference between man and bush, and when confused by this I couldn't stand up for myself. And scuffing my boots whilst learning how to street-fight made me giggle.

Action Man stayed with me, though, like a true amour fou. When I got to uni, while bonding over records, beer and not much else I found myself in the room of who is now one of my oldest friends. He had bedecked it with Action Men. Nine of them, in a variety of uniforms, some of which I'd only ever seen in catalogues, not even on toyshop shelves anywhere. Nine of them. I couldn't believe my eyes, and I felt something like the burning envy of the six-year-old me rising hot inside me. As he explained that he was an only child and was triangulated by aunts, uncles and grandparents from every direction, and that he'd done supremely well out of it, all I could feel was the misery of unrequitable envy. I said so, too – it was the kind of thing that couldn't be bottled up under any circumstances. He also related how he had found a shop with huge numbers of what must have been a very late addition to the Action Man troop – a soldier in an Iranian-Embassy-siege-busting-style SAS outfit, with gas mask and black overalls. Though we became friends, at that moment I wasn't sure I could ever like him. Looking again at this colossal army, I had to admit to myself that the moment had long passed, there was no way of bettering this treasure trove of past play, and the last thing I was going to do was ask if we could take them all on a special mission or something. The envy subsided, but the most recent expression of this true affection for Action Man came when the anniversary dolls were issued. I bought far too many (mainly with the outfits that I'd coveted for all those years, but no Mountie, that would have been cheating) for my daughters and told them to play with them.

8. A spot more Monty

FOR YOU THE TOUR IS OVER

Touring, my chief occupation – in that it's the thing that occupies most of my time – isn't what you might describe as glamorous. This isn't a poor-me whinge, God knows I love playing theatres and I remain ceaselessly amazed, grateful and relieved that people buy tickets and come and see me but as a way of living it creates lots of time to fill, every day different but essentially repetitious. Well, you might say, make some model planes or tanks, you've told us how good they are at filling time, but the main problem is that sitting in a car on the M6 Toll Road (it's quicker and worth every penny and I defy anyone who says otherwise to not actually wanting a series of personal toll roads for wherever they might want to go) going gradually mad doesn't really leave you the chance to get out your paints and while away the time. Also, every day has the departure for the show as well as the show time hanging over it, so sometimes it's hard to get started with anything before my tour manager rings the doorbell, texts me, knocks on my hotel door to take me off to wherever we're going next. It can make the day fractured, bitty. Getting things done, like writing books, is quite tricky. This bit was

163

written in Stoke-on-Trent. Two paragraphs down I was in Manchester.

My tour manager Adam and I get on incredibly well. This is another thing that has me amazed, grateful and relieved. I don't know what he thinks: we're men, British men of a certain age, I'm not going to ask and he's hardly going to offer. We spend what must amount to two-thirds of our time in each other's company and never a cross word. Though there can often be the occasional long silence. Do us a favour. You can't talk all the way from Edinburgh to Aberdeen in the snow taking eight bloody hours. It's impossible. So, needless to say, we have to find ways to occupy our time, ways to laugh. In-jokes evolve, grow, expand, have their moment and then are superseded by others, entire cultures of jokes rise and fall, things that have us crying tears of laughter one week are long forgotten the next: it's all very memey and Dawkinsy (without the religious needle, though). Actual evidence of the in-jokes is harder to come by, though. Until Monty.

Knowing that I had a peculiarly soft spot for Montgomery, my manager[70] had bought a one-sixth – Action Man-sized – poseable model of Monty. A couple of companies in the US make these dolls – they're uncanny likenesses of the people they depict. I'm sorry to say that you can even get Hitler and Goering and the other Nazi top brass in the poseable-action-figure form. I simply can't imagine getting to the till and saying: 'Yes, thank you, the Hitler please. No, no, it's not a gift. It's for my lounge.' Where would you put that doll if you had it?

---

[70] Different from tour manager. I can't stress this enough. My manager actually manages my career (Tim Vine has a great joke which puns hard on 'careering' off a road – you can probably work it out for yourself). Tour managers often get asked if they're an act's manager and, depending what's in it for them, might say yes. Or no.

You'd hide it before a party, surely. ('Darling, where have you put the Hitler?') Or would you? Maybe you'd leave him lying around as a sort of ice-breaker. As it is, the Monty doll comes with a couple of outfits. You can dress him up in battledress – khaki, sober, unadorned but for its general's red tabs, the two-piece outfit that was supposed to meet in the middle at your waist and that British soldiers loathed because it didn't and let in the cold – or in full Field Marshal regalia: braid, medals, peaked hat. Obviously I went for battledress and his famous beret – it's all about the beret with the two badges. He wears a suitably inscrutable expression. You wonder if he's figuring out grand strategy or, better still, how best to jam his foot in his mouth.

We'd found that with a normal digital camera you could line up a background and fake the perspective to make it look like Monty was 'there' – so he came on the tour of the UK with me. We had Monty on the A1 M looking at the Angel of the North, Monty on the beach at Sefton inspecting the Anthony Gormley sculptures. Monty flew to Jersey with us. On at least one occasion life on the road got to Monty. And when we went to the Imperial War Museum at Duxford he took a visit to the fabulous collection at Airspace, posing beside the Mosquito they have there. Did I mention what a great museum it is?

Anyway: here's the Field Marshal:

Monty inspects the Mosquito at Duxford.

Monty inspects Anthony Gormley's art on Sefton Beach.

Taking in modern Health and Safety. His nose is a bit scuffed.

Monty at the baggage carousel.

The sites of the A1 M.

Life on the road gets to Monty.

Interlude

HISTORIOGRAPHY: A (VERY) BRIEF HISTORY OF HISTORY IN THREE Hs

Like anything else, of course, history has a history. It had to start at some point. Not history, you understand, but capital H *History*, not the events themselves and the stuff that happened way back when but the writing-up of those events and the how and the why of the way it gets written up. Prehistoric times are prehistoric because they come before history, but there was also a time before History – all that vague Stone Age, Bronze Age, Iron Age stuff. Nice and vague, no proper dates to learn, lots of guesswork involved. Being an archaeologist seems to me to be a lot like being a detective working in a foreign language on a different planet, trying to solve a mass murder with one thigh bone. Good luck to them: they're all brilliant. But history has a history – and for lots of reasons it is necessarily self-regarding.

In this I think it may be unique: every subject or discipline has a history, but does Geography have its own geography? Actually, it must do – there's probably a study about the sort of locations geography departments find themselves in. I suppose there's a science of Science. Anyway. The history of history, or at least the writing of history is worth jogging through briefly. Philosophically there is the question that if something doesn't get written up by a historian then it isn't history, and therefore effectively never happened. That one is beyond my pay grade, nor really the point I'd like to make in this chapter (he has a point to make all of a sudden!?! gasps the reader). If history relies on written records as sources then there must be whole swathes of the Middle Ages[71] that we don't really know very much about at all. Nevertheless, I'm sure we all agree that history is pretty important, but that we very rarely, if ever, give that much thought to it. Outside your history faculty it rests on lots of assumptions. I can't and so won't offer a comprehensive overview of all history writing ever[72] but if I was to sum up this chapter and the problem it addresses in one crude and clumsy word it would be this: bias.

It might be going too far to say that history is all about bias, but I wouldn't be far wrong. In lots of ways history is like a junkie or a villain saying 'no, but this time I'm clean, I'm going straight, this time I'm going to get it right, be honest' but every generation as it comes to evaluate the past brings its cultural baggage with it.

That cultural baggage sometimes looks like it amounts to little more than an almost adolescent rejection of the previous generation's values. I'd say this is blindingly obvious but not something that always necessarily gets seen or maybe admitted to. Victorian historians when they were establishing history as a professional academic pursuit made many entirely sincere and bold claims about how it could be scientific, objective, properly dispassionate even, as they wrote history that was plainly

---

[71] Historical label alert!

[72] If that's what you're after, though it is a serious read, you could do a lot worse than reading *A History of Histories: Epics, Chronicles, Romances and Inquiries from Herodotus to the Twentieth Century* by John Burrow. And there! I've finally done it, a footnote with a book reference in it!

preoccupied with the world they lived in. And you can be sure that modern historians who get close to the original sources and try their damnedest to read them successfully would say they are as dispassionate as they can possibly be. I'm not saying they're not, either. But history is written in its present, and can only reflect it.

Anyway, I'd say it may be too much or even wrong to expect historians not to write about the past in the context of the present, and that it's got to be worth acknowledging that they do. Sometimes the interpretations are worth interpreting. Often they tell you as much or more about the times they were written *in* than the times they were written *about*. Another problem, if you want to see it like that, is that time doesn't end thus allowing a bold dispassionate summing-up – as cultures change and priorities alter so the kinds of history they write changes with them. After all, history doesn't end. Poor old Francis Fukuyama, he must regret saying that. Points of view – and in this case I mean literally where you're looking at something from – shape even the most apparently clearly defined events.

A good example of this is the notion of the Second World War itself (notion? Has he gone mad? It definitely happened). Depending on your bias, on how you look at it, it began and ended all over the place, not in the tidy version that we Brits might have in mind. After all: do you think of VE Day or VJ Day as the 'end'? Seeing as most of the stuff I've been on about has been in Europe you might be forgiven for thinking that the war ran from 3 September 1939 to 8 May 1945, whereas if you were in the Far East it wasn't officially done until 15 August. I say 'officially': at least, that's when we recognise VJ Day, the Americans see it as 2 September when the official surrender was signed. And tell that to those Japanese men who kept turning up in the 1970s, still fighting for the Emperor. In France the war ended twice – the first time in 1940 when they were tonked by the Germans, and then again pretty much a year earlier than the rest of Europe in August 1944. In Ukraine, nationalist guerrillas carried on fighting the Red Army into the early 1950s. As it is, the Russians don't even call it the Second World War – it's the Great Patriotic War and it started in 1941 – even though they were in the first one (they did lose so maybe that's why they don't mention round one).

If you're Chinese – and as China works its way to being top dog someday soon I'd say it's well worth bearing in mind their huge and hideous part in the war – you could see the war as having started in 1937 with the Japanese invasion, or even in 1931 when fighting first began in Manchuria and ending, most likely, with the triumph of the Communists in 1950. So twenty years or so of struggle. If you're Polish you might be entitled to think that the war didn't end until the last Soviet tanks left in 1989 – fifty years after they turned up in the wake of the German invasion in 1939. Or Germans – central to the whole business – could see the war as having begun in 1914 and ended with Reunification in 1990. Who you are and how you look at something shapes even the simplest, most measurable events: tricky, isn't it? What hope is there of writing anything even vaguely impartial?

When I started learning history at school (and we are talking about a long, long time ago)[73] it's not as if there was ever a discussion about what it was we were learning and why – it seemed that what we were going to learn was what happened and why. It seemed to take its cue from the Bayeux Tapestry,[74]

---

[73] So long ago that it is now officially history. When I started my degree in 1987 history seemed to turn into current affairs or geography around about 1962.

[74] The Bayeux Tapestry is well worth a visit, though the way it is displayed is pretty funny and hasn't changed since I first saw it when I was 9 or 10. You can queue

motte and bailey castles, feudal society's structures, ridged fields, William the Conqueror, that arrow in Harold's eye, the Romans and underfloor heating – these are things I remember with crystal clarity from what must have been primary-school history. So we were learning (roughly) how people lived and what the king was getting up to. We also did a fair bit of RE which was put to us as what you might call history – these things definitely happened – and – as a super-bonus – this is what they mean. We didn't do any other religions at all: don't ask me what Diwali is – I don't know. I don't feel particularly curious about it, either, my head is full up with enough C of E religion junk-knowledge and probably hasn't got room for any more. But at no point did we get told, and certainly no one ever asked, what history might actually be. And what it might be for. If it was even for anything. And why we were learning it. It never came up.

It was obvious that I was fascinated from the start. My godmother gave me a copy of R. J. Unstead's *Looking At History* which is a plain and unadorned telling of the history of these islands from a very orange-squash, Anglocentric point of view (that's the label it'd get but I'd dispute that really, it's more Union-centric). It's illustrated and it follows the lines of: Weren't the Romans interesting with their villas and underfloor heating? Ooh, the Normans were tough but they gave us law! Goodness me, what was Beau Brummel wearing? We invented the railways! It's pretty good – it's worth a read, certainly if you just want to have an idea of the story of the last thousand years. But if you want to date it, and it has dated, you'll find that the emphasis

---

for a fair while, and then trudge along in line with the audio guide looking at the thing, behind glass. And with what I wouldn't ever call a Gallic shrug, at the point of the crucial arrow-in-the-eye money shot there's a join in the glass, so you can't see it properly. Brilliant.

is on Florence Nightingale rather than, say, Mary Seacole. That should tell you everything you need to know. I'd also say that that emphasis is – in my opinion – benign, really, at worst a crime of omission.[75] The difference with *Horrible Histories* is perhaps that in Unstead's book there isn't an emphasis on how ghastly it all was – in describing trial by fire or trial by combat or the Wars of the Roses you were left to work out how grim and ghastly they were. Which isn't all that difficult, if I'm honest.

We did a lot of all this stuff all over again with more grown-up books with added Kings and Queens and dates (bloody dates!) then on to an O level in American history, which means I can drone on in a half-remembered bullshit manner about checks and balances in the US Constitution if you need me to fill a much-needed gap at a dinner party. Oh those Founding Fathers! They had no idea what they were doing! The essay questions would ask why did this, that and the other happen, but there were right and wrong answers. A long-term cause here, a short-term cause there, but definite, locked-down answers.

When we got to A-level history it was becoming clear that these things weren't that simple – at the time we were doing Tudors (I spent a lot of time doing Tudors, in fact there's every chance I spent more time doing Tudors than Edward VI was on the throne – little Tudor joke for you there, and he was one of the little Tudors) and a rising star of Tudor studies in the mid-1980s was J. J. Scarisbrick. Another was David Starkey. Wonder what happened to him. Up until the mid-1980s the industry-standard Tudor-wallah had been Geoffrey Elton, Ben Elton's uncle, which must explain why *Blackadder* is so good

---

[75] At this point, I'm sure, some of you will be throwing the book to the floor and saying 'I knew it all along! He says that character's an act but he believes every word of it!!'

on Queen Elizabeth (mental, bad teeth).[76] Scarisbrick had been digging into new sources from the early 1500s – people's wills, to be precise – and had found a new way of taking the religious temperature of England in the time before the English Reformation. It had been the established view for ages that the reason Henry VIII was able to get away with the break from Rome on a grassroots parish level was because people really didn't like the Church – we had to underline or mark in highlighter the word Anti-clericalism a lot. Anti-clericalism was everywhere and Anti-clericalism explained everything. People hated clerics, priests, they hated paying their tithes, they thought that the Church was corrupt. They laughed at fat rich monks, they thought churches were peopled by the lascivious and venal. They must have done – look at the outcome Henry got. You'd get essay points if you dropped in a healthy dose of Anti-clericalism.

Inevitability is something that historians are supposed to bare their teeth and shriek at like baboons, but the English Reformation is so big, so major, that the feeling seemed to be surely it can't have just happened. But maybe it did. J. J. Scarisbrick had found that people had been leaving the Church lots of money and behaving in ways that contradicted the idea that everyone had lost respect for the Church. OK, so it was people who had stuff to leave, but this discovery was academic dynamite. Anti-clericalism was being run out of town like a knackered nag. This was turning things over in the mid-1980s, this idea, it was earth-shattering, tearing up A-level essays up and down the country; I can only assume it's why so many A-level history teachers were balding in the mid-1980s, they were tearing their hair out as J. J. Scarisbrick smashed up

---

[76] Geoffrey Elton was a big Thatcher fan. Go figure.

their tried and tested standard lessons. Now the truth is that I've had my fill of the Tudors and my curiosity about them thoroughly extinguished chiefly by repetition and Jonathan Rhys Meyers in his mock-Tudor grundies, so there's every chance that this has all moved on since, but when Anti-clericalism was discredited it was all TERRIBLY EXCITING. Something new was happening in the sixteenth century!

So the notion that things might not be as cut and dried as they seemed was falling apart – not even things from 400 years ago, about which surely by now anyone might reasonably expect the dust to have settled. The scales fell from my eyes and I started to wonder, having secured a place to study Modern History at Oxford University, what the point was. These days this whole aspect fascinates me, but when I was 19 it drove me nuts.

Anyway, here, in three Hs, is a rough attempt to get to grips with the thing and its history.

Herodotus: the Father of History

The word History comes to us straight from the man regarded as the Father of History, Herodotus, an ancient Greek. Herodotus was writing history during the period of time we call Ancient History: perhaps he was ahead of schedule – his publisher must have loved him. He was writing, as far as we know, in the fifth century BC. His book *The Histories* – using the Greek word 'historia' which means 'inquiry' – is the first identifiable history book, but not just because he called it that. It also scotches all those jokes or attempts at making a half-arsed point about 'herstory', thank God. Like lots of things – the spoon, for instance – it might seem strange that something we are so familiar with, something we understand so easily, would have needed to be invented. Of course, it may be a fluke of, ahem, history that *The Histories* has assumed its position as the source spring of history: who knows what other writings have been lost? For all we know Herodotus was a hack writer doing what everyone else was doing (probably not) but he's the guy who survives and claims paternity. It's his DNA. It's also worth noting that as well as being called the Father of History, Herodotus is also called The Father of Lies. There are lots of good reasons for this in Herodotus' case, but it pretty much sums up the duality at the heart of the practice of history – what you write, how you write it, what you select to write about, how you go about writing it can be the difference between one person's history and another's set of lies.

Herodotus wrote about the wars between the Greeks and the Persians, and his writing set the mould for (or reinforced? Or quite naturally leaned towards? Or entirely understandably took the form of?) the traditional way that wars are described, even now. It'll seem plainly familiar even at two and a half thousand years' distance. He characterised the Greek states – what we'd call 'Greece', though if we're at all frank it's not a Greece we'd recognise – as fighting for liberty, freedom, against the Persians (Iranians, well, kind of) who were the forces of slavery, despotism, tyranny. Let's not forget, though I doubt we needed reminding, that Herodotus was a Greek. So stop me if you've heard that angle since. If you've seen the movie 300[77] about the defence of the Hot Gates at Thermopylae by the Spartans, it's

---

[77] Even the title reinforces some pretty typical Greek mythmaking. The 300 Spartans were accompanied by their helots – slaves, basically – who numbered around 900 as well as Mantineans, Tegeans, Corinthians, Thebans and other Greek peoples, including Thespians, darling. They totalled something like 5,200, though no one is really sure. They were still massively outnumbered, there were around 100,000–300,000 Persians coming at them.

a pretty good mythic retelling of the battle and fits fairly well with the way The Father of History serves up the Greco-Persian wars: although he does everything he can to try to be dispassionate about the Persians and portray them as human, he nevertheless portrays the war as a battle of civilisations. He set the tone of Western civilisation as a kind of austere clear-headed pragmatism as opposed to Eastern decadence and quasi-effeminacy, a tone that's still with us. Herodotus kicks off *The Histories* by recounting the legends of the rapes of Io, Europa and Medea,[78] reinterpreting them in his rationalist style – in other words, trying to explain them and what they might stand for, and explaining how the Trojan wars were the origin of the conflict between the Persians and the Greeks.

It might seem odd to us that he'd look to mythology to explain or inquire into stuff, but I'd imagine that Herodotus would find it weird that we don't. Well, we say we don't. But the border between history and myth is, at best, porous. Myths don't take long to develop, even about recent history, or even about current affairs. In Germany after World War One the *Dolchstoßlegende* – the Stab In The Back myth – grew up almost immediately. This myth basically stated that the German Army had been betrayed by the political classes who had overthrown the Kaiser's government, Socialists, Bolsheviks, advocates of the Weimar Republic[79] and especially the Jews amongst them (the

[78] I'd spend time telling these stories if somehow I thought it'd help, but they're stories about gods turning themselves into various animals and abducting women wowed by said various animals. They're odd, strange stories that for my money tell us one thing: people back then believed odd, strange things and it's hard to confidently draw any conclusion beyond that.

[79] History label alert! The Weimar Republic, like The Renaissance, The Reformation, The Enlightenment and tons of other historical 'events' wasn't called that at the time. It's a label given by historians. So you could say there was no such thing as the Weimar Republic at a dinner party, but it'll make people splutter/glaze over.

same Jews who were also accused of having started the war for nefarious moneymaking ends – why would they then go on to end it? Y'see, none of that stuff really makes any sense). This version of events got going in 1919, when German general Erich von Ludendorff claimed he'd been let down by the government, and that if only he'd had the support he'd needed the war would have ended differently. Well, ahem, excuse me, general, that particular pork pie is stinking the place up.

If you look even slightly dispassionately at the second half of the last year of the First World War it's amazing that he could have got away with this argument: the Allied blockade had created terrible privations and shortages at home for Germans. The German army which had successfully, though expensively, held on for four years had wrecked itself with its great Spring Offensive in March 1918, and was facing the prospect of a huge influx of American reinforcements on the Western Front. The Allied armies were, in First World War terms, running rampant. The Allies were pushing forward with great momentum in a series of actions known as the 100 Days' Offensive (history label alert!) making the most of the Germans exhausting themselves that spring. In short, the Germans had lost. It might be worth noting that the Spring Offensive has two other names: The Kaiser's Battle or The Ludendorff Offensive. Ludendorff knew perfectly well that the war was lost, and he knew his part in losing it too: as part of the German High Command he had been intimately involved in arranging the Armistice and the transition from the Imperial government to the new Republic.

So he had loads of very good personal reasons for promoting the *Dolchstoßlegende*, and he filled his boots with it. It's worth wondering whether if World War One had ended differently, with an Allied Army in Berlin, with the capital in ruins, it

179

would have prevented the war that followed (the one that did end like that). Almost a century earlier when Napoleon was defeated in 1814 an Allied army (an Allied army with various types of Germans as well as Austrians and Russians in it, in case you were wondering) camped in the centre of Paris and didn't go home until they'd got the terms they were after. Wellington moved into Napoleon's house, took Boney's cutlery and annexed his mistress. Though of course Napoleon, despite being deposed and exiled, did a Glenn-Close-coming-back-to-life-at-the-end-of-*Fatal-Attraction* and had another punt in 1815, lost again at Waterloo, and was exiled even further away and more seriously defeated. You'd have thought that Europe would have learned to make sure that when you won you had to get the message across clearly. At Versailles the wrong message got delivered.

After World War One the Germans found themselves having to come to Versailles and have the terms of the peace dictated to them, even though the Allies hadn't conquered their capital. Symbolism in all this counts for so much – when the French surrendered to Hitler in person on 22 June 1940 he made sure they did it in the same railway carriage that the Germans had signed the armistice in in November 1918. German politicians found going to Versailles to be denounced and dressed down and held responsible for the war incredibly humiliating, and so fed into the *Dolchstoßlegende* by pronouncing that the German Army had never really been defeated in the field (oh yes, it had). The right in Germany wasted no time in smearing the Jews, claiming they'd not fought in the war 'properly', had engaged in profiteering, all the old calumnies. The death of 12,000 Jewish men in the field, the fact that Hitler's lieutenant had been a Jew, a Jew who'd won the Iron Cross First and Second Class, that he'd recommended Hitler for the Iron Cross First Class, didn't stop this element being blended with the *Dolchstoßlegende*.[80] Hitler liked to rail against the 'November Criminals' – the men who'd betrayed the German Army in the field, stabbed them in the back. Cartoons appeared of German soldiers in the field being stabbed in the back by spectral Jews and politicians. With the added burden of reparations, the humiliation of Germany's dismemberment and the demilitarisation of the Rhineland, the *Dolchstoßlegende* offered an easy and entirely distracting alternative explanation for what had gone wrong in Germany. The myth developed momentum; it ran rampant, to the point where it had to all intents and purposes become true, or at least a truth. When the Allies in World War Two were settling on the policy of Unconditional Surrender, they did so very much with the *Dolchstoßlegende* in mind: 'in order to bring home to the German people that they had lost the War of themselves; so that their defeat should not be attributed to a "stab in the back".' From a falsehood to something that international policy had to address in under 25 years: Helen of Troy, eat your heart out.

So if Herodotus was writing a history of how the Allies (fighting for liberty, freedom) found themselves fighting a Second World War against the Germans (slavery, despotism, tyranny) he would have without a doubt started with the *Dolchstoßlegende* just like he looked to the Trojan Wars to explain the roots of the Greco-Persian Wars. He might have treated it as true, because its impact was as concrete as anything that was true. (And what do we even mean by true, anyway? Oops, gone beyond my pay grade again.) And this is how history has been written ever since, though sometimes without even bothering to acknowledge that it's addressing myth. The culprit, of course, is politics.

---

[80] In the end Hugo Guttman had to flee Germany – he ended up in America. If anyone was stabbed in the back it was him.

Don't worry, I'm not going to get into a Michael Gove-style thing about how we all need to know more about Nelson (though I do think we all need to know more about Nelson – I certainly do – but, like Nelson, I get seasick and find I can't quite engage with Navy stuff – sorry, Navy people). But the fact that Mr Gove finds himself saying this over and over is politics (obv, you're thinking, he's a politician). But that's not it. It's the other way round: historians have throughout the history of history found themselves having to negotiate politics – dodge the dodgy, join in with the dodgy, simply be dodgy – and have more often than not ended up writing history that is so saturated with politics that it feels stupid to type it, daft of me even to point it out. The example lots of people are familiar with is my next H in history: Holinshed.

Holinshed, Shakespeare's Wikipedia

Holinshed is the reason why people are still arguing about Richard III, why *Horrible Histories* have to do a song about how Richard III was an OK guy really and how he'd been stitched up by the Tudors. (History label alert!) As with a lot of these early historians, we don't know much about Holinshed at all – but we know from what he wrote, and how it turned out, what the world he lived in was like. He's described as a chronicler, but I think we might as well, what with him being the source of Shakespeare's history plays, call him a historian. Chronicles, because they lack perhaps the 'inquiry' element that Herodotus brought to the party, aren't regarded as proper history, but because they're what people took for history I'd argue we are best off seeing them as such.[81] With the printing

---

[81] I would say that, wouldn't I? They certainly help illustrate my point. Sometimes they're all we've got, though. You're meant to read between the lines, of course,

press as the sixteenth-century internet, Holinshed's work had a far greater reach than Herodotus could ever dream of having. Maybe it was seen in the same way some people might think a film like *Zero Dark Thirty* is a realistic portrayal of what happened. And what he wrote is so drenched in contemporary politics that I think it's only fair to call him a historian. Published in 1577, *The Chronicles of England, Scotland and Ireland* starts like this:

> *What manner of people did first inhabite this our country, which hath most generallie and of longest continuance béene knowne among all nations by the name of Britaine as yet is not certeinly knowne; neither can it be decided fró whence the first inhabitants there of came, by reason of such diuersitie in iudgements as haue risen amongst the learned in this The originall of nations for the most part vncerteine behalfe. But sith the originall in maner of all nations is doubtfull, and euen the same for the more part fabulous (that alwaies excepted which we find in the holie scriptures) I wish not any man to leane to that which shall be here set downe as to an infallible truth, sith I doo but onlie shew other mens conjectures, grounded neuerthelesse vpon likelie reasons, concerning that matter whereof there is now left but little other certeintie, or rather none at all.*

You get the picture. He's admitting that a lot of it is conjecture, he says some of it is quite literally fabulous, he says 'Hey! I'm just reporting this stuff, and don't forget the Bible is all true, regardless of how fabulous it might seem.' Shakespeare made use of *The Chronicles*, not just for his history plays but also

---

but who says people did at the time? Or didn't? Argh!!

for *King Lear* and *Macbeth*, though these are regarded as tragedies. *The Chronicles*, and Shakespeare in turn, tell us how fantastically lucky England is to have a stable (Tudor) monarchy, and how bad things were when stable, just kingship faltered during the Wars of the Roses, climaxing in the chaos of Richard III's reign, when he set out to do wrong: 'I am determined to prove a villain / And hate the idle pleasures of these days.' Henry VII turns up and saves the day, the state, harmony, etc., etc. Hooray for the Tudors. The edition of Holinshed that Shakespeare relied on was from 1587.

1587 was the year before the Spanish Armada, when England was embattled, up against the world's superpower Spain, having religious convulsions (like everywhere else at the time). Backs-to-the-wall time. The Crown, by dint of Henry VIII privatising the Church and making himself CEO (that's one way of looking at it), had extended its power and its remit into what people were meant to believe. Heady stuff. Intrusive. Powerful. Dangerous. A geopolitical can of worms, too. The reign of Good Queen Bess (there, a political label that's made it into history) was a time of a whole country and culture walking on thin ice: with the Queen herself leading the country out onto the ice. Elizabeth, because her father had broken with the Roman Catholic Church and let the religious genie out of the bottle so that he (Henry) could marry her mother, only for the heir he was after to turn out to be a girl, was the embodiment of what many, at home and across Europe, saw as the very particular sort of chaos the Tudors specialised in. So no wonder that Holinshed – who, like Shakespeare, had to get his stuff past the censor – wrote about what a rotten bloody lot the Tudors had replaced. He might even have believed it. It's not like he could consult back issues of *The Guardian*. Or *The Times*. Or any preferred paper of note with the point of view that you might favour. And with publishing being relatively new, it's not like there was an overwhelming weight of material for him to source his *Chronicles*, no Public Record Office, no microfiche, no internet. Shakespeare made use of Holinshed's *Chronicles* because it was what was available to him (and everyone else). It was the sixteenth century's politically correct version of events.

Despite this, the plays were dynamite, because of their subject matter. *Richard II* sees a king deposed. In 1601, when the Queen's former favourite the Earl of Essex was planning insurrection against the Queen, he hired The Lord Chamberlain's Men – Shakespeare's company – to perform *Richard II* in an attempt to stir the people up against Elizabeth, to give them the idea that you could depose a monarch. Risky. She remarked later, 'I am Richard II, do ye not know that.' Essex was executed on 25 February 1601. The play on this occasion didn't so much catch the conscience of the Queen as alert the monarch to what was afoot.

But surely, you're thinking, we don't live in Tudor times any more. There's no way people write history to suit the times they live in. If this comedian can spot this kind of bias, then surely professional university-level historians can spot their own bias a mile off. Surely to qualify as a historian you have to take some sort of Hippocratic Oath, to serve the truth, what really happened, the how and why? Well, no, it would seem not. Contemporary political culture has dominated how history has been written. After WW2 left-wing thought was firmly in the ascendancy and Marxist History was pretty much de rigueur. It gave intellectuals a new way of looking at things, and Marx had done so much to explain the currents and directions of capital-H History. Marx had, in the nineteenth-century style, 'scientifically' decoded the way in which capitalism had come about and its inevitable consequences (many of which are yet to come to pass, oops – or, many of which are yet to come to pass, be patient, the capitalists will mess up and the revolution will prevail, etc.). This meant that anyone of a Marxist bent could apply what Marx had shown about the course of human events to the course of human events and discover he'd been right even about the things he hadn't necessarily spotted himself or used as examples in his writing.

Christopher Hill: History wearing its heart on its sleeve

With Nazism defeated and the Soviet Union in the ascendancy, left-wing ideas (especially given the perceived success of the UK's planned wartime economy) were terribly fashionable – indeed, had been proved right in lots of ways. The UK's planned economy during the war was perceived to have been crucial in delivering victory.[82] Lots of people who'd been Communists before the war found themselves in academia after it; lots of clever people were Communists. History, perhaps because of Marx's emphasis on History, was full of Communists and Marxists (this is making me sound like a particular kind of paranoid American). A star of Marxist History was our third H: Christopher Hill, who wrote about the English Civil War – or, as he preferred to call it, the English Revolution.

Hill had been a committed Communist after going to Germany for a holiday in 1931: he'd witnessed the rise of the Nazis and been radicalised in 1935, he'd been to Moscow to study, he'd tried to go to Spain and fight for the International Brigade – his Communist credentials were impeccable. In the war he'd joined up as a private, but being very clever was commissioned and

---

[82] This has been thoroughly argued with by, um, Tory historians who don't like that kind of thing. Fair enough, though. They're Tories, what do you expect them to like?

then found his way into the Intelligence Corps and the Foreign Office. He was a founder member of the Communist Party Historians Group. I suppose you have to at least credit these guys for wearing their affiliations on their sleeves and not simply pretending that they were impartial, though that's exactly not how you'd see it if you were a believer in Communism. You were right, Marx was right, that gave you the impartiality of truth, of rectitude. Knowing this historian's history you can learn about the history that the historian produced, and its history. We know next to nothing about Herodotus, but we know from what he wrote that he was Greek and proud. Hill's writing, his interpretation of what happened during the English Civil War is Marxist history through and through, summed up by the idea of 'history from below' – ignoring the Great Men of history and looking for revolutionary undercurrents in sources not previously investigated. His pitch was that the Civil War was in fact a Revolution, and, as it happens, the one required by Marxist thought for the release of capitalist forces that would, of course, then set the eventual scene for the revolution of the proletariat (etc.). Also that looking at the surface events – what Charles I did, why Parliament rebelled against the King – just isn't good enough for explaining all this: 'The causes of the civil war must be sought in society, not in individuals.' And that's it in a nutshell, right there. You could remove 'civil war' from that and insert 'problem x' and that would cover leftist history.

Now, one of the problems with this is the scale of it. Society, big thing, really, isn't it? And when your population in the mid-seventeenth century is largely illiterate, how on Earth do you find out what it thought, what it was doing, and therefore where these deeper impulses were coming from? God knows, to be honest. It always struck me as a work-shy A-level student that the Marxist Historians hadn't half set themselves up for an awful lot of homework, some of it impenetrable, and a lot of it that was going to end up not all that interesting to read about. Because inevitably the problem (inevitably? Steady on now, nothing is inevitable except the revolution of the proletariat, etc., etc.) with this kind of history is that it struggles to fulfil the narrative demand that people have of history. They want stories.

Stories, stories with beginnings, middles and ends. For all our sophistication we aren't that far from telling tales around the campfire. Maybe this is why people are so drawn to reading about war, as Thomas Hardy said: 'War makes rattling good history but peace poor reading.' The gradual shift from feudalism through to a more dynamic pre-industrial society by the end of the seventeenth century is all very well, but Shakespeare would hardly pick that one up and turn it into a play ripe for seditious reinterpretation. Brecht might, God help us, and then it could be served up like gruel for A-level English students. Hill has also now been edged out of how people look at the Civil War, the emphasis these days is on religion and how Charles I's attempts to dictate religious practice at the parish level was the straw that broke the camel's back politically – his reach exceeded his grasp, and interfering in what amounted, very directly, to how people lived and ran their lives pissed them off mightily (this is a précis, you understand). It's the sort of history that governments who maybe want to tell us how many chips to eat or glasses of wine to drink should mug up on, perhaps. But it's also the kind of history, in a world where religious revolution has been firmly on the political agenda again since the Iranian Revolution in 1979, that you might reasonably expect to be written these days.

But it's the telling of stories we can't seem to avoid even when, maybe, the story is that there's a new way of looking at something. Orthodoxy is a narrative, overturning the orthodoxy offers a fresh narrative as well as that all too important thing – a reputation: historians are human, they're not automatons coated in some sort of zinc-galvanised objectivity paint, no matter what they might tell you. Popular historians have books to sell, too – books which often make fabulous claims: 'the amazing secret plan that saved D-Day' and the like. And people like stories. And even Marxist History tells a story, one of progress, ultimately towards some sort of utopian workers' paradise. It's a slower story and depends less on personality and exciting battles but it's a narrative nevertheless. Personally, I think you have to admire Christopher Hill for at least being honest about where he was coming from. How people tell stories, or at least how history is put across can save even the driest topics: social history, in other words how people used to live, can offer huge insight into how we live today – especially if you're the sort of person who says that human beings are animals and likely to repeat behaviour. History may not repeat itself, but people surely do. But let this be known: I'd like it entered into the record that I got out on the wrong side of the bed this morning, which is why I am writing in an essentially grumpy, dismissive and offhand manner. I also want it to be known that generalities are something that I like, and in order to make a point I will leave stuff out. Once you take these things into account you can't fault this chapter particularly, even though I've left out the Whig Interpretation of History completely. Thank God.[83]

---

[83] Google it!

9. None but the brave

OOH, YOU'RE SO BRAVE, GOING ON STAGE

Comedians are brave. I know this because I keep hearing it – lots of intelligent, sensible people say it an awful lot: ergo, it must be true. This is after all how things become true like the *Dolchstoßlegende* or those stories about Captain Pugwash. In all honesty I can understand why we might seem to be brave, and I frequently get told how I'm incredibly brave. It's easily one of my top three stranger-at-drinks-type-function questions to have to deal with, not that I mind really. As much as I might try to hum and hah and say 'Well, no, really, not really, you know, I'm used to it and it's what I want to do and anyway coming in in the morning and doing a morning's work in an office looks awfully difficult, ah ha ha ha' I generally can't convince anyone that I'm not incredibly tough and brave for doing stand-up comedy. So I should stop protesting: maybe it's true.

After all: people hate public speaking. Everyone hates public speaking. They can't stand it. Anecdotally it's meant to be the greatest fear known to man, second only to . . . well, I'm not sure what it's second to. Which I'd say suggests that maybe people should get out more, or possibly reappraise their ideas of what's worth being frightened about. Lions. Smallpox. Axl Rose's next album. Whenever the subject of going on stage trying to make people laugh (and I've been doing this so long that I generally hope to skip the 'trying' part of that but you never can be 100% certain) comes up people tend to say, 'Oh I can't bear the idea of being up there speaking in front of that many people.' The old joke that people would rather be in the casket at a funeral than making the eulogy is one of those jokes that, as Homer Simpson would say, is funny because it's true.

Getting up and speaking: well, it is something that's undeniably scary. You're often advised that the best thing to do is imagine that everyone watching is naked. This is – I think – designed to make you feel less exposed, though I can't really imagine a situation in which I'd feel more uncomfortable. I mean, it depends who was in the audience. This is why I'd say Best Man must be one of friendship's shortest straws – not that I've had the pleasure, thank God. Consoling a bereaved relative, coping with a close friend's illness, explaining to a child that they're quite right, I was Santa all along – none of these come close to having to get up and make a load of lame jokes about the groom in front of his family, her family, and your piss-taking mates. So, obviously, it follows, if you don't think too hard about it, that being a stand-up must require iron nerve. Indomitable courage. Steely will. It's incredibly lonely. No one will ever know our courage. For we are the bravest people in the world, we band of brothers (and sisters, of course), we happy few. Etc. And this is before we even go near the business of the telling of 'edgy' jokes.[84]

---

[84] God help us, 'edgy'. The notion that comedy's *actual job* is to push the boundaries is one of the strangest memes to have taken hold of late – otherwise-sensible people

You're probably detecting some sarcasm at this point. This is because, in my experience, most stand-ups aren't at all brave, and going on stage is entirely routine for them. If your idea of bravery involves overcoming some kind of jeopardy, then maybe going on stage – no matter how nervous it might make you – doesn't really involve bravery; there's the reward of laughs at the end of the tunnel. Yes, some comics throw up before they go on, some shake, some pace, some wobble, some have dry mouths, etc., but once you're on stage it all pretty much goes – after all, you have something to concentrate on: the lines, getting it right, listening to the room, all that. I can only speak for myself, but when I'm on the last thing I'm doing is shitting myself. Sometimes, if it isn't going well, a tinge of panic can creep in, but really, you're not in any actual danger, are you?

The wobbliest time I've ever had was when I went on the Royal Variety Show (complete with Simon Cowell and his acolytes prowling the area under the stage, so maybe I really was in danger) and I'd lost my voice – God, what a night that was, but even looking back at it it doesn't make me shudder or sweat or panic, it's happened now and there's nothing anyone can do about it. I felt pretty meek before I went on, glugging more Manuka honey, but the last thing the Queen is going to do is shout 'Get off, you're shit!' It's not as if modern comedians are jesters who could lose their heads telling the slightest misjudged one-liner. At least, not in this country. For now. Though, y'know, watch what you say on Twitter. And don't, on a public broadcaster, upset the *Daily Mail* during a quiet news week. But performing, because it necessarily inhabits strict-boundaried territory, is held together by conventions and

---

like Directors General of the BBC will happily trot this line out without for a minute asking whether it makes any sense at all: pushing the boundaries is nothing more than one of the means at comedy's disposal. Not an end in itself. For pity's sake.

193

rules; it is a formalised environment making it somewhere you can carve out a comfort zone – in fact, that's where the room exists to be funny, tragic, sardonic, deadpan, whacky, whatever. You can say stuff that would otherwise and quite properly get you punched in the face but you don't get hit, simply because there is the division between the stage and the audience.[85] Once you've got on stage, and once you've done it pretty often, there's not too much to worry about. I've always felt like this about performing – except when I end up on the drums and things really do get hairy. But that's not really my performing comfort zone. This comes down to fear and its counterpart, bravery, being all about comfort zones.

Actually, there's only ever been one occasion where I thought to myself gosh, there is an element of bravery to what I do, maybe I am some manner of modern gladiator. In May 2009 I played the O2 arena two nights in a row. To anyone sat at the back, yes, I agree. It holds about 14,500 people in the seated configuration that we used. Which is a lot of people. We'd worked our way up to the O2 via various other arenas – the NEC in Birmingham, the Echo Arena in Liverpool. Playing them is counter-intuitive. With a big screen people can see the bags under your eyes quite clearly: you don't need to get bigger and bigger in your performance at all, you can do eyebrow stuff and that plays well to the back. But with that there is also the problem for the vast majority of the audience of the experience being like watching telly. In an aircraft hangar. And we behave very differently when we're watching telly than we

---

[85] The one time someone has crossed that boundary, in a long-lamented club called the Meccano, it all got a bit peculiar – a very drunk guy who hadn't got a handle on what I was doing got up out his seat, walked up to me, grabbed me by my tie and then realised he didn't know what he was going to do next. The moment passed, as they so often do, and he didn't hit me, he sat down again and I resumed my set.

do when we're in the theatre. For instance, when I watch telly I might talk to the person I'm with, take text messages, eat, fart, scratch my nuts, whatever. And while me and the people at the front who were getting ribbed (yes, 'ribbed', not 'picked on', OK?) were having a fun night, there is always a sense that the folks at the back are maybe wondering about where their next hot dog is coming from. I only say this because that's how I'd behave – it's a million miles from a criticism. At rock shows in arenas going to the toilet or popping out for another pint or hot dog is all part of the deal: you can't do that in the theatre. Steve Martin says in his peerless book *Born Standing Up* that the enemy of comedy is distraction, and he couldn't be more right. Distractions are multiplied into their thousands when you play somewhere with a hot-dog stand and a bar around the corner in the atrium. And stand-up tends not to have lasers and the thudding drums that arena-playing rock bands have that both commandeer your attention and blast out any distracting hot-dog movements. It mainly consists of one person talking. Steve Martin goes on to say that playing an arena is like hosting a party rather than playing a comedy gig – so I suppose if people want refreshments you've just got to live with it.

Lots of comics play arenas now, and fill them too, and the punters seem to keep coming. For me the spark of intimacy with the audience is lost; I'm not sure I'd go to see a comic in an arena. But the O2 was the biggest of the lot, so you might think it could set off some butterflies at least. But it didn't, largely because we were filming the shows for DVD release, and I was taken up with technical discussions about lighting and camera angles. There wasn't time or maybe the emotional bandwidth to be nervous. Preoccupied with the filming, enjoying the novelty of virtually everyone I knew suddenly turning up in my dressing room when they'd previously been nowhere to be seen, least of all in Sheffield, Preston or Plymouth or anywhere, I didn't have the luxury of getting nervous. The second night was much the same story, and anyway, I'd already done one – and experience goes a long way with nerves. We had a suitably lubricated after-show party and everyone said how much they'd enjoyed being in a massive room full of people going for hot dogs while I talked far away in the distance no bigger than an ant.

It was only on the Sunday morning, lying in my hotel bed, that I thought 'SHIT!! 14,500 people!! SHIT!!! Argh!!!!' A wave of proper nervousness hit me, butterflies, sweats. All pointless. I spent the rest of the morning pondering the idea that maybe comics in arenas are somehow distantly related to gladiators. And then I reconsidered. It's bollocks. Perhaps what I do for a living has the element of adventure and glamour in it that war stories had when I was a boy – though I'd argue the main attraction was that it didn't look a lot like a real job. Perhaps I'd parked the fear because it was a sensible and controlled thing to do, or because I'd been distracted, or maybe because there was just no point being frightened. Either way I was in my comfort zone. It might seem weird that appearing in front of all those people could be a comfort zone, but there it is.

The last thing you might describe combat as is a comfort zone. That sentence, looked at from here, the following sentence, is really incredibly trite. Yet some people seem to thrive in the environment of war, wars keep happening despite their infinite ghastliness – people join the army, for Pete's sake. So bravery in this chaotic, hideous, random, un-boundaried and, most importantly, lethal environment is all the more remarkable; it makes just using the word 'brave' about stand-up comics seem even more silly. If that could be possible.

The thought of facing death on a daily basis is something I

can't really imagine. Is that even how soldiers look at it? War movies tend to be full of either gung-ho banter or, if the movie is a war-is-hell job, staring-meaningfully-into-the-middle-distance stuff – of course, what they can't do is get inside someone's head and relay it to you. The US army tried to do this. It surveyed its soldiers during World War 2 and asked them what they were frightened of. During their downtime GIs were given forms to fill in. The questions were direct, their answers revealing. In plain percentages they give you the beginning of a glimpse of what some of it might have felt like. Here's an example. One of the questions men fighting in the Italian campaign were asked was this: 'While you were in combat, did you ever have the feeling that it was just a matter of time until you would get hit?' They were given six gradations, starting at 'Almost always felt that way' to 'No answer'. The results looked like this. Forgive me if I present it in a table, but at least it's not an economic graph, so count yourself lucky.

WHILE YOU WERE IN COMBAT, DID YOU EVER HAVE THE FEELING THAT IT WAS JUST A MATTER OF TIME UNTIL YOU WOULD GET HIT?	% replies
Almost always felt that way	26%
Usually	13%
Sometimes	23%
Once in a while	21%
Practically never	15%
No answer	2%

Only 2% went for the 'No answer' option! Maybe the final 2% were genuine Don't Knows, maybe they just weren't keen on sharing. Maybe putting it down in a tick box didn't feel right. The question, interestingly, is about worrying about getting hit. Not killed.

Coping with this kind of fear is something I haven't experienced. I've been in car accidents, but they're moments of shock rather than long-drawn-out perpetual states of danger and anticipation. The whole time-slows-down thing when you put your dad's new car in a ditch in a rite-of-passage accident seems miles from any of this. After all – you don't get in the car with the express purpose of killing anyone else, after months of training on how to kill or be killed . . . it just happens and you feel like a proper twat and in a strange way are glad you broke your arm because that will temper some of his entirely righteous fury. In the Pacific soldiers were surveyed about how they experienced fear. This stuff is worth looking at. In a table, even. The men in Division A of the South Pacific were asked about what symptoms of fear they had. 2,095 men were surveyed. (I got these figures from John Ellis's incredible classic book about the experience of fighting men in WW2 called *The Sharp End*, in which he goes into this in much greater depth, whilst also not trying to find any jokes in the subject material.)

SYMPTOMS	% reporting
Violent pounding of the heart	84%
Sinking feeling in the stomach	69%
Shaking or trembling all over	61%
Feeling sick in the stomach	55%
Cold sweat	56%
Feeling weak or faint	49%

Feeling stiff	45%
Vomiting	27%
Losing control of bowels	21%
Urinating in pants	10%

These figures are, it's worth reminding yourself, what people were prepared to admit to. 84% experiencing a 'violent pounding of the heart'. I'm no statistician but that's pretty much everyone, isn't it? 'Feeling stiff' came in at 45% – a percentage that can win you a general election in this country. The more outward (literally) physical reactions kick in at 27% with vomiting. Seeing as, I'd guess, shitting yourself is extremely embarrassing the fact that 21% would admit to it is in itself very revealing. I've never shat myself, and if I had I wouldn't tell you anyway. Least of all in a book. I haven't, by the way.[86] Anyway, you can't trust statistics, everyone knows that. It's better perhaps to see what people say about the fear.

This one is tricky. Very often you can ask someone whether they were frightened and they tend to say they were too busy, things were too intense for them to be frightened. When I've asked my dad about what it was like landing at Suez – and we've talked about this twice; once when I was five and it sounded amazing and exciting and there were tanks going bang! and rockets and planes and then again when I was thirty and there were all those same things and it sounded utterly terrifying – he says he was incredibly busy and that basically there wasn't the psychological bandwidth or time to be frightened. He was nineteen at the time, which is of course when you think you're indestructible, so maybe these two

---

[86] I've seen someone shit themselves on stage, but there isn't time for it here. If you bump into me and want to hear the story, ask nicely and I might tell you.

things combined and made him fearless. Maybe it's how he prefers to relate it now. Maybe in the telling you don't want anyone to feel sorry for you, pity you or perhaps you want to shield them from the reality of the situation and how it feels to be in the middle of it. I don't know, and I don't want to ask. He was certainly busy – the landing craft had a company of Marines on it desperate to get onto the beach and a bulldozer with a load of dynamite in its claw. So I'm happy to go with being too busy to be scared.

For example, if you were a member of a tank crew you had lots to do: if you were the commander you were listening in to the troop or squadron radio to find out what was going on, as well as keeping an eye on what was happening around you, if you were the driver you were wrestling with the controls, probably without being able to see out properly, the gunner would be adjusting and 'laying the gun' – all highly technical and complex tasks that required your full, undivided attention. And just being in a tank, for all its armour, gave you plenty of things to be frightened of. It was a dangerous place. It had a magazine of ammunition, fuel, an engine, batteries, all crammed in with you and your fellow crew members. If you were hit by an anti-tank weapon – and this could be a gun on an enemy tank, an anti-tank artillery piece, or a hand-held thing like a bazooka (the Germans had developed a thing called a *Panzerfaust*, cheap and very easy to make, a throwaway anti-tank weapon that, if the soldier using it kept his nerve and got really close, could destroy a tank with one shot) – the interior of a tank would be filled with flying molten metal. Even if the hull wasn't penetrated, shards of white-hot metal from the inside of the tank could detach themselves and bounce around. Your tank could shed a track or break down and become a great big sitting duck. If your ammunition caught fire it would explode inside the tank, and wouldn't wait for you to get out. A tank going up in flames was known ruefully as 'brewing up', the same expression that British troops used for making tea. Sherman tanks – which, of course, we met earlier because they came with their fabulous numerical advantage – were particularly infamous for brewing up quickly and easily. Film of tanks brewing up exists and it makes me want to be an infantryman lying in the mud in a ditch every single time – fire rages out of the hatch on the turret like a chimney, air is sucked in through the barrel of the gun. One witness described a pool of human fat, covered with flies, underneath a tank that had been knocked out on the beach at Salerno. Plenty to be afraid of.

So what's obvious to me is that everyday front-line life required huge amounts of nerve, will, courage, and the energy to prop those things up. Far, far more than going on stage at the O2 to a crowd of people who have actually paid to see you. And then you get to people who were awarded honours for bravery. In the midst of all this you'd have been sleeping in a ditch or under a tree or wherever you could, in the elements, not in a nice warm hotel or B-and-B. Coming down off a gig is a tricky enough business (and bad ones are far harder to get over than worse ones) so God knows how the hell you come down off a day in combat. Medals have always struck me as peculiar – as if they can possibly make up for the stuff that people have been put through (or signed up to be put through) – yet it seems that they can, so I find it hard, again, even to ask about them. When even campaign medals can be controversial – the men of Bomber Command not getting one springs to mind – awards for bravery can perhaps seem to me to be arbitrary. Everyone's brave, aren't they? Why single anyone out?[87] But at the top of the tree for bravery is the VC.

---

[87] I'm only asking. I don't know the answers to these questions at all. Maybe you can tell me.

Citations for something like the Victoria Cross always read pretty plainly, yet tell of stuff beyond my knowing or imagining. It is awarded for '. . . most conspicuous bravery, or some daring or pre-eminent act of valour or self-sacrifice, or extreme devotion to duty in the presence of the enemy.' The VC, instituted by Queen Victoria, was an exceptional medal when it was created in that it didn't recognise rank or class. Also, the medal wasn't always awarded to individuals in particular: if a unit did something particularly valorous then they drew lots for an officer and a man to see who'd get the medal, a practice that only lapsed at the end of the First World War. Only three people have won two Victoria Crosses, or a bar to the Victoria Cross as it's known. This is partly because lots of VCs are awarded posthumously: that's the 'self-sacrifice' part right there. And because very often recipients were seriously injured in the course of the deeds that won them the medal. Of the three men who have won it twice two were medics. The other was Charles Upham.

Upham is one of those people that dares fiction to try harder. From New Zealand, Upham was a sheep farmer. He had been an officer in the New Zealand TA, but when he signed up to fight insisted on starting as a private. It wasn't until July 1940 that he went for officer training. The actions that earned him his first VC were in Crete. British troops were in Crete because of a series of tragic and farcical events set in motion by the *grand farceur tragique* (I've made that term up) Benito Mussolini. Mussolini had sold himself to the Italians as a great war leader and needed to notch up some victories, so he decided that the Italians should invade Greece. Once it was under way, it wasn't long before they were making a terrible mess of it (cue a thousand Italian-army jokes). The Italians had already joined in at the tail end of the German invasion of France in the summer only to find the French army – which had crumbled in the face of the Germans – rather difficult to deal with, but they expected Greece to be easier. The invasion began rather late for an invasion (they tend to require good weather) in October 1940 but things got off to a terrible start for Il Duce: the Greeks held up the Italians and then counter-attacked and forced the enemy back into Albania. Fascism didn't handle embarrassment that well, and so the Germans were drawn inexorably into saving Italian face.

Over the winter the Greeks were able to draw reserves away from their Bulgarian border and shore up their defences. Churchill insisted on lending a hand, and shipped in 57,000 soldiers to help the Greeks, quite a step when a German invasion of the UK itself seemed a daily threat. The following spring it became clear that the Germans were going to join in to finish the job that the Italians had started. The Germans, rather than simply backing up the Italians, were planning to attack through Yugoslavia. This left the Greek troops in Albania who had fought so hard to repulse the Italians outflanked and exposed to the Germans. The British asked the Greeks to withdraw to positions that would make the country more defensible but the Greeks refused, abandoning military wisdom to pride. The Italians began another offensive in April, but it wasn't until the Germans applied pressure that the Greeks changed their minds and began to withdraw from Albania. The retreat became chaotic, the Germans ran rampant. The Greek army's generals decided the very best thing to do was surrender to the Germans rather than the Italians, because surrendering to the Italians would be dishonourable – the Greeks had fought well and they felt they hadn't lost to the Italians. This didn't go down well with Mussolini, but then not much did; in the end the Italians were present at the surrender after he had complained to Hitler.

203

The upshot of this was that the British and Imperial troops that had been rushed in to help the Greeks now had to get out of Greece pronto.

By this point of the war the British were getting pretty good at retreating in an almighty hurry. As well as Dunkirk, we'd left Norway in a great hurry in May 1940. Crete was on the way back to Alexandria, and an obvious stopping-off point. The fallout from the Italian invasion of Greece is hotly debated even now. Some say it delayed the Germans in their planned attack on the Soviet Union – a critical delay which meant that winter was just that little bit closer – that ultimately led to the postponement of the Operation Barbarossa invasion and the Russians having time to get their breath back over the winter. It also meant that British troops weren't available to wrap up things in North Africa, thus prolonging the campaign there (where the Italians had been fighting with a similar degree of skill and resolve). Whatever the outcome, and whatever the points of view it has thrown up, all this meant that Charles Upham found himself on Crete when the Germans decided to invade in May 1941.

Crete is yet another story from the first few years of the war of British collapse, chaos, defeat and retreat. It often seems that if you made a three-part movie trilogy (I know that's a tautology, but it is what people say) about World War Two, the end of part one would be incredibly depressing. In fact, you'd understand if no one wanted to watch part two. By the end of the Battle of Crete the British had been routed by lightly armed German *Fallschirmjäger* – paratroopers – and evacuated with great haste over the mountains to the south of the island to be extracted by the Royal Navy and hustled back to Egypt. Both sides drew different conclusions from the battle: the German losses were so heavy that Hitler decided never to use paratroopers again, the British having been soundly beaten decided they were the way forward. The comings and goings and attendant cock-ups of the Battle of Crete aren't for this book, but they do include us having cracked the German Enigma codes, the Kiwi general on the ground knowing what was coming and when it was coming and still managing to completely fuck the whole thing up. (When people get all triumphant about how we knew what the Germans were going to do next thanks to Ultra code-breaking, this one is always worth bearing in mind.) On day one it seemed that the Germans would be easily repulsed. The descending parachutists were killed in large numbers – some of the British likened it to a pheasant shoot – and the Germans were certain the invasion had failed.

However, overnight the New Zealand troops holding a hill overlooking the airfield at Maleme were withdrawn, taking the pressure off the Germans and making it easier for them to land more men. They crash landed transport planes onto the airfield, so desperate were they to get more men onto the island and into the battle. From there a series of German advances and Allied collapses happened, and seven days later the British and Imperial troops were in full retreat. Again. Crete is one of those battles which has you saying out loud, 'Yeah, but we won the whole thing, right?'

During the course of this, and starting on day two, the day it all went to shit, Upham did the most extraordinary things, leading from the front. Upham was a second lieutenant. If you were an officer in World War 2 you were very likely to be killed or injured; officers took a disproportionate share of the casualties compared with what were called Other Ranks. 'Share' seems like the wrong word, as it happens. In an infantry battalion – the standard unit that infantry fights in – officers made up about 5% of the battalion's strength but typically they might make up 10% of the men killed, and around 25% of the wounded. So Charles Upham had a one-in-four chance of being hurt, a one-in-ten chance of being killed. He must have known it. As his Battalion attacked the Germans on day two, this is what he did. (I won't paraphrase, you're better off with the official account. Warning: contains 'utter indifference to danger'.)

Citation

War Office, 14th October, 1941.

The KING has been graciously pleased to approve of awards of the VICTORIA CROSS to the undermentioned: —

Second Lieutenant Charles Hazlitt Upham (8077), New Zealand Military Forces.

During the operations in Crete this officer performed a series of remarkable exploits, showing outstanding leadership, tactical skill and utter indifference to danger.

He commanded a forward platoon in the attack on MALEME on 22nd May and fought his way forward for over 3,000 yards unsupported by any other arms and against a defence strongly organised in depth. During this operation his platoon destroyed numerous enemy posts but on three occasions sections were temporarily held up.

In the first case, under heavy fire from a machine gun nest he advanced to close quarters with pistol and grenades, so demoralizing the occupants that his section was able to 'mop up' with ease.

Another of his sections was then held up by two machine guns in a house. He went in and placed a grenade through a window, destroying the crew of one machine gun and several others, the other machine gun being silenced by the fire of his sections.

In the third case he crawled to within 15 yards of an M.G. post and killed the gunners with a grenade.

When his Company withdrew from MALEME he helped to carry a wounded man out under fire, and together with another officer rallied more men together to carry other wounded men out.

He was then sent to bring in a company which had become isolated. With a Corporal he went through enemy territory over 600 yards, killing two Germans on the way, found the company, and brought it back to the Battalion's new position. But for this action it would have been completely cut off.

During the following two days his platoon occupied an exposed position on forward slopes and was continuously under fire. Second Lieutenant Upham was blown over by one mortar shell, and painfully wounded by a piece of shrapnel behind the left shoulder, by another. He disregarded this wound and remained on duty. He also received a bullet in the foot which he later removed in Egypt.

At GALATAS on 25th May his platoon was heavily engaged and came under severe mortar and machine-gun fire. While his platoon stopped under cover of a ridge Second

207

Lieutenant Upham went forward, observed the enemy and brought the platoon forward when the Germans advanced. They killed over 40 with fire and grenades and forced the remainder to fall back.

When his platoon was ordered to retire he sent it back under the platoon Sergeant and he went back to warn other troops that they were being cut off. When he came out himself he was fired on by two Germans. He fell and shammed dead, then crawled into a position and having the use of only one arm rested his rifle in the fork of a tree and as the Germans came forward he killed them both. The second to fall actually hit the muzzle of the rifle as he fell.

On 30th May at SPHAKIA his platoon was ordered to deal with a party of the enemy which had advanced down a ravine to near Force Headquarters. Though in an exhausted condition he climbed the steep hill to the west of the ravine, placed his men in positions on the slope overlooking the ravine and himself went to the top with a Bren Gun and two riflemen. By clever tactics he induced the enemy party to expose itself and then at a range of 500 yards shot 22 and caused the remainder to disperse in panic.

During the whole of the operations he suffered from dysentery and was able to eat very little, in addition to being wounded and bruised.

He showed superb coolness, great skill and dash and complete disregard of danger. His conduct and leadership

inspired his whole platoon to fight magnificently throughout,
and in fact was an inspiration to the Battalion.

—*London Gazette, 14 October 1941*

Right, now read that again. This man was clearly incredibly brave, incredibly strong, selfless and, arguably, utterly crazy.

Very often the Victoria Cross has found itself open to political manipulation: battles that go badly tend to have large clusters of medals around them, things that go well don't – there's only one D-Day VC. Rorke's Drift, with its eleven VCs, is a good example (and let's not get into the actual number of Welshmen present). The disaster at Isandlwana the same day – essentially the other *Zulu* movie, *Zulu Dawn* – was something that the British government and military were very keen on diverting attention from. Understandably: 1,300 of the 1,700 force had been killed at Isandlwana and their colours had been taken by the Zulu army; it was all the more embarrassing because the whole adventure had been a barefaced war of aggression on the part of the British. The Zulus had made the British fight to the last bullet and defeated them comprehensively. So Rorke's Drift, with its similar-ish situation but entirely different ending gave the politicians and generals a chance to claw something back from a very bad day for the army. Medals were doled out liberally. This isn't to say that the men who got them were undeserving, I'd never suggest that: it's just interesting when they get given out and why.

Crete was a catastrophe but Upham was phenomenally brave. As if to prove his VC wasn't a fluke or the result of politics, he went and got himself a second one. After Crete the New Zealand forces were brought back into the North African campaign (which by being rushed away to Greece they had been

209

unable to finish). Upham won his second VC at the First Battle of El Alamein. Yes, there were two. Monty's famous victory of October-November in 1943, the 'end of the beginning' as Churchill called it, sealed Rommel's fate and secured Monty's reputation as an Allied general who could beat the Germans. The First Battle ended in stalemate, and was characterised as an Allied failure at the time. But the Germans were, by fighting at the end of a long vulnerable supply chain, at best prolonging their agony. The supply chain was doubly vulnerable because the British had cracked German codes, and knew what was arriving when. By not winning at First El Alamein, Rommel was pretty much destined to lose at the Second.

Upham played a characteristic part. Here's the second citation for the Victoria Cross. You might want to read this twice as well. He'd been promoted to captain by this point.

Captain C. H. Upham, V.C., was commanding a Company of New Zealand troops in the Western Desert during the operations which culminated in the attack on El Ruweisat Ridge on the night of 14th-15th July, 1942.

In spite of being twice wounded, once when crossing open ground swept by enemy fire to inspect his forward sections guarding our mine-fields and again when he completely destroyed an entire truck load of German soldiers with hand grenades, Captain Upham insisted on remaining with his men to take part in the final assault.

During the opening stages of the attack on the ridge Captain Upham's Company formed part of the reserve battalion, but, when communications with the forward troops broke down and he was instructed to send up an officer to report on the progress of the attack, he went out himself armed with a Spandau gun and, after several sharp encounters with enemy machine gun posts, succeeded in bringing back the required information.

Just before dawn the reserve battalion was ordered forward, but, when it had almost reached its objective, very heavy fire was encountered from a strongly defended enemy locality, consisting of four machine gun posts and a number of tanks.

Captain Upham, without hesitation, at once led his Company in a determined attack on the two nearest strongpoints on the left flank of the sector. His voice could be heard above the din of battle cheering on his men and, in spite of the fierce resistance of the enemy and the heavy casualties on both sides, the objective was captured.

Captain Upham, during the engagement, himself destroyed a German tank and several guns and vehicles with grenades and although he was shot through the elbow by a machine gun bullet and had his arm broken, he went on again to a forward position and brought back some of his men who had become isolated. He continued to dominate the situation until his men had beaten off a violent enemy counter-attack and consolidated the vital position which they had won under his inspiring leadership.

Exhausted by pain from his wound and weak from loss of blood Captain Upham was then removed to the Regimental Aid Post but immediately his wound had been dressed he returned to his men, remaining with them all day long under

211

heavy enemy artillery and mortar fire, until he was again severely wounded and being now unable to move fell into the hands of the enemy when, his gallant Company having been reduced to only six survivors, his position was finally over-run by superior enemy forces, in spite of the outstanding gallantry and magnificent leadership shown by Captain Upham.

Finished? It's incredible, isn't it? You might want to read it again.

Now, I have something in common with Upham. Not boundless, almost ludicrous courage, but I've broken my arm – twice, as it happens. The first time falling down the stairs, drunk, after a Sting concert. You don't need to say anything. I knocked the end of my elbow off, so you might say I got what I deserved. The second time was crashing my dad's brand new car. What a twat. I offer in my defence that I was 19 and it almost felt expected of me – I'd have been letting him down if I hadn't stuffed it in a ditch at some point. Needless to say, it really hurts, especially the longer you leave doing something about it. (The first time I went home thinking 'Well, ARGH! I can still ARGH! move it! ARGH!' and didn't go to hospital until the following evening. That might make me sound tough, but no, I was being stupid. I was nineteen, I guess I thought I was indestructible.) But what I didn't do was run about and certainly, once my wound had been dressed, I definitely didn't then run about. I made the most of feeling sorry for myself and then when I got back to college it was a terrific ice-breaker/way to get people to buy me drinks. And it's also fair to say that Upham does a lot of something else I can't do: throw.

Hand grenades are terrifying bloody things if you stop and

think about it. Well, I can only speak for myself: if I stop and think about it they are terrifying, not just because they explode and fire hot bits of metal everywhere but because I have never been able to throw. I don't know why, no one ever sat me down and said, 'This is where you're going wrong.' Perhaps I was ill that week. I'd look with awe on those that *could* throw. It's something that used to really bug me at school – I wish I could play cricket, but when you can't throw (to save your life *or* for toffee) you end up not playing much cricket. At school we'd have a highly regimented system of heats for selecting the best in each category for sports day. One of the events (events makes it sound way too grand, disciplines makes it sound like the exact opposite of what it was, skills is too kind) was throwing a cricket ball. You'd stand in line, throw the ball and your distance on the marked-out field would be duly noted and if you were any good you'd go to the top of the pile – fame, glory, winning would beckon. Once I'd gone round the other heats – and I always felt the long jump was my thing – I'd find myself in the queue for the throwing, deploying my endless good manners: 'After you,' I'd say, 'no, really, you go first.' If spun out successfully this could take the rest of the afternoon and result in not having to face the humiliation of throwing a cricket ball seven to ten yards in front of other listless, bored boys all too ready to take the piss. I don't do throwing. Grenades are therefore terrifying – the thought of something that will blow up and shower me with red-hot iron landing at most seven yards away is . . . surely I don't have to explain that one?

After he was captured Upham eventually ended up in Colditz, as the Germans rather unsurprisingly regarded him as too much of a handful. When the Americans liberated the camp, he broke into the armoury so that he could go hunting Germans. Upham insisted that the medals weren't his and should go to his men. When he got back to New Zealand he turned down money raised after the war for him to buy a farm and put it into a scholarship at the University of Christchurch instead. He returned to farming, and for the rest of his life wouldn't allow any German vehicles onto his property.

This man was brave. So were all the others who never got a sniff of a VC: whoever crossed a start line, manned a gun, flew a plane, sailed the oceans – you get my point. Comedians just . . . aren't. OK?

10. Dumb down, deeper and down

IF IT'S TOO HARD I CAN'T
UNDERSTAND IT

It's an established fact that the world is getting more and more stupider. Established because everyone agrees. Stupidly, possibly. Dumbing down is the kind of phrase that finds itself muttered by middle-aged people who need their kids to fix their laptops. It's easy to say, it sits squarely at the heart of feeling that the world is in continual decline. Has there ever been a time when there hasn't been a feeling that the world is in continual decline? Did Ugg turn to Mrs Ugg and say things have really gone to the dogs since we moved into this cave? Certainly the Romans felt it. Cicero said: 'Times are bad. Children no longer obey their parents, and everyone is writing a book.' So it's nothing new, but it causes huge outbursts of worthy hot air.

But the dumbing down of TV is without a doubt something that is real, has happened and is continuing to happen. Definitely. I'm not just asserting this in the hope I'll be proved right either, like an *X Factor* contestant who just knows she can sing. Don't take my word for it. Critics will say look at Kenneth Clark's *Civilisation* series (which I've never seen), that was what used to be on BBC1. Now look at, say – and I have to be careful here, I might know someone who works on this and get punched on the nose – *Homes Under The Hammer*. *Homes Under The Hammer* is without a doubt unarguably dumber than *Civilisation* – a clever, posh man barking at us whilst standing next to a painting, and all done for our own good. But this doesn't take into account how TV has changed. There's lots more of it. Also, I'm not sure *Civilisation* would work as part of a daytime schedule. They used to just turn off the telly back then; Kenneth Clark would have been up against a test card at that time of day, not exactly a level playing field. But television isn't run by posh clever men in offices full of paintings who know they know best any more. Still, when you're making a history programme it is an issue. After all – what's the point of the programme: to educate, tickle the viewer's interest, tell a story (stories again!) or simply get the viewer through the next half-hour without them turning off or, worse still, turning over? Given that your TV might well be in the living room, next to your hearth, perhaps its job is tell stories by your campfire for you.

You'd have thought this was something we'd have at least talked about whilst making a history programme, but it only really crept up on us whilst making *Road to Berlin*. The story of what happened from D-Day to Berlin is pretty complex – I can't believe I've typed that last sentence, perhaps you can't either, but I'm not dictating this in my hammock on my yacht, chance'd be a fine thing, I'm in my office – and along the way, making the programme, we had had to simplify some things. I've been simplifying things in this book, after all.[88] And I'm not

---

[88] OK, OK, oversimplifying.

a card-carrying historian by any stretch of the imagination. But the question of dumbing down all came to a head on a lovely September evening in Holland. The last week of solid filming was in Arnhem, and the reason it was the last week of solid filming was because I had to parachute for the Arnhem programme and there was an unspoken lurking worry that I might break my neck, leaving us with an unfinished programme that I'd have to narrate from my hospital bed. Or via Ouija board. We'd been in the town for a couple of days' filming, rushing from location to location, and on the second day, a Saturday, had wound up in the town, next to the bridge. And I'd started to worry about whether we might not be dumbing the whole thing down a touch. Maybe I was transferring my worry about the jump the following morning just a little bit. So I started arguing. Perhaps because it was the programme that was closest to my heart, feeling like I'd been brought up on it (and because I was risking my neck), I'd already been wondering aloud whether the title of the programme – inevitably *A Bridge Too Far* – shouldn't have a question mark on the end of it. After all, as an idea it doesn't make much sense and also it's disputed as to whether anyone said it at the time. Anyway.

The early-autumn shadows were growing longer: I'd been getting really stuck into arguing about the way we were presenting the battle at Arnhem, and arguing for a fair while. *Road To Berlin* was made just before recapping became endemic in all programmes (except maybe some that pop up on BBC4) – nowadays it feels like a third of a programme is spent telling you what has already happened. Not to mention the torrent of coming-up-after-the-break stuff that means you could happily wander off and not watch any of the rest of the show. But our argument was all about complexity. Or rather it was about the worry that the viewer might not get to grips with complexity.

217

Indeed, that the viewer might be scared off by it and turn over to *World's Biggest Bikes* or something.

There is obviously a problem when you're making a programme about something complex. Especially a battle. Ten thousand or so men landed at Arnhem over the course of the battle, so there are, from their point of view, 10,000 versions of events. The Duke of Wellington, who said a lot of very quotable stuff about battles, had a good way of putting it: 'The history of a battle is not unlike the history of a ball. Some individuals may recollect all the little events of which the great result is the battle won or lost, but no individual can recollect the order in which, or the exact moment at which, they occurred, which makes all the difference as to their value or importance.' So a ball with 10,000 guests, that could be complex, yes.

The Division's battle was chaotic, fragmented, but not beyond comprehension if you break it down into its phases. Broadly speaking you have:

- The landings and the push to capture the road bridge (I say road bridge because there was a railway bridge that was also an option, which the Germans blew up in the faces of the men from 2nd Battalion The Parachute Regiment who'd been sent to seize it). Some got to the bridge, others didn't – roughly half of those who landed had to stay behind to protect the drop zones for the lifts that were to follow, but those heading for the bridge got held up for all sorts of reasons.
- The battle at the bridge – the men of 2nd Battalion (and others but from the 1st Parachute Brigade – brigades being made up of battalions of infantry and their 'supporting arms') commanded by Lieutenant Colonel John Frost

holding on against heavy odds until finally being overwhelmed on the fourth day.

- The disappearance of the man in charge, Major General Urquhart, who it might be said rashly went forward to find out what was happening and, surrounded by Germans – he shot one himself – got stuck in a loft.
- Days two and three: continued attempts to seize the bridge through the town, attempts that failed – culminating in 'Black Tuesday'.
- Days two and three: attempts by those that landed on day two (remember those who'd stayed behind to protect the drop zones? This is who they were waiting for) to push through the woods to the north of town – to go around the defences in the town that were holding up the attempts in the town itself, a move hampered by the small numbers of crossings on the railway line that dissected the town: yet more 'Black Tuesday'.
- The retreat back to Oosterbeek, the village to the west of Arnhem, where the dwindling remains of the Division then held on in a loose perimeter, less than a mile wide, until they withdrew over the river at dead of night nine days after the initial landings.
- The weather delayed Polish landings south of the river (though for no apparently good reason their supporting arms were landed north of the river on a different day) that saw the Poles literally landed in it.

In the meantime you have the men and machines of XXX Corps (or Second Army, depending on whose accounts you read) trying to get up the single road to Arnhem, making their way up the road held by the two divisions of American airborne soldiers who'd dropped on the first day. This whole thing also breaks down into several phases too, but we needn't worry about them – we didn't on the programme – although they are crucial to what happened to the men at Arnhem: if they'd got there sooner they might have linked up with the men at the bridge. But what happened at Arnhem pretty much stands separate from that – if the battle had run differently at Arnhem, if the bridge had been held for longer, if more men had got to the bridge then the whole thing might have succeeded. Or not. More on that later, I promise.

There, you followed all that, didn't you? You didn't turn off and you didn't turn over. Some of you were a little turned on, no? Seven essential points with a backdrop. Really, it's not difficult. On the TV we had a map to explain it and everything, with a commercial break in the middle. But it's not hard, is it? The fighting in each part of the battle was as critical to the conflict as any other part, the twists of fate were all equal parts of the grander scheme of things – though it is probably fair to say that the die was cast when it was decided not to land directly on or as close as possible to the bridge. The film *A Bridge Too Far* tries to tell the whole story, including the backdrop of XXX Corps, the American airborne divisions and their heroics, but in the Arnhem part of the story it pretty much concentrates (as well it might) on Frost at the bridge, Urquhart in the loft, and the last stand in Oosterbeek. That film is at least two and half hours long. So when you're making a half-hour programme, we are told, something has to give. Fair enough.

So we'd been arguing. I was annoyed, well, miffed, that we were leaving out the push through the woods, the attempt to get into the town by a different route. I was arguing for a sentence, an allusion, something. We were arguing in sight of the bridge – rebuilt after the war, as near as damn it the same as the historic bridge, named for its heroic defender John Frost. The town was preparing for the sixtieth anniversary celebrations. There was a movie screen on the bridge, flags of many nations, a huge parachute drop planned on one of the drop zones, the one furthest from the bridge and the one the men who fought in the woods had landed at, the following morning (that I was going to take part in). The town was thronged with men of every generation wearing red berets. There were old men with medals, middle-aged men with fewer medals, currently serving paratroopers. (The following year I went back so I could visit properly without a film crew and found myself in a bar drinking with men from 3 Para who had just got back from Sangin in Afghanistan, where the government had confidently asserted that they wouldn't fire a shot and where they had found themselves fighting pitched battles with the Taliban. They were voicing the opinion that what they were doing in Afghanistan was one thing, the fighting in Arnhem was another – 'this one was the battle for the galaxy'.)

With my jump in the morning and an abundance of experienced parachutists I'd been amusing myself by going around asking for parachuting tips. It seemed like a good idea at the time. I'd rung my dad and he'd said, 'Feet and knees together, elbows in, chin down' and not much else, except to wish me luck. I remembered him teaching us parachute rolls one summer holiday when I must have been 9, jumping off a wall, feet and knees together, elbows in, chin down. The technique is called a PFL – a parachute-fall landing. The idea is you roll the force around your body, not leaving any one part of your body to take the shock of landing. If you get it right, it's said, you barely feel a thing – one of the guys I jumped with said he'd done a perfect PFL and stood right up afterwards. He was an ex-paratrooper so had at least had some practice, as well as lots of hair-raising stories about parachuting. I hadn't, and now I've only got the one story. I fell heavily on my bum, then flipped onto my face[89] and got dragged along through the heather for what was most likely five seconds but felt like three-quarters of an hour. So rather than not feeling a thing I felt rather a lot, and for several weeks after. I have a hunch that it might all be easier if you don't have great long legs like me that sort of clatter together. Dad's good advice was echoed as I went around asking for tips – however, one fifty-something guardsman in a maroon beret said, 'Simple, chum, close your eyes and hope for the best' which wasn't exactly what I was after. It was a balmy September evening, the sky had been clear all day, and we'd spent the day filming at the bridge. At one point we'd parked our German-registered car on the ramp up to the bridge – we'd been filming in Germany beforehand – so that we could film with its striking arches in the background. It was getting funny looks from Dutch passers-by and we couldn't work out why, until we stopped to consider what some Dutch people might think of the Germans after the Hunger Winter that had followed the Arnhem battle. And it had been a long afternoon.

We had decided to shoot a piece to camera with me on the bridge and the camera down on the riverbank about eighty metres away between the Rijnkade and Jacob Groenewoudplantsoen (Dutch place names, eh? And don't worry, I had to look those up) where the buildings that Frost's men had defended once stood. The buildings had been destroyed. 'Sound' – by which I mean our sound-man, he wasn't a whole department – would catch me on the radio mic I was wearing. I stood by the handrail of the bridge and peered into the lens and tried to deliver a piece to camera, explaining how by the end of day one the bridge had been captured, but that the rest of the 1st Airborne Division couldn't get through. But it was a long piece to camera, and the

---

[89] My instructor had ever so cheerfully called it 'heels, arse, head, hospital!'

walkway on the bridge – as well as the inevitable Dutch cycleway – was very, very busy. There were people making their way to the staging area where the cinema screen was being set up, crew with equipment, people going about their business crossing the river. Lots of people. Bikes, mopeds and gawpers. Loads of gawpers. Gawpers who as they approached me, apparently talking intensely to myself yet into the distance, had to slow down and look at me, look at what I might be looking at, say something, touch me, stop and stare down at the camera. This was somewhat distracting and I couldn't get the words out. At all. We spent half an hour on this thirty-second link (I really had to hit this one right as it was the link that went into the break – a pre-cap rather than a recap). On one of the takes I'd got to the end and realised that one of the gawpers had stopped right beside me and was looking at my right ear, nodding along with what I was saying. I employed some fruity language and could see the sound-man and the director who were listening and laughing eighty metres away, mainly at my expense. We filled a whole tape with this stuff; the take that we finally got ends part one of our Arnhem programme and came with added gritted teeth.[90]

So by the time the light was failing that evening, and we'd got everything we needed filmed, I was feeling pretty ragged, and was becoming increasingly worried that we had got to the end of part one and only covered (really) the first stage of the battle. Of those seven easily digestible chunks we went through earlier. The associate producer – and TV is full of people with seemingly overlapping job titles that are nevertheless both distinct and indistinguishable from one another to the outsider and/or presenter and yet all incredibly vital to the process – was arguing that unfortunately the broadcaster was firm on how the script for this

---

[90] There is a point to all this, trust me, I haven't just slithered into hilarious outtakes anecdote mode. At the wrap party this was on the blooper reel almost in its entirety.

programme couldn't become too complex. But I was adamant: we were leaving out as important a part of the battle as any other, the part where Lionel Queripel won his Victoria Cross during the battle in the woods, where 4th Parachute Brigade, led by its 33-year-old brigadier,[91] John Hackett – who went on to command NATO and write a weird gloomy book about the Third World War – was torn to pieces when it ran into unexpected anti-aircraft guns and armour. Hackett had raised the brigade himself. It had had been two thousand strong before it left England, by the time Hackett and his men had fallen back to Oosterbeek on the third day his brigade numbered something like 150 men.

I was getting worried that we were telling too tidy a tale of the battle (I worry about this sort of thing). One reason for this was Bruce. Jumping with me the following morning on the anniversary of the battle was Bruce, an Arnhem veteran. He was turning 80, and had emigrated to Canada after the war – I think this was how he'd got round all the restrictions that would have stopped him jumping had he still been living in the UK. He had been telling me about his experiences in Arnhem. What he told me didn't fit with any of the history I'd read, but like I said, 10,000 men landed at Arnhem, so it was little wonder that his story was new on me. When 4th Parachute Brigade had landed it had been decided that one of its battalions, the 11th, would be peeled off from the brigade and added to the effort to break into the town and reach the bridge. (I left that out of the seven basic points because it's where things do get complex: there was a huge row at the time about it between the brigadiers at Divisional headquarters, a row about seniority caused by Major General Urquhart having disappeared and ending up squatting in his loft, without having completely figured out how to deal

---

[91] When I was 33 I was farting about on tour, telling jokes. Thought I'd mention that to offer some perspective.

with that kind of absence.) Bruce told me he had been part of an attack that had got within maybe three-quarters of a mile of the bridge, but it had petered out, the airborne soldiers struggling against tanks and the guns in the brickworks on the opposite side of the river. Bruce and his pal laid low, and crept into a boat tethered on the Neder Rhine. Once night fell and the fighting had died down, they slipped the mooring and drifted downstream, the town eerily lit up with the fires from the fighting. The boat foundered on the southern, enemy, bank of the river, they got out of the boat, crept inland and bedded down for the night.

The following morning Bruce and his companion were woken up by a bellowing German warrant officer – on the south bank there were German Marines, the Germans throwing everyone available into the battle. In the night they had crept inside a Marine platoon position – they'd got past the sentries unnoticed. Even though he was doing it in German, it was plain to Bruce that the sergeant was bollocking his men for having let them through. The two men were captured and spent the remainder of the war 'in the bag'. The rest of Bruce's battalion? They had been caught in the open by a mortar barrage as they were forming up for an attack, trying one last time to push into the town, and as the histories say 'ceased to exist'. The survivors fell back to Oosterbeek and fought in Lonsdale Force, who we met earlier with Major Robert Cain, around the church at the southern end of the perimeter, hanging on by the skin of their teeth until the evacuation. Major Dickie Lonsdale made an impassioned speech from the pulpit of the church to his men, about how they had to shoot to kill as ammo was running low. Lonsdale summed up the Germans: 'We've fought the Germans before – in North Africa, Sicily,[92] Italy. They weren't good enough for us then, and

---

[92] Paratroopers with memories of the year before in Sicily knew perfectly well that the business of capturing bridges and being relieved on time was something that

Al Murray

they're bloody well not good enough for us now.' This is the part of the battle that is well documented, but Bruce's story nagged at me: there was more to what had happened than we were telling, and yes, it was complicated, but what of it? Why gloss over that? We trusted the viewers, I trusted my ability to tell the story (hmm, maybe that is what the associate producer was trying to tell me), why not tell them about the fighting in the woods to the north of the town?

We went round and round this, decreasingly good-naturedly, and then I dropped in the idea of 'the man in the pub'. What if, I said, that in a year or two's time I was sitting in the pub, long after we'd completed the programme, long after it had gone out, and all of a sudden someone comes over and says 'I saw your programme about Arnhem'?

'Oh yes,' I'd reply, bracing for a compliment.

'Yes. My grandfather fought there.'

'Gosh, really? How interesting. Which battalion was he in?' I'd say, brimming with interest.

'Not sure, but he was killed in the fighting in the woods to the north of the town.'

'Ah,' I'd gulp.

'The thing is, it wasn't in your programme. You left it out. Why would you do that? Forget the men who fought and died there?' And at that my imaginary man in the pub would turn his back on me and leave, having firmly and fairly landed me in it.

The AP (they get abbreviated these job titles, too) was having

---

didn't run smoothly. Operation Fustian in July 1943, the attempt to seize the Primosole bridge, had seen about 250 men of the 1,900 dropped actually getting to the bridge. They captured it initially but the Germans forced them off the bridge, and the land forces didn't arrive on schedule. You might say that the whole thing went true to form.

226

none of it. He stressed that the thing was half an hour of commercial telly, so, what, 24 minutes at most, and we couldn't fit it all in. That was the way it was and so there. Besides, the viewers wouldn't be able to keep up. The light was failing and it was time for us to head to the hotel which was miles from town and a lot nearer the rendezvous for the parachute jump in the morning. The crew started to pack up the gear so that we could leave. I was about to head back to the bridge to ask more old paras how best to fall out of the sky unnecessarily, when a cutting Ulster voice started barking at us. Heading towards us at a fair rate for an eighty-year-old with a stick was a veteran, medals on his blazer, maroon beret at a proudly old-fashioned angle. He was bellowing at us, 'Hey, you!' He must have meant us; we were pretty conspicuous sitting on the jeep by the river. We mumbled our hellos.

'Are you the BBC?!?' We mumbled our denials, but they didn't register. 'Here you are filming, all you buggers filming!! Bloody BBC! You're always talking about the bloody glory boys at the bridge! That's all anyone's interested in! What about me and my mates? We got cut to pieces up in the woods, but you never film that do you?!??' He waved his stick at us for emphasis and headed for the bridge, still muttering about the BBC. I'd been proved right and told off all in one.

The fighting in the woods at Arnhem – or, rather, outside Arnhem – can be aptly described as the 4th Brigade being 'cut to pieces'. Even their landing had been troubled. On the first day, Sunday, 17 September, the 1st Parachute Brigade had landed very tidily, along with the 1st Airlanding Brigade and their supporting arms who'd come in by glider. Some of the men landing on the day said it was just like an exercise. Of course, the planners had wanted a smooth landing – that's why they hadn't landed near the bridge, for fear of unsuitable terrain and anti-aircraft fire.

The air flotilla delivering the gliders and parachutists to Arnhem alone (not forgetting the drops and landing further south by the US 82nd and 101st Airborne – the *Band of Brothers* lads winning WW2 single-handedly down in Eindhoven) was enormous. 1st Airborne Division was in 475 transport planes, with 320 gliders and their tugs joining them. There was fighter escort, preliminary bombing. Along the way some gliders cast off, one broke up, the sappers in it all being killed. Luckily for the men whose gliders went in the sea, the Allies, controlling the route, had lined it with rescue boats. One glider ditched off the coast of Holland and got into a fight with Russians who'd been conscripted into the German army – they fired over the British soldiers' heads to avoid any bloodshed. The men were rescued by boat. But at Arnhem, 2,283 men[93] parachuted onto the fields some eight miles from the railway bridge. Eight miles. Eight miles is a long walk, yes? Eight miles carrying a rifle, ammunition, grenades, food, the 200 pounds of equipment we met earlier, is a hard long walk. Eight miles with the Germans doing everything they can to stop you, trying to kill you, injure you, hinder you, is an even harder long walk.

Like I've said in this book, the Battle of Arnhem is something I've been aware of most of my life. I went to Arnhem when I was fourteen, as I was doing an O-level history project on it. I went to the National Archive to read the battle diaries – which are heart-rending. I have read many, many books about it. But it's simple, really. Many great minds, brilliant historians, doughty soldiers who were there, and plenty who weren't, have written books about it, sifting through events and accounts for answers. But it's dead simple. If you are landing people from the sky, and your big gimmick is turning up suddenly and unexpectedly somewhere important like the last bridge over the Rhine before

---

[93] One of the men's parachute failed to deploy and he was killed, coming in under the average for a drop that ambitious. Four refused to jump.

Germany itself, and it's all about surprise, then don't land a long, hard eight-mile walk from the important somewhere. Everything comes from this. Much has been made of the problems that 1st Airborne had with their radios. On the first day they found they were having real and major trouble with different parts of the division staying in touch with each other. But 1st Airborne knew they had radio problems, they'd had them before, and – and this is worth pointing out – if they'd all landed on, or near or right next to the bloody bridge they would not have needed the radios.[94]

Much has been made of the radios that didn't work: they feature prominently in the movie, certainly, but British airborne soldiers, unable to take heavy radio sets into battle with them, compromised by using lower-powered radio sets – and seeing as doctrine said that they were supposed to land and operate within a 3-mile radius this compromise could be explained away. Unreliable radios, therefore, were the airborne norm; one of the company commanders in 2nd Battalion didn't trust the radios and instead relied on calls on bugles to run his company, bugle calls that went back to the Peninsular War. Major General Urquhart's disappearance into the battle, desperate to find out what was going on, is attributed to the radio failure and the chaos of this first day. It could also be attributed to him not quite knowing what to do. It is maybe worth noting that one of his predecessors, Major General Hopkinson, had been killed doing something similar, going well forward in Italy and being shot in the chest by an enemy machine gun. Urquhart had attached himself to 3rd Battalion's advance and their memories of what had happened to 'Hoppy' might well have been one of the things that made them hold off continuing that night

[94] The BBC's reporters who'd landed with the Division, Stanley Maxted and Guy Byam, were able to get their reports back to London. Perhaps that's why my old Ulsterman didn't like the BBC so much.

– Urquhart's presence could be the reason why (disastrously) another 600 or so men didn't make it to the bridge. Way to go, boss. But really the only reason there was chaos, and the reason that the three parachute battalions who were slithering in a stop-start advance that, come the evening, had stopped, was because they were having to cover the eight miles there and back. It's simple. It's not complex.

Also. If your big advantage, your unique selling point, is turning up suddenly and unexpectedly somewhere important, surely the smart thing to do is not then hang around somewhere else? That what you really should do is concentrate your effort, your men, your forces on that somewhere important. This is the other thing that makes me boggle, nearly 70 years later. Because so many aircraft were needed to land the troops at Arnhem, Nijmegen and Eindhoven, further 'lifts' were required. This meant that more than half of the men who'd landed on the first day – 1st Airlanding Brigade, the glider soldiers – rather than head into town to seize the bridge had to stay behind to secure and defend the landing and drop zones. Eight miles away from the bridge. So rather than turning up suddenly and unexpectedly somewhere important (somewhere important 60 miles – yes, 60 miles! – behind enemy lines) and concentrating all their effort and force in that important somewhere, the British opted for turning up a fair distance away from the important somewhere, and dividing their effort across that fair distance. And this is before you consider the Germans.

You see, as well as the radios failing, much is made of the fact that there were many more German soldiers at Arnhem when the Airborne Division landed there than they'd been led to expect. That they got a nasty shock when confronted with tanks and SS soldiers is always factored into the explanations of the disaster at Arnhem. But again you might say, this only matters so much if the plan stinks to high heaven in the first place; and, let's face it, the plan that has everyone landing in the wrong place and then splitting up really does pong. The way the British fought at Arnhem, the way that John Frost's men defended the bridge into a fourth day, with something like 740 soldiers fighting tanks and the SS soldiers they weren't expecting to fight gives you some idea of how things might have gone had everyone landed at the bridge instead. Or even if they'd all headed to the bridge and not had to wait behind for the subsequent lifts or if at least another battalion had got to the bridge or . . . you get the picture. It's not complicated.

Similarly, there was a plan for a group of jeeps – calling itself a *coup de main* party under Major Freddie Gough, decidedly ancient at 43[95]– to race ahead and seize the bridge. Gough's Reconnaissance Squadron had problems unloading their jeeps from their gliders and by the time they'd got away, half an hour late, the Germans were starting to react. (As well you might expect them to. A sodding great airborne landing had happened fairly near to a bridge that spanned the Rhine. There was initially some confusion as to where the British might be headed, because they were so far from the bridge, but the man on the ground, *Sturmbannführer* Krafft, threw together the men he could find, and counter-attacked with real vigour . . . but I'm getting ahead of myself.) The jeeps that went ahead ran into trouble, and the *coup de main* was abandoned. Before he'd hared off into the blue yonder, Urquhart had called Gough to report to him – the same Gough who had to get away with no delay. Um. If only they hadn't been delayed, some say, if only they'd got their jeeps away earlier. Balls. If only they hadn't been relying on something so half-baked in the first place – if only they had landed near the

[95] When I was 43 – well, I got the idea for this book. A little bit of perspective for you there.

bridge. Getting jeeps out of gliders was something everyone knew could go wrong – Urquhart had pinned success on something pretty flimsy. A not very well woven plan was unravelling the minute they arrived.

In fact, to explain the complexity of the Arnhem battle, and the tragic (final) defeat that the British Army suffered in World War 2 you can, if you want, dumb down. There is one answer to all the questions thrown at what went wrong. They landed nowhere near the bridge, and then divided their effort. Part of this divided effort, then, was the men of 4th Parachute Brigade, who landed on the second day, at a place called Ginkel Heide. Ginkel Heide is even further from the bridge than the main landing zones, but don't let that concern you, I think I've made my point – in fact, where Ginkel Heide is makes my point for me. The second lift was late, there'd been fog on the airfields and as a result they'd been delayed – and for the rest of the operation bad weather in the UK would plague the planned subsequent lifts. So not only were they arriving miles from where they might have been any use, they were also not just a day late (in my opinion) but four hours late on that day. With the radio failures they didn't know that the plan for day one – the whole of 1st Parachute Brigade getting to the bridge – had misfired. The drop zone was being defended by the men of the 7th King's Own Scottish Borderers who'd landed by glider the previous afternoon. They were under major attack when the second lift arrived, there was machine-gun fire on the drop zone, and the heather had caught fire. When I jumped into Ginkel Heide with Bruce on the sixtieth anniversary he pointed this out as the Dakota banked around back towards the drop zone, having dropped the first 'stick' of parachutists: 'There was a machine gun in that wood there,' he hollered over the sound of the engines.

The brigade landed and rendezvoused, having to do some fighting the instant it hit the ground. There followed some figuring out what to do. One of the brigade's battalions – 11th, Bruce's – was sent into Arnhem. The other two, 156th and 10th, stuck with the plan, and advanced into the town through the woods north of the railway line into Arnhem. The original plan had always called for the whole brigade to do this. Hackett was dismayed that his brigade had been split up, but understood; he'd also been given command of the King's Own Scottish Borderers (KOSB – yes, it's acronym time!) to replace 11 Para. 'Dismayed' isn't really the right word – he was livid, and had a furious row with Brigadier Hicks who had been left in charge. Major General Urquhart had conceived a command structure for his possible absence, designating Hicks his deputy even though Hackett was the senior man – the only problem was that he hadn't told Hackett. However: the KOSB weren't completely at his disposal, they were still guarding the landing zone that the Poles' gliders with the Polish Parachute Brigade (who were landing on the other side of the river. Why on Earth would you land the Poles' support weapons in gliders *on the other side of the river?!*)[96] were going to land on the following day.

So Hackett's men, who set off east into the woods, ran into resistance and came to a halt. It was agreed that night that the following morning there would be a concerted two-brigade push towards the bridge in through the south of the town following Frost's route, and that the bulk of Hackett's hybrid 4th Brigade would go around north of the railway line and head down the other main road, through the woods. So a big attack was going to go in two whole days after the Division had first arrived not exactly near the important somewhere, in what could be called

---

[96] Presumably because you expected the bridge to have been captured and the Germans simply not to be all that bothered about it. If you're looking for a sure sign of overconfidence and/or wishful thinking in the Market Garden plan that's it right there.

– pessimistically – dribs and drabs. With lightly armoured paratroopers who by now knew the Germans weren't the old men and kids they'd expected to be up against. So much for the element of surprise. Or concentration of force. I didn't go to staff college, nor did you, I guess, and while it's easy to be an armchair general – um? This plan stinks.

The attack didn't go well. With its three companies of infantry (numbering about 150 men each) 156 Battalion moved forward. C Company held the battalion's ground, A and B Companies were to push forward and secure higher ground to the east (a variation on the plan hatched back in the UK), where it had been blithely assumed that a second lift could turn up on day two and make its way into Arnhem by a different main road.

One way of looking at what happened at Arnhem is to read the war diaries. Kept by all the headquarters from the top of the Division to the bottom they are a day-by-day record of what happened. During the months preceding Arnhem they all list cancelled operations that came and went. They're full of abbreviations, map references, clipped phrases and muted descriptions. Urquhart's disappearance in the Divisional war diary says simply 'No information as to movements of GOC'[97] – his return the following morning 'GOC returns from 1 Para Bde'. The daily mortaring and shelling that the besieged Division endured was written up laconically on 21 September as '0650 – Morning hate begins.'. The 11th Battalion war diary ends like this:

Tuesday, 26th September 1944

I cannot say how 11 Bn fared. I was blind with blood and

---

[97] General Officer Commanding.

field dressing and lost touch with my men in the darkness, crossing the river myself with 1st Bn personnel.

The 156th Battalion war diary describes the initial attack like this – the long numbers are map-grid references, 'coy' means company, S.P. guns means Self-Propelled Guns (tanks to you and me):

0830 – A Coy put in an attack on the line of defence on the rd running from 702805 to 699792. The axis of advance was along the track running from 693778 to 700798. The coy met very heavy opposition including S.P. guns and armd cars and was brought to a standstill, after suffering heavy casualties including all the officers along the line of the track running from 699802 to 700797.

This rather dry write-up tells you what happened, but nothing about what it was like. A Company were making for some high ground at a place called Lichetenbeek but had advanced into a German defence line that was along a road called the Dreijenseweg, with a bank that concealed the Germans as well as protecting them from artillery fire. The Paras overran the front of the German positions, but the Germans had half-tracks armed with anti-aircraft cannon covering their defence line. The fire was merciless, the Germans making the most of being on higher ground and the heavy weapons they had at their disposal. Major Pott, commanding A Company, made it, with six men, to Lichtenbeek where he held on for an hour before they were captured. B Company moved up, oblivious to what had happened to A Company, putting in their attack half an hour later. This is how the diary puts it:

*0900 – B Coy put in attack on the same line of enemy
defence, moving round the North of A Coy, and met the
same heavy opposition. B Coy Comd was then fatally
wounded and heavy casualties were sustained.*

As it was, A Company's commander wasn't fatally wounded
– he was shot in the groin by a sniper. As he'd gone forward
he'd seen the roadsides of the Dreijenseweg littered with the
dead of A Company, including a whole platoon headquarters
that had been killed. The anti-aircraft guns struck again, their
exploding shells shattering the trees around the men and filling
the air with deadly splinters. 'Me and my mates were cut to
pieces.' Only C Company was relatively unscathed.

10th Battalion were experiencing similar problems. I can't quote
from their war diary because it was lost on Wednesday, 21
September, when the battalion was overrun. But their experience
of 'Black Tuesday' was all part of the day's pattern – confusion,
chaos, carnage. There is some confusion as to what the orders
were that they'd received, whether they knew about 156's
movements or not, but they found themselves fighting the same
German armour, facing the same anti-aircraft gun fire. Doubtless
the Germans on the ground didn't know which battalion was
which, just that these lightly armed Brits kept trying and kept
running into their blocking line. They were able to disengage
from the Germans, using smoke. At around quarter past three
that afternoon the order was passed on that the 4th Brigade would
'cut its losses' and head back towards Oosterbeek. Here their
troubles really began. The Germans had scented success and were
counter-attacking strongly, mortaring the British, and at four
o'clock the Polish gliders began to land. The Germans reacted to
this ferociously as well. In the chaos the 4th Brigade found the
only way to get out of the woods (and rarely has this expression

cropped up in such a wrong place) was across the railway line. This was no problem for the infantry who were able to scramble up and down the embankment. But the Brigade's vehicles, laden with ammunition (and worthless radios) had to get across the railway. As well as a level crossing at a place called Wolfheze a drainage tunnel under the railway line had been discovered that was big enough for a jeep. In the confusion and while being shelled and mortared the Brigade did what it could to withdraw in an orderly manner.

10th Battalion's A Company was holding a strip of woodland that defended the Brigade's retreat. Captain Lionel Queripel and his men hung on through the night but in the morning they were under too much pressure. He was wounded in both arms, but carried on – he'd been wounded in the face the previous day while carrying a wounded sergeant to an aid post. Queripel's Victoria Cross citation explains:

> Disregarding his injuries and the heavy mortar and machine gun fire, he continued to inspire his men to resist with hand grenades, pistols, and the few remaining rifles. On at least one occasion he picked up and threw back an enemy stick grenade which had landed in the ditch.

As the Germans applied even more pressure, Queripel ordered his men to withdraw – he insisted on staying behind, covering their withdrawal with his pistol and some hand grenades. That was the last anyone saw of him. He was awarded a posthumous VC, the fifth won at Arnhem. He was 24.

This is the story of the men 'cut to pieces in the woods'. It's not difficult to follow. Once they had fought their way out of the woods and over the railway line, the 4th Brigade had to fight the remaining distance into the perimeter at Oosterbeek. On the

237

Wednesday morning, Brigadier Hackett himself had led a desperate charge of about 150 men to seize a hollow about 400 yards from the Divisional perimeter. They held out all day, the Germans unwilling to get too close; when night fell, with half of the 150 injured, Hackett roused the survivors and in a wild bayonet charge broke out for the perimeter. Once inside the perimeter, 156 Battalion was down to enough men to defend one large house. Hackett's 4th Parachute Brigade had been destroyed in less than 48 hours. But again, had they been landed on the first day at least within reach of the bridge, things might have turned out very differently for them. I don't think it's dumbing down to say the whole thing turned on one giant, howling error. They didn't land near enough to the bridge to seize it immediately, and all else followed. Maybe even if it had been decided to leave the 4th Brigade in the UK, the men who'd had to wait and guard further landing zones wouldn't have had to do so, and could have been used to seize the bridge: effort wasn't concentrated – and so couldn't be committed effectively. But the mindset seems to have been: we have a whole Division, we should use it all.

You might say, well, yes, this is all very well with hindsight, and besides, didn't you say at the start of this book that hindsight is a nonsense and doesn't really get us anywhere? And, yes, you'd be right. You might even say history is what happened, not what might have happened and what could have been done. But what's so odd about Arnhem and the landings is that only four months previously, in June, on D-Day, when needing to capture another bridge – the bridge we now call Pegasus Bridge – they landed three gliders just a hundred feet away. They turned up suddenly and unexpectedly somewhere important, and with great success – the British airborne establishment knew how to do what it was trying to do, had done it before – yet somehow when it came to Arnhem the essential business of landing the soldiers in the right place got forgotten. Or put aside.

General 'Windy'[98] Gale, who had commanded 6th Airborne and had formulated the plan for capturing Pegasus Bridge as well as capturing the lesser known Horsa Bridge up the road from Pegasus Bridge and knocking out several others, was asked to assess the plan for Arnhem and said that he would have insisted to the point of resignation on a glider *coup de main* at the bridge. Brigadier Hackett put it like this: 'The airborne movement was very naive. It was very good on getting airborne troops to battle, but they were innocents when it came to fighting the Germans when we arrived. They used to make a beautiful airborne plan and then added the fighting-the-Germans bit afterwards'. Not that Hackett was on record as having objected before the event. It wasn't so much a bridge too far as a drop zone nowhere near the sodding bridge. If you'll forgive my (possible) oversimplification. It worked pretty well in my O-level history project. I remember leaving out the fighting in the woods in that and still got an A*. Ah, well.

But – and there's always a but – in telling this tale I have made the fatal error of the overexcited would-be armchair general and historian. I haven't taken the other side properly into account.

---

[98] Top-notch nickname, yes?

11. Two sides to every story

WOULD YOU RATHER BE RIGHT OR HAPPY?

My brilliant and pithy account of what the British did wrong in the preceding chapter misses a little something. Fans of *A Bridge Too Far* might well recall the scene in which Gene Hackman, playing the Polish General Sosabowski says, 'The Germans, what about the Germans?' (With a hard 'Guh' G; it's a great moment, but then all moments with Gene Hackman are great moments.) Sosabowski is portrayed as deeply sceptical of the plan, of his superiors, of everything, the wallpaper in the briefing room too, probably. His parachute brigade, unlike its British equivalents, didn't consist of volunteers: 'Why should only the brave die?' he reasoned, not entirely unreasonably. Some of his men had been on hunger strike the previous month in protest at not being dropped in to help their fellow citizens fighting the Germans in the Warsaw Massacre. Sosabowski and his men had a different, more aggressive attitude to the enemy. They weren't about to underestimate the Germans. And in my oversimplified round-up of what went wrong at

Arnhem I did just that: I hardly credit the Germans with winning. In fact, in a rather British way I'm all too ready to credit us with the loss and take it on the chin and crack on with the glory of noble defeat and struggle. But what about the Gg-ermans?

Obviously this question applies across the board in history. Not just 'What about the Gg-ermans?' specifically but what about the other point of view? 'The other side of the hill' as Wellington used to call it. Alexander the Great might well be the Great from the point of view of those who think he's great – Greeks and Macedonians, for instance – and certainly if you look at what he achieved in conquering the known world, overthrowing the Persian Empire, you might well think 'Wow'. But what of the peoples he invaded, conquered, bent to his will? In Persian literature he is known as the 'accursed' (*gojastak*) and is accused of destroying temples and other religious crimes – ways of pointing out how bad he was, as if conquering and killing wasn't bad enough. Given that he conquered Persia this is a pretty much understandable point of view, but from the Western perspective he won't lose the 'The Great' tag too easily. His achievements, regardless of how brutal they might be (he famously killed his best friend in a drunken brawl, nice guy, must invite him to my next dinner party) are just too, um, Great. Historical accuracy aside, when a man has been deified by his culture – even during his lifetime, as we're told by Plutarch – it is going to be pretty hard to write a revised history of his achievements, which have pretty much always defied the firmest attempts to flick historical Vs. Besides, we get the bulk of what we think of Alexander via the filter of the Romans who thought that his all-round conquering imperial military antics were just peachy. As well they might.

Again, if you look at the Battle of Waterloo from the point

of view of Napoleon, a man also virtually deified by his culture[99] mainly because he'd so modestly insisted on it, it isn't so much a battle won by Wellington as a battle not won due to mitigating circumstances. Putting aside Wellington's steadfast army and its excellent tactical handling, the Coalition's overall strategy, as well as perfect Prussian timing, gallons of Gallic ink have been spent on finding reasons why the French lost or, rather, why they didn't win: Napoleon was poorly on the day, it rained wrong, um, er, Boney's piles were playing up, etc. Similarly, German argument and interpretation has centred on what time the Prussians arrived on the field at Waterloo, blunting Wellington's and his multinational army's achievement in holding off the French that day – the earlier they arrive the less impressive Wellington's feat of arms becomes. That's the answer to Sosabowki's question in this instance. And here's the thing: history gives us the chance, with the passage of time, to look at both sides of something, a chance we rarely get in our everyday lives – so, why not? What about the Germans?

Well, from the German point of view the airborne landings on Sunday, 17 September, and the days that followed, were so close to the Reich – Germany itself – that something resembling panic set in. I remember when dad and I visited Holland in 1983 we took a wrong turning somewhere around Nijmegen and found ourselves at the German border. Indeed, the repeated airlifts – which I so sternly criticised in the previous chapter as a division of effort – felt to the Germans like constantly renewing pressure, a bottomless pit of surprise and resources at the Allies' disposal. Every time a new lift came in the Germans thought that the Allies had regained the initiative. They didn't know which way to turn. But shock had quickly turned to resolve

[99] Visit Paris, look at Napoleon's tomb at Les Invalides, and tell me (a) he didn't think he was great and (b) the French aren't mental.

and the Germans decided that the most crucial part of the battle lay further south – if they could cut the corridor made by XXX Corps, or the Second Army, then what happened further north at Arnhem would be academic. In other words, the Arnhem battle, which we have been concentrating on, was, in the German assessment, not the most important part of the whole campaign. (I did promise I would get to this later!) As one German officer said:

> 'The biggest mistake historians make is to glorify and narrow-mindedly concern themselves with Arnhem and Oosterbeek. The Allies were stopped in the south just north of Nijmegen, that is why Arnhem turned out the way it did.'[100]

Oops. Well, that's me told. The British landings at Arnhem would be contained, and the men trying to reach them along what became known as 'Hell's Highway'[101] would be delayed, held up, their momentum stymied until they ground to a halt. Simple. And this is pretty much what happened. The Germans won because they had figured out what to do and went ahead and did it, not because we lost, not because we had radios that didn't work or a somewhat hare-brained divisional commander driving around in his jeep looking for trouble. It's already not such a good film.

So the German reaction to the Allied landings, which wasn't what had been expected at all, was the deciding factor. Not landing nearer or further from the bridges, either. 1st Airborne landing so far from the bridge (my main gripe in the previous chapter) confused the Germans on the ground – it took them

---

[100] All of these quotes come from Kershaw's book.
[101] Perhaps the antithesis of Harry Secombe's old show.

several hours to figure out what the hell the British might be doing: after all, the Germans reasoned, if you wanted to seize a bridge in a great hurry and with maximum surprise why the hell would you land eight miles away from it? (The law of unintended consequences in full operation right there.) However, once they'd figured it out they reacted aggressively and ruthlessly. It could be – and it has been argued – that landing next to the bridge itself would have been met with just as aggressive and ruthless a response, if only because the Germans had earmarked the bridge as a possible target for an airborne assault: the British would have landed nearer the infantry from 9th SS Panzer Division. 9th SS Panzer Division had trained for how to deal with airborne landings too. This is all covered in an excellent book called *It Never Snows in September* by Robert Kershaw which tells the story of the Market Garden battle from a German perspective. It's the kind of book that busts apart, indeed vaporises, any armchair approach to this battle: it's the kind you need to reread after confidently asserting what could have been done differently by the Allies. The what-ifs that surround the battle are dispatched one by one. Digging deep into battle diaries, personal accounts and reports, Kershaw got the other side of the story.

Robert Kershaw's book wasn't published until 1990, long after the established way of explaining the battle had taken hold of people's imaginations. Hollywood movies can do that. But the question of 'the Gg-ermans, the Gg-ermans' and what they'd done to thwart the Allied attack was one that Kershaw, and lots of other people, felt needed addressing, what with the Cold War at various points in the 1980s seeming not very cold at all. (I remember a debate at school along the lines of 'Would you rather be Red or Dead and Red?' with Red winning despite lots of people voting for Dead. Debates were a way of meeting girls, so you'd sit through pretty much anything for the chance to grin at girls sheepishly. My genius tactic to impress them was to get up and say something stupid. It still doesn't work.) It's an interpretation we don't really have to interpret; *It Never Snows in September* is very much an example of someone asking the direct question 'What can we learn from history?' – and 'plenty' was Kershaw's answer. He'd written it to address some of what NATO had thought it might face in the event of a Soviet invasion of West Germany.

Soviet doctrine for how to fight had evolved from a pre-war concept called Deep War – the idea of a huge rolling front that would break through deep into enemy territory and seize logistic troops and reserves before they could be deployed. Part of this would be done with airborne soldiers, paras, helicopter forces. Airfields would be seized, headquarters attacked directly, as would key communications points like, um, bridges. The Soviets, who had been the first to experiment with parachute troops between the wars, had tried this twice on a large scale during the war on the Eastern Front. It hadn't gone well. In January of 1942 a corps-sized airborne operation had taken place in the battles around Vyazma as part of a Soviet counter-offensive against the German salient (or bulge) near Moscow. They landed behind enemy lines, went to ground and linked up with partisans. They held out for four months, taking heavy losses – about 4,000 out of the 14,000 dropped were killed. Rather like at Arnhem, because the land forces that the Soviets were meant to link up with failed to break through, the Germans were able to mop them up at leisure. The second, at the Dnieper River in August 1943, ended in utter disaster, with the Soviet airborne soldiers overwhelmed and their units completely destroyed by the Germans reacting swiftly and ruthlessly. Though there's no movie to commemorate their heroic struggle, mind. In fact, it's pretty hard to find out anything much about those operations – everything I've written about them may well be a load of cobblers, and although Russian archives have opened up since the end of the Cold War I'm not the man for this job. Despite this chequered track record, by the 1980s the Soviets were supposedly keen on landing airborne soldiers deep behind enemy lines and while, as Kershaw admitted in his book, much had changed between 1944 and the late 1980s, maybe there were lots of lessons to be learned from how the Germans had defeated the Allies in Operation Market Garden. Lessons that NATO could itself apply if the worst happened.[102]

The main – cheery – conclusion seems to have been that if you didn't care about the cost in terms of lives, you could thwart pretty much anything, even élite airborne soldiers, if what you did was hold them up, harass them, wear them down any which way you could. An 'all hands to the pump' sort of thing. The Germans had used men who weren't yet trained, cadets, older men and men from 'Ear and Stomach' Battalions. Ear and Stomach Battalions were made up of men who were otherwise not fit enough to serve, because they had health problems. The men with the ear problems were particularly vulnerable: they couldn't hear the orders they were given, and wouldn't hear incoming enemy shelling. That's fairly funny, I'm afraid. Ahem. But these men, with 'stiffeners' in the form of experienced NCOS – sergeants and corporals – were able to fight fairly effectively, and hold up, delay, stymie the Allies' efforts. The dwindling advantage that the British had gained was squandered fighting a ragtag of people thrown together (and you might say thrown away) with the exact aim of getting the British to squander their meagre advantage. The conclusion that Kershaw draws from

---

[102] The introduction contains a disclaimer – this book is all my opinion, not that of UK high command. Imagine being able to write that in your intro! Ha, ha.

this was that Soviet troops could be stopped, held up, harassed and worn down by anyone – old men, schoolboy cadets (help!!) or the TA – if they were applied properly and ruthlessly and without much care for the cost. Great. The German losses at the Arnhem battle were very heavy: they lost something like 1,300 men fighting in Arnhem, comparable with 1st Airborne Division's losses, which, given the Germans' advantages of tanks, supplies and time, show how ferociously the British had fought. 'In the best traditions of the British Army' without a doubt, though, in similar tradition, not necessarily brilliantly led.

Kershaw also points out how well organised the Germans were. (Finally! a stereotype we can rely on!) German command structures, even when they referred to what were essentially armies that existed merely on paper, were hugely flexible and well understood, and above all they worked. I suppose also that the fact that the Market Garden offensive, if successful, would have threatened Germany itself would have concentrated minds rather a lot. By being able to make quick decisions, stick to them, and organise their men in an ad hoc way (with all that that implies when we are talking about Nazi Germany) the Germans were able to repel the Allies' elite troops despite what looked like, on day one, a demonstration of overwhelming Allied superiority. Similarly, Operation Goodwood was pored over by Western military thinkers – maybe it offered clues to how to defeat the Soviets with their 3-to-1 numerical advantage? How had the Germans, after being bombed heavily, held off a numerically overwhelming force of tanks on the plains to the south-east of Caen which aren't unlike what used to be the West German landscape, so effectively? Anti-tank guns that knocked out tanks before they got too close, good command structures, motivated soldiers. The German side of the story had lots of potential lessons to offer your Cold Warrior. It also had the advantage of making the Germans feel valued by their NATO Allies. Either way, the other point of view takes some getting used to. I expect if this book had been around when I was doing my O-level history project I'd have shoved it under a chest of drawers or something.

The German perspective is initially strange to read about if you're familiar with the way the story is usually told. All the units and names familiar to the modern British reader with his British perspective, maybe with a cultural trace memory of Sean Connery and Anthony Hopkins at the back of their mind, fade into the background. The arrows on the maps point in a different direction, they contain different emphasis. The opposite perspective makes the whole thing turn upside down. The urgency in everything the Germans were doing is in striking contrast to the way the British conducted themselves, even once you've fenced through all the rather studied officerly grace under pressure and cups of tea. Once they'd figured out what was going on the Germans organised their response accordingly, creating blocking lines preventing the rest of 1st Airborne reaching the bridge, whilst another force dealt with containing the men at the bridge. The Tiger tanks which arrived on 'Black Tuesday' and roamed around blasting houses were sent by Field Marshal Model himself: his headquarters would send out a couple of Tigers to units that were deemed to be underpowered, a prime example of the German command structure's ability to look right at where the crisis points were and make the most of their advantages. The Arnhem Bridge needed to be cleared not because the Germans thought that XXX Corps would arrive, but because they couldn't use it freely while it was being held by the British.

Away from the bridge, once the battle had shifted to Oosterbeek with the British on the defensive it's interesting to discover the reluctance with which the Germans approached the fight, preferring instead to let the British run out of food and ammunition rather than have to take them on. The battle oddly offered the initiative to the defenders, in that they didn't have to figure out how to fight or probe for weak points. The Germans called Oosterbeek 'Der Kessel' – the Cauldron. German descriptions of the fighting are illustrative of the fact that they were throwing everything they could into the mix. *Sturmbannführer* Krafft who from the very start of the Arnhem battle had done everything he could to hinder the British (though after the battle he wrote a glowing report for his superiors full of fibs about what a great job he'd done) said of the fighting in the Cauldron:

> *'the concentrated British forces fight desperately and ferociously for every house and every position. The attack has little success because our troops have little experience in house and wood clearing.'*

The British had been told to expect old men and Hitler Youth, and they'd got that, but with SS troops backing them up as well. Most tellingly, perhaps, while British accounts like to say how we lost because we muffed the whole thing, the Germans on the ground had a different view. SS-Corporal Wolfgang Dombrowski[103] – another account that Kershaw found of Arnhem – said of the end of the battle:

> *'We had fought non-stop for 10 days and nights. Coffee and Benzedrine had kept us awake. After it was all over we were as exhausted as the British; we slept and slept.*

---

[103] Nice German name there.

All the Wehrmacht battalions that fought in Arnhem got a special 10-day leave from Hitler. It was our last-ever victory. But not the Waffen-SS. Himmler said we would get our holiday after the Final Victory!'

For all the cries of 'they started it', uttered in jest or not, the German soldier's hard fight at Arnhem isn't all that different from the British soldier's, though there is the unanswerable question of what they thought they were fighting for.

Given the numbers, you'd hope they thought it was worth fighting for. 41.1% of German males born in 1920 were killed in World War Two. The figure for 1926 through to 1928 – soldiers who would have been sixteen in 1944 – is 33%. In the final eleven month phase of the war, between June 1944 and May 1945, 80% of German casualties were on the Eastern Front. One of the oft-remarked characteristics of the Arnhem battle is that both sides treated each other's wounded, and even arranged a two-hour ceasefire for an evacuation of the wounded from inside Oosterbeek. On the Eastern Front medics and hospitals weren't safe. When Frost and his men were finally captured on the Wednesday – smoked, burned, shelled, starved and outgunned out of the houses around the bridge – the SS officer who took his surrender was heard to remark on what a nice proper battle it was as he handed out captured British smokes to the survivors. If they had been Red Army men it is unlikely there'd have been much conversation. Dombrowski again:

'The battle for Arnhem was something completely new for us. We were used to dealing with Russian 'human wave' attacks where there was no regard for human life. Hand-to-hand fighting was normally required to stop the fourth or fifth wave because we had run out of ammunition. The

251

Americans had been our main opponents in Normandy. Their aircraft had often shot up medical columns, we had fought against the Poles at Falaise and they had been brutal. The British were an unknown quantity.'

Other soldiers said they had no hatred for the British. Isn't that nice to know, eh? Or just mad. Or chivalry, perhaps? This weird contrast becomes stranger still, I think, as our culture gets further away in time from the 1940s – does any of this make any sense to us? Can we relate to any of it at all? A war in which we were fighting an enemy, made up of soldiers who'd grown up in Nazi Germany – now in our culture the very watchword for evil (and fair enough) – who thought that there was a sort of kindred spirit with Britain? Like most things to do with World War Two it is mind-boggling. But what was understood on the battlefield, where the lines were drawn was a matter of life and death – if the view from the German side meant that the British were less of an enemy than the Russians, if that became the custom – then who am I to argue or question it? It'd be bad form, old chap. Would you like a cup of tea, old boy?

12 Always use the butter knife

'DO AS YOU WOULD BE DONE BY'

Manners. Something from a bygone age – the past, from history. Kids spitting on the street (I'd never have done that). The gentleman holding a door open for the lady. The lady bloody well saying thank you when the gentleman holds a door open. Each age, each generation has its customs, its ways, there's the ever-shifting sands of mobile and social-media etiquette that's around today, the coded language of fans fluttering in Georgian times, whatever Romans would have done in a Roman bath – I don't want to know, thank you. Manners and customs at a historical distance can seem absurd – they can seem absurd close up, too. Dad was always big on 'elbows off the table' when we were kids, it was a common refrain. Sometimes he'd threaten to biff the offending elbow with a spoon. It never happened and, please, no one call Childline. I still for the life of me don't really know why having your elbows on the table might matter or why it might be worth being bopped on the elbow with a spoon: at the time – and maybe now – it seemed to exist purely to give him something to bust us up over at mealtimes. Apparently you can put your elbows on the table if you're an uncle or an aunt, but even though I suspect he made that up I'm quietly relieved to now be in the clear.

Military institutions are tangles of etiquette, protocol, port-passing, rank displaying, waggle dancing and manners. A few years ago dad invited me to a dinner at his regimental mess, to celebrate the safe return of one of their squadrons from Iraq and its expansion to meet its new duties. At these events I wear the look and attitude of the interloper: amazing strong handshakes and steely gazes abound, and I feel like my essential soft-handed show-business-layabout nature is waiting to be exposed. Actually, everyone is very nice to me, which makes it even worse. Poor me, you're thinking right now. At dinner where we were toasting the squadron I tried to take the port from one of dad's contemporaries and found myself in an ever so subtle booze-based arm wrestle with a septuagenarian. He'd been telling us all sorts of fascinating stories about how as a subaltern on his National Service because he spoke French he'd found himself attached to the French Foreign Legion and consequently at the battle of Dien Bien Phu[104] – 'they were pissing on the machine-gun barrels to keep them cool'. A recent book published about the battle was 'wrong, all wrong, it was nothing like that', but in telling the story he'd neglected to pass the port and I'd become thirsty, but I couldn't prise it from his steely grip

---

[104] France's catastrophic defeat in Vietnam in 1954. The French decided that they would set up a huge forward base behind enemy lines, supply it by air, and the Vietnamese would destroy themselves attacking it. As it was, the Vietnamese, who'd had a lot of help from the Chinese, destroyed the Legion base – its various features named after the French Colonel de Castries's mistresses, Beatrice, Gabrielle, Anne Marie, Dominique etc. The Legion at the time was made up of lots of Russians who'd escaped Stalin and SS men who had needed to disappear. With this defeat France quit Vietnam, the country was split in two and we all know how well that worked out. What was remarkable about dad's friend being there was that he hadn't mentioned it before: 'I was one of the last out.'

and in the end I decided to bow to etiquette and let him pass me the port when it was my turn. And I don't really like port that much. Clearly I was no gentleman.

However, dad's greatest mannerly admonishment – and it's one you can't really fault him for except when he's reaching for the elbow spoon – was 'do as you would be done by'. And this rule, also known as the Golden Rule, is one that I think entirely underpins a great deal of the etiquette, manners and customs of warfare. A good example of this is a Drum Head Auction, where men ceremonially auction off a dead colleague's possessions to raise money for his family – it's an expression of how they look after each other, and how they'd like to be looked after themselves. I've been to one, at Stonehouse Barracks in Plymouth, and it was very moving, the banter, the money raised, the high emotion and the sergeant major dressed in drag. It was a real privilege as an outsider to witness this – the Marines in the dead man's section were determined to get things like his water bottle, his boots, his webbing – and like at my father's regimental mess, I thought I was due to be found out any minute. I bought some stuff that I gave back right away – it felt wrong to take anything but right to contribute. I tried to 'do as I would be done by'. But the other side of the Golden Rule, how 'you would be done by' by the enemy is the basis of customs and actual rules about how you behave on the battlefield; rules that have been around a lot longer than the famous Geneva Convention.

A lot of people, and a fair chunk of them Christians, it has to be said, think that the Golden Rule is uniquely Christian. It's what sets Christianity apart. In its Christian formulation 'Love your neighbour as you love yourself' it gets wheeled out as Jesus's true message, a distillation of what he had to say, putting aside all the other stuff about the meek, peacemakers and the rest; it also appeals to those who don't want any of the Holy Spirit-type mumbo-jumbo stuff. For all its centrality to Christianity it's not in two of the Gospels, but then there's no snow or donkeys in the New Testament either. It makes its appearance in the Matthew and Luke Gospels, and is known by the sort of people who know these sorts of things as The Great Commandment. It's pretty cheeky of Christianity, really, as the Golden Rule has cropped up all over the world and in various shapes and sizes, in all sorts of religious and philosophical formulations since people started writing stuff down.

And little wonder – it's an idea that smacks of basic human decency, restraint and common sense. Perhaps, rather than it being simple ignorance of other religions, where Christianity has a right to claim the rule as its own is that Jesus went to the trouble of defining who 'your neighbour' is. He tells the story of the Good Samaritan to answer this question. Though I don't know, I've often wondered whether that parable's main job isn't so much to make the Samaritan look good as to make the priests and Levites look like complete and utter shits. Then again, I never was much good at parables: I always thought the son with the Talents who stayed home and played safe was the one who'd done the right thing, and that the Prodigal Son could do one.

I'm not much interested in theology – or this book might be called *Pulling Apart Sermons With My Dad* – but what you have to bear in mind historically with Jesus is that what he is reported to have said always has to be placed in the context of him and the Gospel writers being very familiar with Jewish scripture – like they were swimming in it – as well as the crucial context of his role in fulfilling prophecies in that scripture. That's why where he was born, what his lineage is, where he turns up, what happens where is all so important in the Gospels. If he'd been born in Acton proving he was the Messiah would be more difficult. By ticking these essential boxes he has the right to reinterpret and reflect on existing scripture. He knew his stuff. And lo and behold, it's right there in the Torah – 'You shall not take vengeance or bear a grudge against your kinsfolk. Love your neighbour as yourself: I am the LORD.' This caps-lock moment is in Leviticus along with all the stuff about shellfish and homosexuality being bad, but there it is, the Golden Rule nestled in alongside Bronze Age hygiene regulations and a predictive revulsion with lax twenty-first-century mores. It also rather tellingly sits alongside how you should treat your slaves, who often were prisoners of war, people captured during inter-tribal conflict. No matter how prescriptive of lifestyles in general (and in the highly clean/unclean specific) the high priests of Judaism might have been, they nevertheless had room for the simple down-to-earth common sense of the Golden Rule. Jesus giving the Golden Rule a nod and adding it to his philosophical quiver shows what an all-round wise fellow he was.

But Jesus was beaten to it by several centuries, not just by his own people but by amongst others Buddha. Siddharta Gautama – who lived from 563–483 BC (around the same kind of time that Leviticus was coming together-ish, no one's entirely sure) – said 'Hurt not others in ways that you yourself would find hurtful'.[105] Snappy, but the same thing really: I know we're meant to find the East all mystical and mysterious and somehow deeper than our shallow Western ways, but that's the same dead-ahead unarguable common sense, isn't it? I wonder what he said about slavery, shellfish and homosexuality. Whatever it is I'll bet my bottom Western prejudiced dollar that it's much

---

[105] As you have doubtless deduced I've had to look all this up. Kids these days know all this stuff. They don't know they're born. When we did RE it was thinly disguised religion masquerading as an O-level literature paper.

groovier than anything we've got here in the West. Similarly, Islam is very keen on the Golden Rule – it crops up both in the Qur'an five or so times and in the Hadith (the collected sayings of the Prophet)[106] another five times; pithiest, perhaps, as 'That which you want for yourself, seek for mankind.' That's Islam there (though Sharia-paranoaics might say – 'look, there it is, right there! They want Islam for mankind! See?!?') Of course, the Qur'an, like the Bible, also contains other stuff that contradicts the Golden Rule pretty square on – smiting, etc. – but it's in there and you might well say that it's the Greatest Commandment, if only because it's cropped up everywhere. And it *is* everywhere – Confucianism, Taoism, Sikhism, Jainism, Hinduism and Platonism amongst others. But the thing that strikes me is this: all the societies that produced these religions were intimately familiar with war and its effects. The Bible makes it perfectly clear that the Israelites were at war a great deal of the time: the Israelites were either fleeing enemies, eyeing enemies up, blowing trumpets at enemy cities, putting enemies to the sword, selecting their kings via trial by single combat or being carted off by enemies into exile. The Old Testament has more war in it than *Commando* comic. It's little wonder that the idea of doing as you would be done by should have come up, because where it applies most absolutely – especially in a supposedly and self-consciously Christian culture like Europe's – is warfare and the taking of prisoners.

'Taking no prisoners' is something that gets said about performers – it means you're really going to go for it. And what does it really mean? It means killing even those who surrender. In cold blood. No matter how much 'Hande hoch', 'Kamerad', 'For you the war is over' you do, you won't be making your

---

[106] Really, I had no idea. I expect a lot of you had no idea too. There are lots of Hadiths, the Prophet had much to say about a whole range of topics.

way to somewhere where you can form a committee and start digging a jolly tunnel. It can, did and surely still does happen in the heat of battle. Imagine someone who a few moments ago was trying to kill you, and maybe killed one or more of your mates, suddenly putting his hands up and coming out and saying 'Leave off, will ya?' and you, with all the excitement of the situation, then not pulling the trigger.

Killing those who surrender, especially those who have surrendered and are being moved away from the lines, is the kind of thing that, putting it mildly, might cause far more problems than it solves – especially if the battle is fluid, the front constantly moving and any bodies that have obviously been murdered might be readily discovered. A good example of this is what happened between men from the Canadian Army and the 12th SS Panzer Division 'Hitlerjugend' in the days following D-Day.

12th SS Panzer Division 'Hitlerjugend' soldiers were exactly what they sound like – Hitler Youth who had been recruited and enrolled in an SS tank division. This idea had been dreamt up by *Obergruppenführer* Gottlob Berger (convicted of war crimes at Nuremberg) who passed it up to Himmler (in charge of the Holocaust) who loved it so much that he simply had to tell Hitler (I don't need anything in these brackets) who was predictably very keen on it. You can imagine him dancing one of his grim jigs and patting his dog gleefully at the news that the division had been raised, the youthful 'Heils!' bouncing around in his head. Ugh.

With a pedigree like that the unit was bound to be extra-specially Nazi. The division was made up of soldiers born in 1926 (that year when 33% of German males born were killed in the war) – some of the men or boys were so young that they weren't issued with alcohol and tobacco rations but with sweets.

As they were 'ideologically sound' they probably didn't mind too much about that. They excelled at fieldcraft, and had been trained differently from regular German soldiers[107] or even regular SS men. With experienced officers brought in to train the Division, it had done a lot of training with live firing. These officers were men who had fought on the Eastern Front, in what had been called the *Rassenkrieg* — it means race war, but you'd figured that out. To put it simply, they were young, indoctrinated, and really, really into it. They wore their hair long and had what military people call a very strong *esprit de corps*.[108] Three months before D-Day the Division had been sent to Normandy and the (young) men – oh, who am I kidding? boys – spent their time getting familiar with the ground around Caen. When the landings began on 6 June, the first thing that 12th SS Panzer were sent to deal with was an attack that turned out to consist of dummy parachutists – a successful Allied deception plan (one of many) designed to have the Germans chasing at shadows and to draw tanks away from the beaches. But once they were engaged properly in the Battle for Normandy it was how these youngsters treated their prisoners that became notorious, and haunted them for the rest of the war.

It was D-Day + 1 (7 June 1944 to you and me) that the 12th SS Panzer was ordered to attack the advancing Canadian forces and drive them back into the sea. 'Driving the Allies back into the sea' was a regular German refrain at the time, though the German command itself was split about what to do. Not knowing where the landings were going to come (and when

---

[107] The SS, of course, was the Nazi party's own military and security wing. It had its own uniforms, its own equipment, and its own ethos – probably best described as really very Nazi. 12th SS Panzer Hitlerjugend offer perhaps an idea of what Germany and Germans might have ended up like had they not lost the war.

[108] Nothing like *esprit de l'escalier.*

they did come the Germans had been amply fooled by the simple fact of the proximity of Dover and Calais, as well as things like dummy parachutists, false armies, false fleets and the bombing of absolutely every possibly useful target in all of Northern France) had led to divided opinion about how best to respond; there was considerable disagreement between Rommel[109] – who'd been put in charge of defending the French coast as head of Army Group B – and General von Rundstedt, Commander-in-Chief West. Rommel set about preparing defences, putting up tank traps and doing a lot of posing at gun emplacements for propaganda films – publicising the formidable Atlantic Wall defences. He had poles put up to stop gliders from landing that were nicknamed Rommel's Asparagus. But the disagreement about what to do rumbled on between Rommel and von Rundstedt.

This was entirely like Hitler, to have two people doing roughly the same job – it meant they put their efforts into arguing with each other rather than with him. Rommel – who had lost in North Africa because, as he saw it, of Allied superiority in the air – wanted to keep pockets of tanks and other armour near the beaches so that he could respond immediately to any landing where it happened. Von Rundstedt saw it differently, and wanted to hedge his bets in case the landings came at Calais, holding his tanks inland to dispatch them decisively in a killer blow when he knew where they were needed. This, of course, left them vulnerable to air attack. Everything major and increasingly everything local had to be run past Hitler as he sought to micromanage the war, so decision-making at the highest level

---

[109] Erwin Rommel – the legendary Desert Fox – had been out of a job since being chased out of North Africa. The Germans had a slight propaganda gap between the reputation of his invincibility and his being beaten, so he'd been twiddling his thumbs for a while.

was at best constipated. Hitler couldn't decide which of these policies to pursue, so the defence of the French coast's chief characteristic, in command terms, was indecision and division before the Allies even got started. The fact that Rommel was at home celebrating his wife's birthday when D-Day itself came was pretty much incidental – no one was able or allowed to decide anything quickly or easily anyway.

12th SS Panzer spent the whole of D-Day trying to get to the beachhead but had problems moving because of relentless Allied air attack. Rommel can hardly have been pleased to be proved right, though human nature programmes pretty much everyone to enjoy saying 'I told you so'. They were sent to the west of Caen. Caen sat the eastern end of the area of the beachhead, and had a river and a shipping canal; it was a major communication centre and Montgomery had made it clear in his plans that he intended to take it on the first day of the invasion – D-Day. The fact that the city wasn't captured on D-Day became hugely controversial, during the campaign within Allied upper echelons as well as in the newspapers, and afterwards in people's accounts and then amongst historians. It remains so. 'Phase lines', lines on a map that were used at a briefing to demonstrate the planned progress of the Normandy battle, have become the focus of historical debate about Caen. Characteristically, Montgomery stuck his oar in in his memoirs by saying that the grand strategy of the battle had played out exactly according to plan – which seems pretty bold given the fact that Caen wasn't completely liberated until 18 July (and by then had been destroyed), six weeks after D-Day – but it is true that things had worked out broadly as planned, and Paris fell ahead of schedule. It's worth noting, like they tend not to in lots of history books, that the Americans were meant to take Saint-Lô on D-Day as well but didn't: that took similar time and effort and lives. So who's right? Both, probably. Either/or doesn't really do this situation justice.

On D-Day + 1 (a day after Caen was meant to have fallen) Canadian soldiers were trying to push south from the beaches and on to Caen. They had landed the day before, their uniforms would have still been wet, they had slept out in the open that night. The D-Day landings' success had stemmed directly from a previous landing's failure. The raid on Dieppe[110] in August 1942 had been an abject failure – 60% of the men who got ashore were killed or wounded, and most of them were Canadian. The Dieppe Raid – which ended in an ignominious retreat being sounded less than six hours after the landings had begun – had taught the Allies bitter lessons about landing on a heavily defended beach: basically you did what you could to avoid it, and if you did do it you made sure you were incredibly well prepared. You could say that these lessons belonged to the Canadians. Though it must seem scant consolation, and it'd be a hard-hearted bastard who would say that the Dieppe raid was all worth it, their tragic failure had been turned to success, even if it didn't exactly match Monty's phase lines.

The fighting that afternoon saw the SS holding up the Canadians – men from the excellently named Nova Scotia Highlanders – but quite unable to drive them back into the village of Buron from which they'd advanced, let alone the sea. This was an early indicator of the German command's false and operationally muddled expectations. The young German soldiers fought very well, holding their fire until the advancing Canadian

---

[110] What a 'raid' was meant to be in this instance is even now very hard to work out. The idea was to, um, land at Dieppe, and then, well, no one was sure; there's every chance it was to make the man in charge, Lord Mountbatten, look like a man of action who got stuff done. Like lots of things without a clear aim it turned out to be disastrous.

forces' flanks were exposed, and their boss Kurt 'Panzer' Meyer was delighted with how they had handled themselves. But. During the fighting the Germans had taken around 150 prisoners. And it was in how they handled these prisoners that the Division – for all the tactical brilliance of its fighting that afternoon – made its reputation. For killing around 156 Canadian prisoners of war. Possibly more. No one can come up with a firm figure.

After the war, Panzer Meyer found himself condemned to death by a Canadian military court for colluding in the prisoners' deaths. As it turned out his sentence was commuted as the evidence against him seemed to be circumstantial. Meyer (like a lot of SS officers) was lucky really, in fact he was really lucky: he'd been involved in murdering Jews in Poland in 1939, so to get off on this charge was extremely jammy. Twenty men who'd been shot in the head were found at the site of his headquarters the year after the invasion. The Germans claimed that the Canadians had orders not to take prisoners – certainly, advancing as swiftly as they were the armoured Canadian soldiers had problems in handling and guarding prisoners, they weren't far from the beachhead, the front was congested and infantry were precious – and there was an incident when three German officers were tied to a tank and beaten up, but nothing the Canadians did matched the SS for ruthlessness. Word got around that the SS weren't taking prisoners and the fighting between them and the Canadians was particularly bitter for the rest of the Normandy campaign.

Because this is how it works in warfare – the Golden Rule isn't just about helping old ladies across the road, or not pulling your sister's hair, or not screwing someone for interest, or taking out insurance (even) or not helping yourself to the last of the roast potatoes. It's not just 'Love your neighbour as you love yourself', it's 'Don't kill our lads when they surrender so we won't kill yours.' This rule has applied since people started chucking rocks at each other. Breaking this rule is incredibly provocative. Yes, it's been enshrined in international legal convention and all that now, but it can be little coincidence that every major religion has come up with it along the way, especially as religions all too often have sent people marching off to war with their blessing. If you break these rules you've done the wrong kind of killing and you're a war criminal. Of course, who wins and who loses also comes into these definitions – victor's justice.

War has long been about limits or at least attempts to make sure it had some; indeed, it's notable that the expression 'Total War' is a pretty new one. Aztec warriors made a point of not killing one another – it was the fact that they could have done so that counted. Like settling international disputes with a paintball competition. Medieval chivalry saw prisoners spared, if only so that they could be ransomed. Knights in their heavy and expensive suits of armour wouldn't be able to get up once they'd been unseated from horses so they'd be collected and sold back to the other side. Think of the orphans spared, the not-bereaved wives not crying, the lack of military funerals and scarcity of memorials. These are also pretty recent developments: the dead at Waterloo – not the officers, mind – were buried in a pit there and then. The fields were ploughed over eventually and the bone-rich earth shipped back to England as fertiliser. Should you ever go to Waterloo the big memorial mound[111] at the battlefield is where a Dutch Prince was knocked from his horse by a musket ball; know your place, everyone.

---

[111] The Duke of Wellington was furious with this development – 'They're ruining my battlefield.' The Duke's relationship with the epochal fields outside Brussels is worth all the books that have been written about it. He had been for a look the year before, just in case he needed to defend Brussels. When asked who the greatest general of all time was he said Napoleon – who he had beaten of course.

So manners, customs, the Golden Rule really matters. Do as you would be done by. Understanding this simple idea might explain why Afghan people aren't that keen on us – how would you feel about a JDAM[112] bomb being dropped on your local school? And bad manners are unforgivable. There's no excuse for them. And maybe there's no excuse for dropping a JDAM on a school. But I grew up with my elbows off the table, trying to be polite. So how did I, someone raised to use a butter knife when I was on my own, to hold a door open for a lady, even find myself considering refusing to shake hands with someone? Like some sort of petulant premiership-football moron. At the time it seemed like a reasonable question. I was going to interview the last man out of the Führerbunker, Rochus Misch. Rochus Misch was the last man to leave (according to his account). He died in September 2013 but up to that point he was the last person from the bunker who was still alive. He's been portrayed in films – he pops up in *Downfall*, though not in one of those scenes where Hitler rages about his Xbox 360 subscription.

We had decided to film Herr Misch at the site of the Führerbunker – where else? The site of the bunker is nothing much – it's a dog-shit car park at best. Tufts of grass and that paving that has small concrete squares spaced out so you can trip on a new one with each pace you take, and more than its fair share of dog dirt. Maybe the locals don't pick it up as some sort of statement. You wouldn't know that the bunker was there if you weren't looking for it, or if you hadn't been brought up on war films like me. It's in sight of some flats that were built for the top echelons of the East German Communist Party, and they're as lovely as they sound. If you go there now it is within

---

[112] JDAMs are what you might call 'smart' bombs that used to be 'dumb': they're regular bombs with GPS and other hi-tech stuff attached that make them more guidable than bombs you simply drop.

a short walk of the Memorial to the Murdered Jews of Europe that sits between the site of the bunker and the Brandenburg Gate. The site was in the Eastern sector before reunification: that part of Berlin had been devastated after the war and was left in ruins for a long time, being very close to the Internal Border – what we'd all call the Berlin Wall. The bunker itself had been sealed off by the Communists and was left like that after Reunification, the idea seemingly being to make the scene of Hitler's death ordinary, unremarkable, dreary; not hidden but not made anything of, either. They'd certainly pulled that off. With lashings of dog mess.

Our problem was that we just didn't know how to greet someone who had been a member of Hitler's personal bodyguard. Misch had been in the SS, been wounded badly in Poland and then recruited to be part of the *Führerbegleitkommando* – the section of the SS whose task was taking care of Hitler's personal security. Bodyguards mainly, but when not guarding Hitler the men would work the switchboard, take Hitler hot-water bottles and the like. For all Misch's protestations about not being a Nazi, I am going to stick my neck out and assert confidently that if you were a member of Hitler's personal bodyguard then you were a Nazi. A proper one: a heel-clicking, Sieg-heiling, Fatherland-and-Fuhrering Nazi. I'll go further – he knew what was going on. How could you not? He answered the phone, for Pete's sake. If you're the sort of person who referred to Hitler as 'my boss, a good boss' you knew what was happening. You may even have liked what was happening, hoped it would all work out, if only to keep the boss happy. So that morning there was debate amongst our little party at breakfast about whether we should shake hands with Herr Misch. After all, Misch had shaken Hitler's hand, no doubt many, many times. Did we really want to shake hands with him?

267

Breakfast in our hotel was taken up with this urgent debate. The day before I'd driven around Berlin in the programme's jeep; up and down the Tiergarten, feeling more and more conspicuous with every pass. I felt like I was bringing up something the city had long forgotten about. The Soviet War Memorial halfway down from the Brandenburg Gate has a faded melancholy – the guard party left when the Soviet Union ceased to exist. The pair of T-34s is about the only reminder in the bustling, clean and urbane centre of Berlin of the city's final fate in 1945, as the Red Army sliced the place in two with its competing pincers. I would drive up the Tiergarten and back – dropping off the cameraman sometimes once he'd done the over-the-shoulder shots or I'd done a piece to camera. We'd been over to the old Olympic stadium and filmed where German men had been shot for 'desertion' and a man walking his dog had come over and told us all about being a boy in the city in April 1945. Even though the Russians were at the heart of the Reich he'd seen a jet plane fly past – most likely an Me 262 – and thought 'Ah yes, we will win, the Fuhrer's wonder weapons will save us!' At the end of the long day's filming we hadn't given a moment's thought to Rochus Misch and how we'd deal with him.

The argument basically went: he's a Nazi, you can't possibly shake hands with him. Um, well, maybe that is so but surely you go in with courtesy and then if he acts like a Nazi or in a Nazi way we can then deal with him accordingly. Not sure what that meant, I don't remember anyone proposing forming an impromptu tribunal. I didn't really see the need to be rude to him, but then, um, he *was* a Nazi. There was an argument that it was all a very long time ago, and that, well, he was an old man, and that you shouldn't be rude to anyone, not even a Nazi. After all – it's one of the reasons we are better than them.

Though in war films and in plenty of accounts there are loads of Nazis who pride themselves on their manners, conduct (non-evil) and generally cultured manner. Breakfast rumbled on in this inconclusive and faintly fractious manner and we failed to figure out what on Earth we were going to do.

After he'd fled the bunker Misch was captured by the Red Army, who were understandably interested in him and what he might have seen – specifically, Hitler's death. The NKVD,[113] the USSR's internal political-control organisation and an all too concrete manifestation of Stalinist paranoia, interrogated and tortured Misch, then somewhat bizarrely went as far as re-enacting events at the bunker, watching Misch and other survivors for their reactions, convinced as they were in paranoid Stalinist mode that the Germans were all lying. The Soviets hadn't known that the bunker existed – no one had: when Hitler killed himself the official communiqué said he'd died heroically in the fighting – so they were suspicious of tales of the end of the Third Reich. Then he was carted off to Siberia to a labour camp, along with lots of other Germans. He didn't get back to Berlin until 1954 when the Russians released him (and lots of other Germans, including plenty of unsavoury ones who might have thought they were never going to get back to Germany – plenty hadn't). Once he was back in Berlin Misch found himself helped out by philanthropists who set him up with a painting and decorating business. Lucky chap, I wonder who they were.

Misch has been known to court controversy – the year after I interviewed him he called for a plaque for the Goebbels

---

[113] It stands for Narodnyy Komissariat Vnutrennikh Del, meaning the People's Commissariat for Internal Affairs. Their political officers were sent into Red Army units and kept an eye on soldiers' and officers' political motivation, i.e. shot them if they retreated, stuff like that. Such nice people, our allies.

children, who were murdered by their mother right at the end of the war. Mrs Goebbels, fearing what the Russians might do when they arrived in Berlin and found the top-echelon Nazi children, had decided that murdering them would be the better option. She had the doctor in the bunker inject them with morphine, then crush a cyanide capsule between their teeth. The eldest girl, Helga, had bruises on her jaw when her body was found that suggest she was forced to bite down on the capsule. It's hardly surprising that the Goebbels family ended up doing this: firstly, as Nazis – and the Goebbels family were big fat top-end bastard Nazis – death had been their prescription for a wide variety of problems, people and situations; and secondly, besieged Berlin, and those trapped in the bunker, had been given plenty of warning as to what the Russians had in store for them. The Russians had made it very plain that they were going to repay the Germans in kind for their conduct in the Soviet Union – Germans had been doing everything they could to escape the Red Army and surrender to the British, American and French armies: refugees were fleeing west in their millions. In Berlin there were stories about the Russians phoning the centre of the city from the suburbs and speaking directly to their enemies – one phone call went roughly like this: 'Hurry!' cried a German down the line. 'The Ivans are coming!' The voice on the other end replied, 'This *is* Ivan!' One (apocryphal, might be true) tale has the NKVD being put through to Goebbels in the bunker ('Can I speak to Goebbels, please?') and describing in grim and vivid detail exactly what they were going to do to him and to his family.

Misch denies this last story – and he did work on the switchboard – but he knew the Goebbels kids well, and brought up the idea of a memorial to them when he was asked about the building of the Memorial to the Murdered Jews of Europe within spitting distance of the Fuhrer-dogshit-car park. That went down as well as you might expect. In interviews he has been known to cling to the idea – the same notion that Hitler had in the final phases of the war – that if only the Allies could have seen sense they'd have joined the Germans against the Russians and 'rolled all the way to Moscow'. Hitler had convinced himself that this would happen, and when news of President Roosevelt's death reached Berlin he clutched at it as a straw sent by Providence – surely the Allies would change their minds? Hitler would sit and muse over exactly this kind of turn of fate: Frederick the Great of Prussia had been saved from almost certain defeat in the Seven Years' War when, in January 1762, Empress Elizabeth of Russia had died and the anti-Prussian alliance had collapsed. Misch, at one time during the last days of the war, came across his boss in silent reverie pondering Frederick the Great's portrait. All this really shows is how detached from reality Hitler had become. So Misch – similarly at odds with the universe – presented us with a quandary. Do you shake this man's hand? Would you?

As it was, the decision was taken out of my hands. We arrived at the location – it was a beautiful sunny day – mused upon the scumminess of the location, discussed the pieces to camera we were going to do and what I'd ask Herr Misch. This huddle around the back of the production van was then interrupted by a tall old man who solicitously yet rather humbly shook everyone by the hand and told us how nice it was to meet us all. We all responded similarly: how could you snub such politeness? Of course, it was Misch. After all that fuss we'd been ambushed, by a polite Nazi. The only thing he didn't do was click his heels together. We felt stupid, thwarted. I felt like a decision I hadn't yet made and was deeply ambivalent about had been taken out of my hands. Those damned pesky Nazis!

Misch went on to give an interview of well-rounded anecdotes and polished phrases – sixty years is what you might call plenty of time to rehearse a story. He told his story of how he'd got the job – Hitler had hidden behind the door during his job interview (mmm, mature). When he was satisfied with Misch's answers he said something like, 'I think we have found our man', swung the door shut and . . . 'There he was,' Misch said, 'neither a monster nor a superman, but a regular human being like you and me.' Um, no, thanks. That was at best an awkward moment. Misch told me about one of the other men in the bunker saying, 'The boss is dead!' and him going to look at the bodies of Hitler and his wife moments after they had killed themselves. And as he described the flames rising from Hitler and Eva Braun's bodies, he let out a sigh and said 'And here the Third Reich ended.' That pretty much said it all. And I'd shaken his hand, and therefore, kind of, Hitler's. Good manners: look where it can get you.

13. Watching war films with my kids

SEEING THINGS IN BLACK AND WHITE

Next year, 2014, sees the 100th anniversary of the outbreak of World War One. It'll be 70 years since D-Day as well. Events that, when I was a lad, had touched people's lives directly and hadn't yet entered into myth but stood firmly in people's memories are now slipping further into the past. They're sliding away further back into time now, the khaki drill, tin hats, puttees and Lee-Enfield rifles that belonged to the Tommies of both wars exist in a black and white world in every sense – on film and in moral terms.

Growing up, the only colour film of either of the World Wars was in movies, World War Two was mainly in black and white. The Vietnam War, the Falklands War – they were in colour, and it seemed to me that they were more complex for it. When I see footage of WW2 in colour I find it incredibly arresting: colour film of the BEF embarking for France somehow makes the events seem more real, more poignant, less quantifiable as mere history, as something simply to be interested in, fascinated by. The events certainly no longer seem to be the kind that small boys find thrilling. In living colour, it is perhaps less glamorous. In colour what happened to my grandfather and his generation becomes all the more real. For all its complexity and ghastliness, in black and white it is perhaps contained, stylised, dealable with.

And maybe this explains ultimately my untroubled fascination with military history and World War Two. It is history in the sense that it is done. It lets us define ourselves and, because it's in black and white, for all the horror, for all the controversy that can swirl around it, it leaves us fundamentally untroubled. Our minds are made up. We fought on the side of right and it's there on screen in black and white. Churchill has pretty much become someone you can't question, his every decision part of the grand drama of saving our country and with it democracy. I have to admit framing it in these sort of terms teeters on the bombastic, maybe this is because George W. Bush was so determined to riff on this stuff during the last Gulf War and some of it feels a little dog-eared as a result. Nevertheless, the famine in Bengal in 1943, the alliance with the Soviet Union, the area bombing of German cities – they're all long enough ago, and the end result satisfactory enough (unless you're the kind of swivel-eyed loon who would rather the Germans and the Russians had been allowed to get on with it while we 'held onto the Empire') for it to be something you can be interested in but about which maybe you really don't need to think too hard.[114] Arguments about command are just that, arguments, they're not something we have to face today, thank God, they're repetitions of controversies of old, echoes of debate long since laid to rest. It's far easier to deal with than modern politics,

---

[114] You'll notice I'm using lots of maybes and perhaps-es in this bit. That's because I'm sticking my neck out here and it's not at all comfortable.

modern conflict, which now all seems so complex, so thorny. In other words, maybe it's something I could put aside, grow out of, without too much trouble.

God knows I've tried. A few years back a primary-school email asking for books for the school summer fair seemed like a chance to do something about it. My bookshelves were groaning with WW2 books, Hitler's baleful eyes staring out at me from enough covers and spines for a new visitor (or passing burglar) to wonder if I might be a fan or at least mildly obsessed. I went round the house trying to pick the books that had to go, that I could part with. It wasn't easy but I dropped off at least 30 books – some of them duplicates I must have ordered on Amazon when I couldn't find something I really needed to read – when I went into the school. At the school fair I wandered over to the bookstall and there they were, Hitler's sulky gaze fixing me as I browsed the unwanted cookbooks and discarded novels. I wondered if anyone else browsing the second-hand books could tell which were mine: they were like a coal seam through the rest of the donations. It gave me pause, and like anything that might be revealing I hoped no one else had spotted it – I hung around guiltily, the books knew, they seemed to be sniggering at me. Perhaps the other parents were simply hanging on to their dissections of the Third Reich, and were understandably more concerned with getting Jamie Oliver's gormless mug out of their kitchens. I took a circuit or two of the playground, checked my kids hadn't run off and/or helped themselves to any half-drunk Pimm's and ended up back at the bookstall. I bought back probably half a dozen of the books I'd donated. I had to. Just in case. I might need to double-check some half-remembered stuff when, say, writing a book.

Another thing that draws me back like a magnet is, of course, my dad. I can't remember a Sunday lunch at mine when he hasn't disappeared somewhere in the house, found a book about the war and proceeded to snaffle it up. His memory and his reading are astounding, encyclopaedic, broad. Exhaustive and, as any guest who's found themselves sat next to him at lunch might attest, often exhausting. I love it, though. He can talk general or specific about pretty much whatever you like – there's been a lot about the Glider Pilot Regiment and its origins lately, how it was organised, recruited, the tension it ran into with the RAF over resources and training pilots. It's fascinating stuff. I could digress into it right now in some detail, but we're getting near the end and you've probably heard enough of that. But even then, there are times when I wish we could talk about something else. Sometimes I think we're just like those blokes who talk about football in order to avoid having to talk about anything else, especially personal stuff. There are times when I envy people who can simply drop into how Arsenal are doing when that gap in the conversation comes up. So we talk WW2. Certainly it's easier to talk about than politics. Or my job. So thank God for that.

The last time I really tried to put it all aside and be interested in something else was two summers ago. Perhaps it was a growing realisation that it might not be a bad idea to engage with the real world rather than the black and white one. That no matter how many times I reread what happened at Arnhem it wasn't going to change: I sometimes think my fascination with the explanations and re-examinations of the battle is in some way trying to will this to happen – I do wonder if I'm not the only one. For all the advice and interpretation which historians can lob back at the protagonists nothing can change. That might seem obvious to you but there are times when I find myself shaking my head and willing the rest of 1st Parachute Brigade to hurry up and get to the bridge.

Perhaps I shouldn't put it aside, perhaps I should take it all more seriously. Six years ago I went to Hazebrouck in northern France where my grandfather's battalion made its last stand. The Bucks Battalion were Territorial soldiers, butchers, bakers, candlestick makers, part of the Oxford and Buckinghamshire Light Infantry, a classic English county regiment. My grandfather James, a banker, was the battalion adjutant – organisation and admin says the definition, part of the battalion headquarters: BHQ. There was one professional soldier in the battalion, the regimental sergeant-major. They had been in France since the war began and had a typical Phoney War experience, lobbing turnips instead of grenades on exercise, waiting for the Germans to take the initiative as the French and British governments remained paralysed, sclerotic, doing nothing to help Poland who they'd gone to war for.

This thumb-twiddling had done little to prepare them for what was to happen in May 1940. The British army fell back from its ill-fated advance into Belgium – having fallen plumb for the German feint into the Lowlands – and was now fighting for survival as it tried to find a way out at Dunkirk. Two weeks after the Germans had attacked (on 10 May, my birthday, no wonder I remember it), exhausted from their advance into Belgium and back again, the battalion was part of the barrier intended to hold up the German attacks towards Dunkirk. It's strange writing about this, placing my grandfather onto the map with all the arrows, putting him into one of these scenes, like the other stories in this book. As kids all we knew was that he had died before mum was born. We didn't know where he fitted on the map, which arrow – going backwards like in the *Dad's Army* titles – he was. He was on the pointy bit of the last Union Jack in France before the Union Jacks all end up back in the UK.

The Germans were astonished at the success of their thrust through the Ardennes and the subsequent surprising collapse of the French army but they were beginning to run out of steam, and – because they hadn't really thought the Allies would fall apart so quickly and easily – didn't have a coherent plan for what to do next. The British had counter-attacked at Arras on 21 May and taken the Germans by surprise: Rommel, who was at the head of his column, wrote a majestically exaggerated account of how many British tanks had attacked from the north and how he had beaten off the attack despite overwhelming odds and because of his undeniable energy and decisiveness. On 23 May Hitler ordered a halt for the following day: a source of endless debate even to this day – why? Was it to let the British off the hook and show that his intentions were honourable, as some generals argued after the war? Was it because the terrain was 'unsuitable for tanks'?[115] Was it because Goering had convinced him that the Luftwaffe could finish off the British in their bubble around Dunkirk? Or was it, as at least one German historian has suggested, so Hitler could show his generals, flush with success and full of momentum, who was actually in charge?

The Germans got going again on 25 May – released from the halt order. The same day the Bucks Battalion arrived in Hazebrouck. Hazebrouck, when I got there, reminded me of Leighton Buzzard. There's a market square – French forefathers had the foresight to make space for pay-and-display parking in the middle of town – a grand church or two. The mayor's joint is rather impressive: French civic buildings always have that bit

---

[115] This – of all the reasons that get thrown up – is probably the thinnest: the German advance through the Ardennes that had caught everyone out and simply not been spotted or molested by the French was in defiance of the prevailing wisdom that the Ardennes was 'unsuitable for tanks'. It's a lousy excuse, I reckon.

more grandeur and seriousness than ours do, even though theirs are just as concerned with bins and dog-poo. But I don't think I'm being unfair if I say Hazebrouck is unremarkable. To the north-west of Hazebrouck is Cassel, a town on top of a prominent hill – on the Eurostar on the way down to Paris you can't miss it, it's on your left with its windmill poking up through the trees about ten or fifteen minutes after you exit the Channel Tunnel. As the German panzer forces pushed south and west from Belgium, as well as north from the space they'd forced between the Allied armies, into the British Expeditionary Force (hastily rearranging itself as it had been outflanked while retreating) my grandfather's battalion organised itself for the defence of Hazebrouck.

They were bombed and strafed from the air until 27 May when the German 8th Panzer Division attacked the town. By the evening the Germans had infiltrated the town successfully, their tanks and infantry forcing the battalion platoons to the point of disintegration. The battalion headquarters fell back into the grounds of the town's orphanage. It's a large, institutional, unmistakably French building, made of brick and stone. The following day, 28 May, the Germans sought to finish off the rest of the battalion and in the afternoon headquarters decided that it was time to break out. About 200 men of the Bucks Battalion made it back to England in dribs and drabs. The high walls in the orphanage grounds meant that escape from there was fraught with danger but the men of battalion HQ did what they could to fight their way out, every man for himself. It was here in these grounds that my grandfather James Richie fell in the defence of Hazebrouck.

It was in May 2007 that the plaque to the men of the 1st Bucks Battalion was unveiled, all of 67 years after the events it commemorated. Dad had spent a great deal of time wrangling with the translation on the plaque as well as with politicians on both sides of the Channel (he muttered a fair deal about ours being far more useless than theirs: go figure). I took my eldest daughter to the unveiling. Men from the Rifles, the regimental heirs of the Bucks Battalion, were there, as well as veterans. Regimental standards, the mayor, representatives of the town, relatives of the men who fought and died in Hazebrouck, all were there to pay tribute. This simple ceremony was unspeakably moving. We met a man who remembered my grandfather, and as we put flowers on the graves of the men buried in the town cemetery he told us how James had made him tea back then in that fateful summer of 1940. That my eldest met someone who'd known my grandfather was very, very moving.

It was a weekend heavy with remembrance, but also, in the May sunshine, sweet with the peace that men like my grandfather had fought for and won. We'd come to France on the hideously named Le Shuttle – brought under the sea to France, to a Europe that has put aside the kind of catastrophe it seemed to be drawn into irresistibly over and over again. The unveiling was poignant, solemn, grateful and mournful, and it seemed a million miles from the glorification or the glamorisation of war. But the story of what had happened to these men drew me back, again, to the history that always fascinated me. A story that was shifting and changing as those left behind were able to give their impressions of what had happened, as superior officers' reputations didn't need preserving any more. Old rivalries between county regiments characterise some of the reports, claims about who ran away and when, gaps in the account of the battle find themselves filled – artillery actions that went unrecorded in bigger accounts, units getting detached and reappearing elsewhere . . . history's complexity always revealing more, even in events that might seem exhaustively written about.

As the years have passed this has been exactly what has happened to the history of the fall of France. Right from the start, in the aftermath of the collapse of France, everyone was looking for answers (even the Germans – they didn't really know how they'd got away with it). The French historian Marc Bloch, a medievalist and a founder of the Annales school of history, who believed in looking at things from the bottom up rather than in Great Men, was vexed by the issue of how France had failed. He wrote a book, *Strange Defeat*, in 1940. It wasn't published until 1946 – Bloch had died at the hands of the Gestapo in 1944, captured and killed for membership of the Resistance. *Strange Defeat* found fault in French society, its moral collapse, and – for all Bloch's antipathy to the idea of men at the top having any influence – in its leadership.

The Germans drew huge confidence from what had happened, putting down to their judgment a great deal of what had actually been luck. This was a mistake, fuelling Hitler's and his generals' feelings of omni-competence and invincibility. In essence, this version of events, with changes in emphasis along the way, has pretty much held. The French military, caught in a defensive mode of thinking (which had, after all, won them the First World War) misread what the Germans might do and played firmly into their hands – the lassitude at the top of the French army possibly reflecting a sense of political paralysis in the country itself. The British didn't do much better. The British and the Germans credited Blitzkrieg with what had happened. The Germans, who knew no such thing existed, should have known better, but they had achieved in a few weeks what they'd taken four years to fail to do before: defeat France. There have been attempts to revise this pretty much settled version of events, but they mainly seem to be about emphasis, stressing French intelligence failures, or German luck, or downplaying the sclerotic state of French politics and the Allied command structure.[116]

You can keep peeling layers off this historical onion, and doubtless people will.[117] The Fall of France – and one or two moments of the battle, the Germans getting across the Meuse pretty much unopposed, the halt order – these are all enormous turning points of history hingeing on the actions of a few. But at this unveiling these complex truths fell away – it wasn't generals and divisions and battalions, long-term causes, underlying currents, short-term causation – it was about men, men like me, men in my family, a man in my family about my height, who my mother never knew, who we all grew up without. History's footprint, right there, on our lives. Realising that is a far cry from being the thrilled five-year-old playing with his Action Man and saluting at no one in particular, which, after all, is where this all started.

After the unveiling my father took some of the Rifles on a tour of a part of the battlefield. The German tanks had pushed up a road into the town, and the Bucks Battalion, light infantry, had tried to hold them off. The Rifles discussed how they'd have dealt with that same situation. They have a weapon called MILAN – it is wire-guided, meaning it has a wire that pays out behind the rocket after it's launched, back to the operator who guides it onto its target. Being wire-guided it can't be jammed.

---

[116] That's overdoing it really – there wasn't one.

[117] The wonderful Dan Snow, a veritable puking geyser of historical knowledge and enthusiasm, made a point a while back over one of many whiskies of how different the war will come to appear as China grows more powerful in the world. His point – and there is single malt between me and recalling it entirely clearly – is that millions of Chinese died, the Americans intervened and backed the wrong side, and that an event like the battle of Britain could be reinterpreted as pretty small beer by comparison. (I may have got this wrong, much whisky had been consumed, but it's still a good point.)

The lads from the Rifles discussed where they'd have placed their MILAN in the same situation, facing an attack by tanks. The Bucks Battalion had no such gear: they had a long, heavy rifle called the Boys Anti-tank Rifle, that required the man firing it to get very close to his target, leaving him vulnerable to enemy infantry. The Boys was notoriously unreliable as an anti-tank weapon, in that it wasn't very good at going through tank armour. Discussing this with the men from the Rifles it came home again – this wasn't arrows on maps, platoon positions and so on – it was men, like me, like the Rifles, holding our nerve as the tanks came closer. A modern infantry battalion with its modern equipment, holding out against a modern tank division, would have done well to last a day and a half.

So this long day in Flanders, this day of remembrance, made me think long and hard about my fascination with the history of the Second World War. It was of course good to have commemorated what had happened in the town, but perhaps even better to be properly reminded what it all meant, to have the names on war memorials come to life. If history is something we are going to learn from then we need to do more than remember, we need to remind ourselves of its lessons, otherwise it's little more than a way of doing well in a pub quiz. Like geography or something. And that is no fate for the lives of men and women. Hazebrouck's reminder for me was of how close to home this all was, how the adventure of war is no more than tragedy waiting in the wings. I read up about the Fall of France, wanting to find and place these county-town men in the chaos (they don't come up much, frankly) and then decided to put the books down and think about something else, resisting, as best I could, the gravitational pull of the subject.

I managed for a while. A holiday in Crete didn't help. Looking at the map for a water-park I noted mentally it wasn't at all far from Maleme airfield, or the scenes of Charles Upham's incredible heroics. I managed to sneak in a visit to the Commonwealth War Cemetery, the white headstones dazzling in the Cretan sun, the ages of the men buried there providing moving reminders of who they were – lost futures, what could have been. In my luggage was 1990s Tory bad-boy Alan Clark's best-selling account of the battle as well as Anthony Beevor's book about it and Crete's subsequent occupation. I gave up on Clark's book – I didn't want to know what that grimly louche chancer thought about what had happened on the island. The cemetery's eloquence did better than either book. The headstones are white: World War Two's monochrome putting us on the side of the angels, again.

But the time I decided finally to put this stuff aside, to try to find something else to be interested in, for pity's sake, was in Normandy. I took my daughters and my then girlfriend to France. My eldest is – at the moment, though we've now entered the rapids of the teen years so who knows where we will end up – fascinated by history. She is good at asking difficult questions, questions that draw on my deepest bullshitting resources to answer. I thought that Normandy, with its clearly marked-out beaches and bridges and mercifully explicable sites would be a good place to start. We drove up from Paris after several days of goggling at paintings: the Louvre made my mind up quite firmly that I need never see another Madonna and child, and that the Renaissance painter without PTSD from churning out yet another grimly sadistic crucifixion must have been in the minority. I had found a hotel near Arromanches, smack in the middle of the area *de debarquement*. Normandy is beautiful: the villages which had been flattened have been painstakingly restored – the N13 dual carriageway that runs along the south of the invasion area, dipping down south around

Bayeux, has probably left a deeper scar through the area than anything else. It has all the stuff you'd expect nowadays – ring roads, warehouse retail on the ring roads – but the long stone walls, the cattle in the fields, the corn blowing in the summer breeze . . . summer in Normandy now doesn't seem to be that different, maybe, to how it was during that tumultuous summer of 1944.

Arromanches is a good place to start in Normandy, because it has the clearest evidence of the invasion right there, on the beach. The remnants of the Mulberry Harbour lie on the sand, the outer ring of 'Phoenix' stands further out to sea. The Mulberry is like something out a Marvel comic or Bond movie, a huge artificial harbour, designed, manufactured and then assembled in secret, sidestepping the need to capture a port: they'd brought their own. And there were two of them! The contrast with the chaos, defeat and disillusionment of four years earlier in Flanders couldn't be more marked. The museum at Arromanches has a model I remember seeing when I was nine in 1977, it's of a whole strip of Mulberry from the outer ring of breakwaters to the roadways leading onto the beach, with model jeeps driving down it – the sea goes up and down and the pontoons with it. Standing on the sea wall at Arromanches you can, I think, picture the activity, the hustle and bustle around the place, an echo of the two and a half million men and the half a million vehicles that were landed there. Anyway, it was a good place to start with the kids, and with a steady supply of crêpes on hand the holiday got under way pretty smoothly. I did what I could to explain what had happened in Normandy, and then my eldest would ask yet another tricky question and I'd do what I could to answer it.

We went to Pegasus Bridge on the Caen Canal, captured by men of the Ox & Bucks, my grandfather's regiment. I explained how the gliders had landed at night, in bad weather, how the men in them had come to moments after landing and seized this crucial bridge. Doing my best to make it come to life, I got the kids to run from the plaque where the first glider had landed to the bridge itself – it took them 12 seconds. Hopefully, I was thinking, another generation astounded by what happened that night. We went across the bridge to the Café Gondrée, the first building to have been liberated in France. It has a large plaque saying so, it does a roaring trade as a shrine to British airborne forces: and, you may say, why not? There's been a long history of fallings-out amongst the Gondrées, and between the men of the Gondrées and the Ox & Bucks – sometimes the veterans found themselves having to drink in Les Trois Planeurs (The Three Gliders) over the road from the café. Arlette Gondrée, who owns the café, was there on the night of 6 June 1944. She was two, I think. We walked into the café, hot chocolate firmly on the agenda. The café is full of regimental coats of arms, maroon berets, scarves, model gliders dangling from the ceiling, books long out of print and other paraphernalia. I started eyeing up the books, the girls were rather more concerned with getting themselves hot chocolate.

Behind the counter was an elegantly coiffed lady in her seventies, exactly as you'd imagine a well-heeled French lady to be, with her grace, poise and perfume. We settled down at a table and I asked the girls what they wanted to drink, and it dawned on me that the lady must be Arlette Gondrée. I told the girls who I thought she was. They didn't believe me, so when I went to the counter to order our drinks I dragged my youngest with me. I ordered our hot drinks and then, apologetically, asked if she was '. . . um . . . Madame Gondrée?'

'Yes, of course,' she said in impeccable English.

'Girls,' I said, 'it is who I thought it was.' They murmured their astonishment. A breakthrough, seeing as we were just entering the world of whatever with the eldest. 'Madame Gondrée was here when the gliders came.'

'Yes, I was here that night. My father owned the café,' she said. 'We were hiding in the cellar that night.' Her English was perfect, lightly but deliciously accented. 'My father had buried the champagne to hide it from the Germans. It was not nice living with the Germans here, you know.' She raised an eyebrow. She'd meant that last bit. She went on: 'My parents were from the part of France next to Germany so we understood what they were saying, you know. We did not like having them here.'

My daughters were dumbstruck. At least I think they were. I was in awe. She asked if we'd seen the glider at the museum up the road at the 'Memorial Pegasus', her (fairly recently established) local commercial rival – they have the original bridge complete with bullet marks.[118] She told us it was nowhere near as good as the one that was being built at RAF Shawbury, she even gave me directions – 'along the M54 towards Shrewsbury, then you turn right up the ring road, you know? It is much better than the *toy* they have up the road.' I didn't tell her that we were on our way there once we'd finished our hot chocolate.

We went and sat back down again. I bought a book (an out-of-print book about 6th Airborne Division's war in Normandy, full of photos I hadn't seen before)[119] and boggled at what had

---

[118] It was replaced in 1994 by a stronger, more modern bridge. This caused kerfuffle in the papers at the time, but at least the original bridge wasn't scrapped. The museum is very good, they do an excellent presentation of how the bridge was taken, using footage from *The Longest Day* though they rather huffily point out – like I might, or my dad might – that they didn't approach the bridge from the angle shown in the film.

[119] It's called *Go To It* and is very hard to come by. Madame Gondrée usually has some copies if you're passing, worth pausing for a hot chocolate and buying a copy.

just happened. History had come to life right here in front of us, the occupation, liberation, the aftermath (and the gift shop). We drove over to the Merville Battery, a few miles north of Pegasus Bridge, scene of the most incredible night attack, but it was shut. Unlike the men who stormed the battery that night despite only a quarter of their strength having made it to the rendezvous, I turned the car around and went to find somewhere to eat.

Normandy is bucolic and beautiful, lush green fields, hedgerows and plenty of signs telling you where the *plages de debarquement* are. As you head west of Bayeux and into the American sector outward signs of Normandy's invasion heritage become more and more pronounced. By the time you get to Sainte Mere Eglise you'd be forgiven for thinking that the Second World War was fought and settled in the town square. Sainte Mere Eglise is the centre of where the American airborne divisions landed early in the morning of D-Day, at the same time as the British were seizing the eastern end. It's where, as famously depicted in the film *The Longest Day* (oh God, the Messerschmitts in that are ALL WRONG) one of the men got caught on the church tower and hung there all night as the bells rang, deafening him. Private John Steele watched the firefight in the town square, saw two of his comrades land in a burning house and get killed as their grenades exploded, and played dead until the Germans cut him down in the morning and took him prisoner. On the church tower today there is a canopy hanging where Steele got caught.

There are gift shops, cafes, military-memorabilia shops that sell decommissioned weapons, German bucket helmets, the works. These places leave me staggered: who on Earth could possibly want to dress up as a Wehrmacht man? If you come to Sainte Mere Eglise in early June you could be forgiven for thinking that the landing had happened all over again. The town is busy with American tourists (fair enough) but not just tourists, people dressed as men from the 101st and 82nd Airborne Divisions, all dirt-green uniforms, high boots, field dressings taped to their helmets. They cruise around in jeeps, often in fleets, and one summer when I was in Normandy there was a camp on the road into the town, huge green tents. The museum at Sainte Mere Eglise makes the Memorial Pegasus look polite and retiring with its saved-from-scrap bridge. There is a Sherman tank at the gates, inside there's a Waco glider, smaller than the British Horsa but every bit as terrifying. In the larger building they have a C-47 Dakota. It's a fantastic collection, no doubt.

But it was at this museum that I had a moment of solid doubt. Part of the collection, and it's really arresting, is the letters and personal effects of men who had fought as part of the American airborne landings. Things like cigarette lighters, ration packs, trading cards. But also: letters. Letters to moms and dads, sweethearts: letters written by unknown soldiers to be sent who knew when. They're heartbreaking. I'll be home soon. We are fighting with God on our side. Please, don't worry about me, I'll be fine. These letters, again, remind us. It's not about the dirt-green uniforms, high boots, field dressings taped to their helmets, the M1 carbines, the Garand rifles. It's about 18-, 19-, 20-year-olds writing home, trying to keep their spirits up, trying to reassure their families as they went to war. These lie under the glass along with the ammunition clips, grenades and badges.

But as you work your way around, for all the poignancy of these letters the museum seems to lean towards flags and standards and uniforms. As I made my way round the second hangar, next to the Dakota, I realised I couldn't do it any more.

I'd had enough. It all felt bombastic (I'm not saying don't go, this is just how I ended up feeling at the time, this could have happened in any museum), it felt like it was glorifying war. I was suddenly sick of it all – sick of the flags, sick of the uniforms, sick of the minutely detailed weaponry, sick of the idea that any of it could possibly be glorious. The flags are meant to make you remember, but it's the letters that are a true reminder, a reminder of the young lives lost in the mud, lost in their prime. I shuffled around the rest of the museum, disgusted at the flags, uniforms and weapons, but mainly disgusted with myself. I loved this stuff. I'd dragged my kids and my girlfriend to northern France for this stuff, for pity's sake. Oddly, I think we all felt it.

Driving away from Sainte Mere Eglise – after a quick and delicious crêpe lunch, obviously – I said to myself that enough was enough. No more World War Two. Time to put it aside finally. It was no adventure: it was death, mud, blood, fear, carnage.

The next day we went to Falaise, birthplace of William the Conqueror. He seemed far away enough in time to be containable, dealable-with. He's not even in black and white; he's in profile on a tapestry, an embroidered bloodthirsty cartoon of a king. The castle at Falaise is proud and ancient, and intriguingly restored. Medieval life seems to be so alien, so distant, that we might as well have been discussing *Game of Thrones*. William the Bastard's rise from his brutal, rejected childhood to the English throne was certainly easier to talk about than teenagers in the 1940s going to their deaths. And him being called the Bastard got a delighted naughty squeal from the kids that we hadn't heard for a few days. We went back to Paris and looked at more paintings and I decided I was done with D-Day.

And I was. I found other things to talk about. Music, for instance. But gradually it crept up on me. It crept up on me because that's the way I'm raised, and it's something I'm known for. This means I get invited to lots of military-related things. Last year I went to the launch of the London Taxi Benevolent Fund's annual trip to Europe with veterans. 160 veterans were taken by black cabs to (yes, you guessed it) Arnhem. They left from the Union Jack Club in Waterloo, a services club, where they have regimental standards, badges and they celebrate those who've won the Victoria and George Cross. It's mind-boggling. I did a photo-call with lots of Chelsea pensioners and we got talking – they all wanted to know where my pint was, I asked them about their medals (they all had tons of medals). Then Boris appeared.

Boris Johnson: well, let's not get into that. Apart from, at one point, he shot me a look and said 'Were we at Oxford together?'. No, I replied, oddly relieved. 'When were you there?' I told him. 'Ah!' he blurted. 'I'd gone by then.' I said that Michael Gove was Oxford Union[120] President when I'd arrived and that Duncan Grey (important telly person) was running for the Presidency that term too. 'Ah yes,' he chuckled, ' I made all those buggers!' Boris was chattering away, and as we had more pictures taken – me leaning out the cab, me giving them the thumbs-up, Boris looking interested and so on – one of the Chelsea Pensioners started telling us about Sicily, how he'd found himself behind enemy lines, was captured and told by an officer 'and his English was very good, perfect' that England would lose the war within the year. His account was

---

[120] It's not like a normal student union, it's a debating society, with disproportionate influence (historically, at least). Famously in 1933 they debated 'This House will in no circumstances fight for its King and Country' and the motion was passed. It caused a worldwide sensation. These days they get in the likes of Jordan to talk.

self-deprecating, measured, funny, and seemed almost tinged with disbelief. And, most importantly, it shut Boris up.

And the other big problem has been writing this book. I set about writing it as part of the process of getting over my interest in military history. And it meant I had to reread a lot of stuff to make sure that what I'd half-remembered was right. And a lot of it is fascinating. Argh! And having taken my kids to Normandy, and roused their interest, and my dad coming for lunch and not really being able to talk about anything else . . .

So it was, four weeks ago, I decided that maybe, having written about it so much, I should watch *A Bridge Too Far* with my kids. I had to trick them into it. It was a Sunday evening and there wasn't anything decent on, so I decided to brush up on the film and see what the kids thought of it – to see how they handled watching war films with their father. They were sceptical. I did the old 'let's watch 10 minutes, see how you get on with it.' I joked about how they were much better off watching it with me rather than with Grandpa. It starts with a whistle-stop précis of the state of affairs in early September 1944, that's good enough, though it contains one too many Monty vs Patton cracks for my taste, and it sets the scene well. I made sure I'd pause it if they didn't know what was going on, explain who was who and what the main points were but resisted all other temptations. The story is carried well, told clearly, the stars in it – to a 13-year-old and a 9-year-old – having none of the baggage that they do for me. Bloody hell, it's long. And a long time for me not to say 'He didn't say that!', 'That's not really the case!', 'Yes, but . . .' and the rest of the stuff you've been putting up with in this mercifully slim volume. We got all the way through it: the ending, when the wounded soldiers left behind in Arnhem sing

Abide With Me, had my youngest saying how sad she thought the film was. I don't think the bug has bitten her. Despite my very best efforts.

But that Leopard tank! NOOOOOOOOOOO!!!!!

Index